A CONCEPTUAL COMMENTARY ON MIDRASH LEVITICUS RABBAH
Value Concepts in Jewish Thought

Number 126
A CONCEPTUAL COMMENTARY ON
MIDRASH LEVITICUS RABBAH
Value Concepts in Jewish Thought
by
Max Kadushin

A CONCEPTUAL COMMENTARY ON MIDRASH LEVITICUS RABBAH
Value Concepts in Jewish Thought

by
Max Kadushin

Scholars Press
Atlanta, Georgia

A CONCEPTUAL COMMENTARY ON
MIDRASH LEVITICUS RABBAH
Value Concepts in Jewish Thought

© 1987
Brown University

Library of Congress Cataloging in Publication Data

Kadushin, Max, 1895-
  A conceptual commentary on Midrash Leviticus rabbah.

  (Brown Judaic studies ; no. 126)
  1. Midrash rabbah. Leviticus--Commentaries.
I. Title. II. Series.
BM517.M67K33   1987   296.1'4   87-4868
ISBN 1-55540-175-9 (alk. paper)

Printed in the United States of America
on acid-free paper

Contents

Foreword

This commentary by Professor Kadushin to Midrash Leviticus Rabbah, an early rabbinic interpretation of Leviticus, may be viewed as a companion volume to *A Conceptual Approach to the Mekilta*. Kadushin's annotations and expositions in both of these works exemplify and substantiate the original principles, perspectives and conclusions which he had formulated and elucidated in his classic studies of rabbinic thought.

In this book Kadushin examines each rabbinic text or sequence of homilies in order to uncover specific value concepts which are reflected in them either explicitly or implicitly. After skillfully revealing these value concepts, he proceeds to elucidate them in light of the midrashic context under consideration, and then discusses their meanings and significance within the entire rabbinic value complex. These explications, based upon Kadushin's conceptual approach, clarify the frequently obscure nexus between the biblical citations which initially served as verbal stimuli and the rabbinic comments which appear to be so far removed from them. Furthermore, particularly when analyzing rabbinic texts in which biblical conceptual terms are employed, Kadushin adroitly demonstrates the similarities and differences in meaning and nuance between the distinctive levels of usage. In addition, Kadushin's notes underscore the organismic relationship and interdependence of all rabbinic value concepts, highlight the indeterminacy of belief and the genuine emphatic trends that distinguish rabbinic Judaism. They also call attention to the special character of the rabbinic religious experience which he had earlier described as normal mysticism.

For further exploration of Kadushin's terminology and methodology, I refer the reader to the introduction to *A Conceptual Approach to the Mekilta* where they are summarized, and to his detailed discussion in the volumes listed on page vi.

Avraham Holtz

Preface

This commentary attempts to describe the role played by the rabbinic value-concepts in Midrash Leviticus Rabbah, a book consisting largely of Haggadah but which also contains a number of halakic passages.

The way the rabbinic value-concepts functioned in haggadic literature reflects the way they functioned in everyday life. In other words, Haggadah is a literary expression of the value-concepts. But the value-concepts are experiential, and hence they are fluid and dynamic, just as the situations and potentialities in life are fluid and dynamic. Haggadah not only allows us to recognize these qualities of the value-concepts, but also possesses kindred qualities of its own, a quality for example, such as indeterminacy of belief, which we discuss here in the Introduction.

Haggadah consists in the main of rabbinic interpretations of the Bible. They are obviously seldom attempts at exegesis. Instead, they are new, original ideas stimulated by texts of the Bible and informed by the rabbinic value-concepts. The rabbinic interpretations thus represent, as we have phrased it in the Introduction, fresh impacts of the Bible on the complex of rabbinic concepts. These impacts are possible because, as we demonstrate there, the Bible and the rabbinic concepts are in the same universe of discourse.

This commentary is pegged to the critical edition and commentary of *Midrash Wayyikra Rabbah* (5 parts, Jerusalem, 1953–60) by Mordecai Margulies. We have assumed that the reader will use this commentary side by side with ours, and therefore we do not usually take up matters dealt with by Margulies. However, our commentary is not altogether tied to the Margulies edition. Because every one of our comments is prefaced by the chapter number and paragraph number of the rabbinic statement to which it refers, our commentary may be used together with any edition of this Midrash.

The date and composition of the Midrash, and similar problems are discussed by Margulies.

We refer to our earlier books by the following abbreviations:

TE: *The Theology of Seder Eliahu: A Study in Organic Thinking.* New York: Bloch Publishing Company, 1932.

OT: *Organic Thinking: A Study in Rabbinic Thought.* New York: Jewish Theological Seminary of America, 1938. Paperback edition—New York: Bloch Publishing Company, 1976.

RM: *The Rabbinic Mind.* 3rd edition. New York: Bloch Publishing Company, 1972. (First edition, 1952.)

WE: *Worship and Ethics: A Study in Rabbinic Judaism.* Evanston, Ill.: Northwestern University Press, 1964. Paperback edition—New York: Bloch Publishing Company, 1975.

CA: *A Conceptual Approach to the Mekilta.* New York: Jewish Theological Seminary of America, 1969.

Hebrew commentaries are referred to using the following abbreviations:

יפה תואר	=	יפ״ת
ר׳ זאב וואלף איינהארן	=	מהרז״ו
מתנות כהונה	=	מ״כ
ר׳ דוד לוריא	=	רד״ל
ר׳ שמואל שטראשון	=	רש״ש

To explain how we designate a statement or passage of the Midrash, we shall give the following example:

I.4 (13:2 ff.)

The Roman numeral **I** refers to the chapter number of Midrash Leviticus Rabbah. The Arabic number 4 immediately following refers to the paragraph or section in that chapter. The notation (13:2 ff.) is to be read thus: Margulies edition, page 13, line 2 and continuing on the following pages. Throughout the commentary, a notation such as 13:2 *without the name of any book preceding* designates page and line numbers in the Margulies edition. A notation such as :2 (with no number preceding the colon) indicates a line number on the page that was most recently referenced.

Introduction

In the Bible, the forty years of wandering in the wilderness is represented as a punishment. "And your children shall be wanderers in the wilderness forty years, and shall bear your strayings until your carcasses be consumed in the wilderness. After the number of the days in which ye spied out the land, even forty days, for every day a year, shall ye bear your iniquities, even forty years, and ye shall know My displeasure" (Num. 14:33-34).

But the Midrash gives an entirely different reason; it accounts for the forty years in the wilderness in a manner so different as to make the rabbinic reason practically contradict the biblical reason. "As soon as the Canaanites heard that the Israelites were about to enter the land, they arose and burnt the seeds, cut down the trees, destroyed the buildings, and stopped up the wells. God, then, said: I promised Abraham to bring them not into a desolate land, but into a land full of good things as it is said: 'And houses full of all good things' (Deut. 6:11). Therefore I will make them go round about through the desert forty years, so that the Canaanites will arise and repair what they have spoiled" (Mekilta, ed. Lauterbach, Vol. I, p. 172, lines 36 f.).

When we consider the concepts embodied in the two reasons given for the long wanderings on the road to the land, we are aware that the reasons are not only different but definitely contradictory. In the Midrash the concept embodied is *Middat Rahamim*, God's love, and in the Bible it is God's justice (*Middat Ha-Din*, in rabbinic terminology). But how can such a contradiction to the Bible be entertained? We learn from this and from other such contradictions, some even more unequivocal, to recognize a pervasive feature of all haggadic literature. Haggadic literature as a whole was accepted with what we may call indeterminacy of belief, a kind of qualified belief, shadings of belief, an attitude of mind which is neither complete assent nor complete dissent; indeed, that is what is implied by the term Haggadah. This attitude of mind is made strikingly evident at times, especially when there is a clear contradiction between a midrash and the Bible.

Indeterminacy of belief is elicited by Haggadah because the rabbinic concepts imbedded or named in midrashic literature are themselves characterized by indeterminacy. The abstract rabbinic concepts are never defined, which means that these abstract concepts are not delimited. Instead, they are pragmatic as well as indeterminate, possessing a drive to be made determinate, or to be concretized, in a situation or in a statement or in a law. For example, *Middat Raḥamim*, embodied in the midrash we quoted, and interpreting there the forty years in the wilderness, also interprets or gives meaning to any number of situations, from the dawning sun to a morsel of bread.

A midrash in Leviticus Rabbah (ed. Margulies, p. 542) affords another illustration both of indeterminacy of belief and of the indeterminacy of a rabbinic concept. Resh Laḳish derives from a word in Judges 4:18 the idea שלא נגע בה אותו רשע, that Sisera did not cohabit with Jael. But this interpretation patently contradicts the biblical verse, בין רגליה כרע נפל שכב (ibid., 5:27). Margulies, in his commentary, points out this contradiction and is puzzled by it. However, to us this is only another striking instance of indeterminacy of belief.

This last midrash also demonstrates another way in which an indeterminate concept is made determinate. *Rasha'*, the term used by Resh Laḳish, is an indeterminate concept, for it refers to a person who is capable of any number of wicked acts, such as killing, stealing, etc. Here it is made determinate by the imbedded concept of *Ni'uf*. Ordinarily, the midrash implies, this *Rasha'* engaged in *Ni'uf*, but he did not do so here. We shall call attention to indeterminacy of belief in other midrashim where it ought be reckoned with.

The rabbinic concepts endow events or situations with significance or value. We have therefore called them "significance-concepts" or "value-concepts." Following, is a list of some of these value-concepts: חלול השם, קדוש השם, גמילות חסדים, צדקה, תורה, מצוה, גזל, תלמיד חכם, צדיק, אונאה, etc., etc. They have several characteristics:

(1) No sensory experience is involved in the value-term, sensory experience such as is involved in terms like tree, chair, high, round. Concepts of the latter kind, those crystallized out of sensory experience, must be named when used. On the other hand, value-

concepts are sometimes named but are usually imbedded in a situation or statement as, for example, the concept of God's love in the *Berakah* on bread.

(2) All the value-terms are *noun forms* found in rabbinic literature. Some of them are also found in the Bible, but in rabbinic literature these terms usually have different connotations.

(3) Some of these value-terms or concepts are what we call religious concepts and some are ethical concepts. (See the Foreword to the 3rd edition of *The Rabbinic Mind.*)

Value-concepts are not related to each other logically. They are not logically connected, so that there is not only *one* possible combination of given concepts—for example, the concept of *Rasha'* may be combined with the concept of the Nations of the World, but it may also be combined with the concept of Israel. Instead of being logically connected, the concepts interweave with each other. Notice how in the first midrash cited as an instance of indeterminacy of belief, the concepts of God's love, *'Abot* (Abraham), Nations of the World (Canaanites), and Israel interweave, and how in the second midrash cited, the concepts of *Rasha'* and *Ni'uf* interweave. To give one more example, in the *Berakah* on bread, mentioned above, the concepts of God's love, *Malkut Shamayim* (the Kingship of God), *Berakah,* and the concepts of Man interweave.

What allows rabbinic concepts to interweave? They have a unity to start with, not a logical unity in which concepts are placed in a hierarchical order, but an organismic unity in which each concept can combine with any other concept in the entire complex. In other words, they are elements of one organic whole. In fact, in every situation or event, the whole complex is involved, and the concepts concretized are the maximum number that can be concretized in view of the particular circumstances in that situation or event. We have called the utilization of such concepts, whether in actual life or in rabbinic literature, organic thinking or organismic thought.

The rabbinic concepts are, in every instance, *rooted in the Bible;* there are always biblical antecedents for every rabbinic concept. But the conceptual terms themselves, the names of the concepts, are often lacking in the Bible. It is this fact, and its large implications, that make for the difference between the rabbinic concepts and their biblical antecedents. The conceptual term enables the rabbinic concept to have a much wider application, to carve out a much larger world than that of the Bible. Compare, for example, the manifold concretizations of *Ķiddush Ha-Shem* with its biblical antecedent in Leviticus 22:32; and the concretizations of *Ḥillul Ha-Shem* with its biblical antecedent in that verse. (On this matter, see RM, pp. 289 f., and the references there.) In short, the rabbinic concepts represent what we certainly can call a development out of the Bible.

The complex of rabbinic concepts constitutes a new organismic level which emerged out of the Bible. It must have emerged from the very beginning as an integrated complex, for had the concepts emerged singly they could not have possessed that organismic unity, which they exhibit in rabbinic literature. Since not only are most of these concepts new, but their integration new as well, this integrated complex of concepts is a new organismic level.

Although with respect to the Bible, the rabbinic concepts constitute a new organismic level, the rabbinic concepts and the Bible are in the same universe of discourse. This is especially evident when the Rabbis occasionally employ some concepts as they are employed in the Bible, despite the difference, ordinarily, between the rabbinic and the biblical usages of those terms. For example, although *Żedaķah* in the Bible usually means righteousness or justice whereas in rabbinic literature it usually means charity or love, there are occasions when in the Bible, too, *Żedaķah* means charity and, on the other hand, there are also instances when the Rabbis definitely retain the predominant biblical usage of the term as justice. Similarly, in rabbinic literature, *'Olam* ordinarily means "world" whereas in the Bible it refers to time, yet there are instances in rabbinic literature, too, in which *'Olam* refers to time. There is, indeed, a passage in this Midrash in which *'Olam* is used once in its biblical meaning and several times in its rabbinic meaning (see RM, p. 288). But the common universe of discourse is to be recognized not only when the Bible and the Rabbis use the same conceptual terms. When the conceptual term concretized in a statement is purely rabbinic, the proof-texts from the Bible are often completely congruent with the rabbinic idea, so much so that the proof-text itself can be taken as a concretization of the concept imbedded in that rabbinic idea (see RM, pp. 288 f.).

Midrash Haggadah is, as a form of literature, apparently without any parallel. If that is so, then it is because the relationship between the Bible and the rabbinic concepts is itself unique, the Bible making fresh impacts continually upon the rabbinic complex of concepts. To the creative mind, or rather the creative imagination, the plain meaning of the Bible provides a stimulus for the expression of new ideas embodying rabbinic concepts. There is always a connection, to be sure, between the biblical text and the new rabbinic idea, but the connection is often tenuous in the extreme. Moreover, since the connection between the text and the rabbinic haggadic statement is not a logical one, the same biblical text can act as stimulant to other rabbinic interpretations, can give rise to multiple haggadic interpretations. All this is to say that indeterminacy characterizes the very process of haggadic interpretation. That is why philosophical, allegorical interpretation presents no parallel to haggadic interpretation. Allegorical interpretation is anything but indeterminate and is, indeed, in an entirely different universe of discourse. There may perhaps be a kinship between Midrash Haggadah and the interpretations of the Dead Sea Scrolls, but the latter does not seem to be characterized by multiple interpretation.

Without expanding on the point now, we ought to say that just as the process of rabbinic interpretation is unique, so too are many of the rabbinic ideas unique and especially so are the rabbinic concepts embodied in those ideas.

PART ONE

Chapter I

I.1 (1:2 ff.)

[1] ‏חנילאי פתח‎ (2:)—A ‏פתיחה‎ is a compositional form which unites several haggadic statements. It consists of different interpretations of the same verse, usually one taken from the Ketubim, so given that the last interpretation leads directly to a verse in the lection from the Pentateuch; here the verse given various interpretations is Ps. 103:20. Each of the interpretations is an independent entity, and what unites them is a form which organizes these independent entities. What does unite the midrashim in the ‏פתיחה‎ is, in fact, a unifying *form*, not a unifying idea. In general, the function of a form in rabbinic literature, whether in Haggadah or Halakah, is to build a larger structure out of what are primarily discrete entities; in Halakah, see for example Megillah I.5.

[2] ‏מלאכיו . . . אם בתחתונים . . . ד׳ ברכו‎ (2 f.:)

‏בעיליונים‎ (3:)—Refers to angels. Angels is a cognitive concept, not a value concept; angels are thought of as possessing bodies (wings, feet, etc.). They always act as background in the concretization of value concepts, here as foil for the concept of man.

‏בתחתונים‎ (4:)—Refers to men. The concept of man is a universalistic concept, and so are ‏עולם‎ and ‏בראשית‎, all of which emphasize universalism.

‏אלא עליונים . . .‎ (2:1)—Angels always carry out commands of God. These commands relate ordinarily to their function as agents; the word for God's commands is ‏תפקודיו‎ (2:).

אבל בתחתונים (2:)... —Many men are not able to carry out commands of God. Again the word is תפקודיו (3:) but now these commands are מצוות (4:3) and are intended for man. The men who do carry out His commands, however, are designated מלאכיו (3:). The concepts concretized here tell why; angels are holy and thus concretize the concept of קדושה. When carried out, the מצוות confer קדושה on men, and thus such men (Israel) are קדושים (אשר קדשנו במצוותיו). The value concepts here are: Man, מצוות and קדושה.

[3]   ... ד״א נקראו (4:)

ד״א (4:)—The term implies not only that this interpretation is "valid," but that the preceding one is also valid. In other words, in Haggadah there is multiple interpretation of a verse and this means that the belief demanded by any given interpretation is an indeterminate belief. (On indeterminacy as a characteristic of organismic thought, see RM, pp. 131 ff.)

נקראו ... מלאכים וכו' (4:)—Num. 20:16, employing the word מלאך (4:) is taken to refer to משה (5:) obviously because it was Moses who was sent, and this indicates that the prophets are called מלאכים (6:).

ר' יוחנן (3:5 f.) ... הנביאים ...—The function of מלאך and נביא is the same; both are messengers of God and hence prophets are called מלאכים (5:). This is derived from Haggai 1:13 which is to be regarded as the basic text in this matter.

[4]   ... עושי דברו (5:2)—The resolve of עשייה (3:) even before שמיעה is "strength." Concepts of מצוה, Torah and Israel are involved; גיבור, a neutral, purely descriptive concept is here given a valuational quality, cf. above, 4:1.

[5]   ויקרא אל משה (5:4 f.)—The capacity to "absorb" דבור at Sinai was beyond the power of the 600,000 men of Israel; only Moses had it; hence again ויקרא אל משה (6:2). The concepts here are: מתן; דבור; תורה; Israel and נביא.

הדיבור (6:1)—Perhaps הדיבור here is also an appellative for God, notice לא קרא הדיבור (1:), and following that ויקרא אל משה.

אבינו שבשמים, מקום, שכינה, הרחמן, רחמנא, הקב"ה) Appelatives, etc.) are expressions of reverence and love; all of them refer to God's nearness, *not* remoteness. Notice here קרא הדיבור, were it meant to be "mitigation" of anthropomorphism, would there be "calling," a decided anthropomorphism? In medieval philosophy, where no anthropomorphism is acceptable, דיבור is a Divine Light, a new Platonic idea, created by God.

I.2

[1] ... ר' אבהו פתח (6:3)

הגרים (4:)—A rabbinic concept. Biblical גר comes from גּוּר; rabbinic גר comes from גַּיֵר. Note organismic development out of the Bible—גר is emphasis on universalism. See RM, pp. 290–93.

גרים (5:)—נעשו עיקר כישראל are authentically ישראל.

חביב עלי שמותן של גרים (7:)—Exalting of גר. Concepts are: God's love and גרים.

שמלבין עוונותיהם וכו' (7:2)—Derives from לָבָן. Concepts are: עוון; כפרה ;ישראל; note interweaving of concepts.

I.3 (7:7–8:1)

[1] ... לא ניתן (8:1)—Midrash Haggadah, according to these authorities, is not solely a rabbinic product, but *inherent,* as a method, in a book of the Bible. Apparently the many lists of names, as here, seem to be otherwise irrelevant. In דרש, biblical words act as stimulus: פשט is stimulus for דרש and דרש is a *creative* matter utilizing *any* kind of association of ideas. (RM, pp. 116 f., 132).

[2] יהודים בעולם (4:)

Notice that יהודי relates to *religion,* not to a people here; thus בתיה is היהודיה because she converted. Biblical antecedent is perhaps דעת אלהים (Hos. 6:6).

[3] ילדה ... המים וגו' (4: ff.)—Following are interpretations of names as referring to Moses. In these names of Moses and in others, there is

an emphasis on the individual. Moses' character is enriched as against the biblical—ירד (5:) brought down the שכינה to earth by building the Tabernacle.

Notice, this interpretation of ירד is introduced by ד"א (9:1), i.e., it is *another* interpretation by the *same* authority (ר' חננא 8:5)—a striking example of indeterminacy of belief; see RM, pp. 72, 105 for other even more striking examples. Note the multitude of concepts here and above: גלוי שכינה; פורענות; תורה; נביא; רוח הקודש; עולם (5:) = Israel; God's love (5: ,אבינו שבשמים) עבירה.

I.4 (13:2 ff.)

The פתיחה here is unusual in that the separate interpretations of Ps. 89:20 are connected through the concepts of דיבור (3:) and חיזיון (4:). Yet these are also separate statements. מכירי on the verse has each statement introduced by ד"א.

Concepts of דבור and חיזיון are rabbinic subconcepts of גלוי שכינה. Here they classify, group together three men. But, as rabbinic concepts they have a wider range than the biblical antecedents. In the case of David, even the verse quoted (II Sam. 7:17) shows Nathan the prophet to have experienced the דבור and חיזיון, but David did not (and see v. 4).

All three men are characterized as חסיד, an ethical qualification, as well as גבור and בחור; each of the three is the "first" or "chief"—Patriarch, Prophet, King.

I.5 (16:3 ff.)

[1] שאם . . . גואלם (17:6)—Moses is a גואל—an example of the larger range of rabbinic concepts.

A rabbinic concept is a generalization; it must have more than one concretization; משיח is also גואל; so are Aaron and Miriam; so is Elijah (Pes. R. 13a). In regard to כפרה too, the concept has many concretizations: e.g., צדיקים נתפסים על הדור (Shab. 33b); a son is to say: אני כפרת משכבו (Kid. 31b); people say to the High Priest: אנו כפרתך (Sanh. II.1) etc.

ענווה (.6 f:)—בים . . . אל משה of Moses is enlarged upon—emphasis on individuality in rabbinic literature.

I.6 (18:7 f.)

[1] דיעה (9:)—A trait or property of man, and belongs to the first phase of דרך ארץ, a neutral concept (see WE, p. 39 f.).

[2] שדיבורך (19:4)—דבור of man—again a trait of man—the first phase of דרך ארץ.

I.7 (19:7 f.)

[1] Parable—as always a parable is not a complete analogy; (see CA, pp. 51, 252, 255). Here in the נמשל Moses does not write on the posts and walls the name of God as in the משל.

[2] Notice the implication that כאשר צוה ד' את משה (20:8) was, in each instance, concerning the משכן, written by Moses himself. A parable always adds something. Here these words, כאשר וכו' are characterized as giving כבוד to God. Concepts are: תורה; כבוד; מדת הדין (reward of Moses); קדושה (משכן).

I.8 (20:10 ff.)

[1] שבשדרה . . . (21:1)—A reference to the bowing in the עמידה (י"ח). The תפלה is במקום קרבן in the משכן or better, the bowing in the תפלה is related to גלוי שכינה in the משכן.

[2] למה הדבר דומה (22:6)—There is no element of love or reward in the parable, but only of concern for the state of affairs: the king seeking information turns to his אגרנומון.

In the נמשל, the importance of Moses in respect to Israel's daily sustenance.

Moses did not originate the instructions to Israel, yet he is given credit for them. The agent in an act is the "efficient cause" of the act.

God's love, not for Moses but for Israel (God does not seek information) *combined* with מדת הדין (reward for Moses—also the
concept of דיבור).

Note: Concepts are often fused as here: God's love and justice.

I.9 (23:5 f.)

[1] When God speaks with Adam, Noah and even Abraham, it is because
of a definite "homely" specific relation to each of them—not so in
the case of Moses. Even Abraham is no more than the "host" to
God (:6-7).

[2] Moses is of higher rank than even Abraham. But nowhere is there any
idea that Moses is "the perfect man." Highest rank does not spell
perfection. Moses is the superlative נביא: he is אבי הנביאים, as a
midrash here says. The concepts are: Man (Adam, Noah); Patriarchs (Abraham); דיבור.

I.10 (24:7 ff.)

[1] תורה וכו' . . . (:7 f)

Torah, apparently all of it, already at Sinai! If this was "theory"
why do the Rabbis emphasize it? Because *all* of Israel *heard* it
there; hence every individual heard it, not as with אוהל מועד
when only Moses did; therefore the Rabbis could say: (Shebu'ot
III.6) מצוה שהוא משבע עליה מהר סיני; also (Mekilta, ed. Horovitz,
p. 253) אוזן ששמעה לא תגנוב והלך וגנב היא תרצע מכל אבריו.

[2] Notice again that the parable is not a complete analogy. אהל מועד
(25:1) is not really a public square (בדימוסיה; 25:2), quite the
opposite; but the point is made that the הוראה (:5) was for all
Israel. The concepts are: מתן תורה. הוראה; ישראל; מתן תורה is
modified by the concept of תורה.

I.11 (25:6 f.)

[1] אהל מועד (:6)—is always within Israel, a particularistic institution,
but it has a universalistic aspect for it saves אומות העולם (:6).

[2] The דיבור (26:2) is described here in terms of the *otherness* of God. If it is a דיבור, it is nevertheless unlike that of man; its sound is unbearable, throwing the non-Jews from their palaces. They are therefore safe only when the דיבור is in the אהל מועד and so קול נפסק (27:1) is there.

Here (4:)דיבור (קול, 2:) gives life to Israel who accepted the Torah and death to אומות העולם who rejected it—apparently refers to עוה״ב.

[3] The concepts here are: פורענות ;דיבור ;אוה״ע ;) אוהל מועד) קדושה ;ישראל ;(סם חיים) מדת הטובה ;(סם מות) (ונתרזין).

I.12 אומות העולם . . . נבואה (27:2)

There were Gentile prophets, especially בלעם (and others, e.g., Job and his four friends—see Ginzberg *Legends* s.v. "Prophets, Gentiles") but they still remained Gentiles, were not converts. The idea is: Nations cannot say they were, so to say, shut out since they had prophets.

[1] אחזתיו ולא ארפנו (3:)—Once Israel had גלוי שכינה in the אוהל מועד, she refused to give it up. The idea is that גלוי שכינה and נבואה (2:) are related and used here interchangeably. נבואה was not often a comfort but conveyed prophesies of doom and punishment, whereas בלעם (4:) prophesied after the אוהל מועד was established, yet was allowed to be a prophet because his prophesies were לטובתן של ישראל (4:).

Israel prized נבואה because it was the word of God, not because of happy tidings.

I.13 (27:7 f.)

[1] The נביאי אומות העולם (7:) were Gentiles and remained so, not converted to Judaism despite having experienced דיבור; hence they were regarded with opprobrium, even called רשעים (29:1–2). The Rabbis recognized them as נביאים because, *in the Bible*, God does speak to them (especially to בלעם) though in the Rabbis' own day there were no נביאי אוה״ע.

[2] קדושה (28:6) and טהרה (6:)—are both the obverse of טומאה. טומאה is one of the concepts which have two obverses.

[3] אנשים . . . אמ' ר' יוסי (29:5 f)—Secret, almost surreptitious quality of דיבור to Gentiles (as when men are separated, not wont to meet).

ר' חננא . . . עם אוהבו (8 f:)—In this interpretation of Job 4:12, ר' חננא has the verse complete the idea: Those who are not אוהבו (30:1) speak with Him through a curtain, not directly, by stealth as it were, whereas His אוהבו speaks with Him directly and these are the נביאי ישראל.

I.14 (30:10 ff.)

[1] ר' יהודה . . . (10 f.:)—Apparently through many איספקלריות (31:1) the view is fainter and that is what the rest of the נביאים saw; whereas Moses saw through one איספקלריה, a much sharper vision—but this kind of vision is the same, "As in a glass darkly" (I Cor. 13:12).

[2] לפי שבעולם הזה . . . וראו וגו' (32:1)

גלוי שכינה (2:)—היחידים is not a concept within the experience of man or Israel generally; it is experienced by only a few individuals. In my terms, it is not a pure value concept, for cognitive elements are involved. But the name *Shekinah* often does not refer to גלוי שכינה but is an appellative used in *normal* mysticism in contexts telling of God's nearness, as in those of prayer, תלמוד תורה, etc.

I.15 (32:5 f.)

[1] תלמיד חכם שאין בו דעת (5:)

דעת here means "sensibility" and relates to manners, the third phase of דרך ארץ.

From the example of Moses, a man's achievements do not entitle him to override common courtesy.

[2] בסנה הפסיק . . . לדבר (33:4)

God called Moses, then told him: אל תקרב הֲלֹם and only then: ויאמר.

Chapter II

II.1 (34:2 f.)

[1] סכלות מעט (7:)—In this midrash סכלות מעט is laudatory, may refer to
a noncalculated "foolish" act as a departure on occasion from a
man's normal careful behavior; a "simple" act on the part of a
wise man. The concepts: דעת, תבונה, סכלות belong to the first
phase of דרך ארץ, traits of man, and so does עושר (see WE,
pp. 39 ff.).

[2] ד"א . . . זה עמרם . . . (35:7 f.)—Apparently the progenitor of Moses
had to be the צדיק of his generation; again אפילו יוכבד (8:); also a
צדקת, but not quite like Amram (עמרם).

ד"א . . . זה משה . . . (8: f)—Moses was *the* צדיק of his generation, and notice: no אפילו here.

[3] ר' א' . . . דלתותיהן (36:1-2)

A view describing women as *superior* to men, in contrast to the
preceding views, the concepts are: Israel; מצוות; *'Arayot*.

[4] משפחות משפחות וכו' (5:)—The כנים and ערב belong to God and in
sending them on Pharaoh, God gave them up to him. In themselves, these משפחות have a worth as God's creatures.

II.2 (37:1)   לי—כל מקום . . . ולא לעוה"ב

[1] לא לעולם הבא (1:)—עוה"ב is a dogma—a concept in a seriatim series,
connected in consecutive order; pure value concepts are never
connected in consecutive series.
    The series is: (1) עוה"ז, (2) ימות המש', (3) תחית המתים,
(4) עוה"ב.

[2] Further, it is a dogma because מודה and כופר are applied to it.

But not pure dogma for there is room for different views (RM,
pp. 362 ff.). In our midrash, for example, Israel, Sanhedrin, priests

etc. function in עוה"ב, whereas ר' יוחנן (Sanh.. 99a) insists that only God knows "what He worketh for him that waiteth for Him" (Isa. 64:4). וּמֵעוֹלָם is interpreted as עוה"ב there.

עוה"ב is obviously regarded here as taking place on this earth for Israel, Sanhedrin, priests, Levites, etc., are regarded as *continuing* in עוה"ב.

II.3 (39:3 f.)   אם ילד שעשועים

[1] For Me to punish him justly by rebuking him is enough; and I cannot actually punish him (רד"ל) כי המו מעי לו) Combination of the concepts of מדת רחמים and מדת הדין; דיבור (תוכחה) and Israel.

II.4 (40:3 ff.)

[1] שהן דבוקין לי (41:5)

The verse (Jer. 13:11) embodies the concept of God's love; and Israel alone being the subject of God's commands to Moses is regarded as indicating God's love, but the concept of מצוות (that Israel performs) is also implied, and that means that Israel, too, has to do something. If Israel must deserve such love through acts, can the midrash be taken as expressing the idea of the Chosen People? Were it simply a matter of being the Chosen People, Israel would not have to *do* anything.

[2] אמ' ר' אבין . . . ימלוך וג' (41:6-42:5)—Again, Israel deserves God's love.

שהמליכו אותי על הים (42:5). The concepts are: מלכות שמים; Israel; God's love and justice combined.

[3] שקבלו מלכותי בסיני (:10)—Again, Israel deserves God's love—זקן (:7), scholar, lawgiver, hence בסיני.

In both [2] and [3] here there is the implication that by accepting מלכות שמים, Israel can be expected to perform מצוות; just as [1] implies the concept of מצוות. In other words, God's love is only one aspect, the other is God's justice. A combination of the concepts of God's love and His justice, and not an idea of the Chosen People; also מלכות שמים.

[4] ישראל . . . אמ' ר' יודן (43:1)—Frequent mention of name indicates almost involuntary expression of love.

Association of ideas (God's love and Israel) and not an interpretation of דבר אל בני ישראל (6:).

II.5 (43:3 f.)   ישראל . . . אמ' ר' שמעון

Question addressed to בן ביתו in (4:): ספרא . . . אכל ברי. Here the interpretation embodies the concept of God's love but the concept of מצוות is not implied, for the parable indicates that it is a matter of solicitous concern only—כך בכל יום ויום היה הקב"ה מצוה את משה (5:); the emphasis is on בכל יום ויום in the נמשל.

[1] אתפאר . . . אמ' ר' יהודה (43:6–44:3) Another interpretation of דבר אל בני ישראל—This is understood not as referring to מצוות at all but to praising, glorifying Israel (probably אֶל here = עַל). Not as a pedagogic device but what Israel will deserve in the future. The concepts are: God's love and justice combined. The idea here concerns Israel's destiny, but a destiny marked by their character (עבדי אתה) and not simply an undeserved boon.

II.6 (44:4 f.)   הכתובים חלקו כבוד לישראל (4:)

[1] אף הכתובים—Concept of Torah (הכתובים), but personified: כתובים חלקו כבוד. Personified and thus an example of indeterminacy of belief in a poetic metaphor.

כבוד, a value concept; קרבן a subconcept of קדושה, hence the context of the verse is כבוד and thus the verse speaks of מכם (Israel).

לדבר אחר (5:)—Note the delicacy of expression (in contrast to today's "literary" language).

[2] ר׳ שמואל . . . הארץ (7:)—A midrash that builds on the preceding one, not at all an uncommon form. The idea in common is אף הכתובים וכו׳ (4:)

[3] הקללה (45:2)—A value concept, literally consists of words.

פורענות (3:)—A sub-concept of מדת הדין; לעולם—a value concept, here refers to Israel in view of the biblical context, as in Avot VI.6: האומר . . . מביא גאולה לעולם.

צדקים (3:)—A value concept; this emphasis on פורענות is not something deliberate. The very presence of צדיקים prevents פורענות from taking place.

Idea of *corporate personality*—Presence of צדיקים in Israel averts the punishment deserved by the rest of Israel.

II.7 (45:5)

[1] אמר לו הקב״ה לאדם זה (5:)—An expression often used, which is itself an indication of indeterminacy of belief, despite the halakah here.

[2] אדם הראשון (6:)—Adam, but called הראשון, a usage which indicates that אדם here is conceptualized, means "man" in general, emphasis on universality.

[3] החמסין (7:)—Taken by force, a form of גזל; the latter is a negative value concept. קדושה is קרבן which is impossible with a גזילה.

II.8 (46:1 f.)

[1] ד״א אדם זה לשון חבה . . . רעות (1:)—אדם is a concept emphasizing universality, but it also has connotations of love, brotherhood, friendship (רעות, חבה, אחוה). Perhaps the connotations of the word "humanity" (compassion, universality) derive from this.

[2] שמא תאמר . . . ממקומו (47:3 f.)—Concept of קדוש השם—but by angels, not man. Outside of the קדושה of the Amidah which states that Israel imitates the angels, קדוש השם by man in speech occurs in ברכו and קדיש (WE, pp. 135 f., 141 f.).

Indeterminacy of belief; in the קדושה of the יוצר, the angels say: 'קדוש וג, and אופנים וחיות הק' respond antiphonally with ברוך וג' (continually every day)—קדושה of the angels is therefore no dogma—and there are other versions.

"Angel" is a cognitive concept. Angels give dramatic background to value concepts; here to קדוש השם.

[3] מבעטין אתם בייסורין (6:)—You object to ייסורין, chastisements, sent to correct and purify. ייסורין is a subconcept of both God's justice and His love—the exile and the troubles before it (the proper attitude to these ייסורין is expressed in saying: ומפני חטאינו גלינו וכו').

למען . . . אבל . . . (6–7:)—Concept of חלול השם. What might be חלול השם by God, ח"ה being the *effect* of action, or refraining from action, on *others* (לעיני גוים [in the verse]). The idea here is that not only can there be קדוש השם *by* God, but also ח"ה. Notice biblical antecedent here in Ezekiel, practically the same as rabbinic.

II.9 (48:1 f.)

[1] אדם להביא את הגר . . . (3:)—Concept of גר is a universalistic concept, and notice that it is associated with אדם, also a universalistic concept. גר in the Bible is a "sojourner," in rabbinic literature it is "convert"; the rabbinic emphatic trend to universalism—the rabbinic concept is always of wider range than its biblical antecedent. The conceptual approach helps us here: קרבן is קדושה, or a subconcept of קדושה; since only Israel of all the nations are קדושים and since קרבן is in some sense a projection of the individual or of the צבור, only קדושים can bring a קרבן. But a גר, a *convert* also embodies קדושה and hence can also bring a קרבן.

[2] מכם . . . מביא עולה (3:)—מכם—Exclusive, not all of you. גוי may bring עולה, but אינו סומך—this halakah exhibits a trend to universalism, but not an emphasis on it. An *emphasis* on universalism occurs when a number of *concepts* embody it (מלכות, אדם, גר, שמים, etc.). A law (or statement) may exhibit only a *limited* trend to universalism—probably not true of other emphatic trends—but

סמיכה symbolizes the relation of the מקריב to the קרבן. It is a projection, symbolically, of the מקריב, even perhaps the symbolic substitution of the קרבן for the מקריב. Since גוי does *not* embody קדושה, קרבן is not a projection of him; he ought really not be allowed to bring a קרבן, but so *strong* is the trend to universalism that he *is* permitted to do so. Moreover, סמיכה even for the Jew is not an absolute requirement.

[3] גוי (3:)—In the Bible refers to "nation" and so to Israel as well; in rabbinic literature it refers to an *individual* non-Jew; this change marks an emphasis on the individual—yet the biblical meaning is not lost for the Rabbis since they use the term occasionally with regard to "nation."

גוי is not a pariah in relation to Israel—he has real association with Israel. Notice that although the whole idea of קרבן is biblical, the *halakot* governing it embody rabbinic concepts.

[4] שהביא עולתו וכ׳ (4:)—Notice that if a גוי has not provided נסכים, they are provided by the צבור (i.e., Israel). Israel thus encourages the גוי, even shares with him—the trend toward universalism is not so limited after all.

[5] אמר רשב״ג (49:1 ff.)

נביאי אומות העולם—Function of (2:) ז׳ נביאים עמדו לאומות העולם is to exhort or warn the Nations to accept the Torah, to convert. Concepts: נביא; אוה״ע; Torah. גהינם (2:) is a subconcept, usually of עוה״ב.

אוה״ע refers to the Nations as a collective personality, whereas גוי refers to the individual non-Jew.

גר is a term for God, and שכינה (4:)—להכניסו תחת כנפי השכינה, like Israel, thus belongs in a special sense to God, i.e., is holy like Israel! Furthermore, the Nations cannot claim לא נתנה לנו תורה גרים (3:) ועדיין לא העידו בנו. The very fact that they see גרים indicates that anyone can accept the Torah—the "invitation" is always there.

Again, an emphasis on universalism. The Nations are not neglected by the Rabbis, they are reached by the *normal* functioning of Judaism as the Rabbis see it.

[6] . . . חוץ . . . מקבלין . . . הבהמה (:6 f.)—Properly, they ought not to accept זבחים from רשעי ישראל (:7); the latter are not holy, since מצוות make Israel holy and רשעי ישראל do not observe them. Not embodying קדושה, they are ineligible for קרבנות, which are קדושה.

רשעי ישראל (:7) had קדושה but lost it, hence they are like בהמה, of lower status than "neutral" human beings.

רשעי ישראל (:7), for there are, of course, רשעים in אוה״ע. The opposites are parallels too—צדיקים and the term צדיקי אוה״ע (e.g., יתרו, Antoninus etc.).

[7] כדי להכניסן תחת כנפי השכינה (:7)—This expression is used for a גוי when he becomes a גר. No divine immanence as a principle is permanently within Israel.

When one of רשעי ישראל wants to bring a קרבן it may mean that he has a twinge of conscience and needs encouragement, the feeling that not all is lost.

חוץ מן המשומד . . . בפרהסיא (:7)—All three are apostates; yet, of course, this does not mean that they can no longer repent. But they must make their own way.

II.10 (49:9–51:3) מן בקר . . . דרכו

For each biblical character here there are numerous other sources. Each statement is therefore basically an individual statement, but they are united by the same theme, namely, that each of these characters observed a biblical commandment, although the Torah had not yet been given; hence all could be gathered together— שלא . . . והם . . . מאליהן (51:1).

[1] The connection is not only with the sacrifices of בקר וצאן of the text, but also with the first example, אדם (50:1), which relates to אדם כי יקריב (48:1).

[2] ברוך . . . שספר עצמו . . . (49:10)—"He counted Himself with," as Albeck says. A softer expression is "associated Himself with"; the implication here is made evident in the conclusion of the passage.

צדיקים (10:)—The term refers to *superior* צדיקים עם הצדיקים הראשונים, higher than the other צדיקים. "הצדיקים הראשונים" were חסידים, חסיד being higher than צדיק (Abot de R. Nathan, A, VIII, p. 38). The term הראשונים means not only earlier in time, but greater, e.g., חסידים הראשונים in Ber. V.1, whose practice could not be excelled. The full implication is given in the conclusion of the passage—they were "perfect" or near-perfect.

Since excellence consisted in observance of the Torah, the צדיק in general is he who observes the laws of the Torah.

[3] והשליך עצמו (50:3)—Isaac was a *voluntary* sacrifice, hence the concept of זכות אבות is associated with עקידת יצחק, the deed of Isaac rather than that of Abraham.

[4] יוסף קים . . . לא תחמוד (5:)—Leaves out the proofs given in Seder Eliahu; perhaps they were assumed to be well known.

[5] דרכו . . . לפי אהבם (51:1 f.)

. . . והשוה (2:)—"Equated." Only of perfect men could this be said.

תמימי דרך (2:)—Interpreted as "perfect," and thus associated and equated, too, with הצור תמים פעלו, and even more clearly by means of the verse האל תמים דרכו, where the phrase תמים דרכו corresponds to תמימי דרך.

The idea of "perfect *men*" is a *rabbinic* idea, but it is not the idea of a Perfect Man.

A great number of concepts in the passage: צדיק; Torah; קרבן (קדושה); זכות אבות (יצחק); עבודה זרה (יעקב), the various concepts in the Decalogue (כבוד אב, etc.), God's love combined with God's justice (והשוה); אבות.

II.11 (51:4 ff.) ושחט . . . מעידני . . . לפני ה'

[1] איל (4:)—Reminiscent of איל sacrificed by Abraham in place of Isaac. The כבשים, (6:) תמיד (תמידין), morning and evening to "remind God" of עקידת יצחק (7:). תמיד is made a symbol; concept of זכות

אבות is embedded. Involved is the idea of corporate personality. What Isaac has done brings reward to his decendants—they are not separate from Isaac.

[2] חורבן after the ,"Or read this verse"—(6:) וקורין את המקרא הזה (יפ״ת)—the verse is a surrogate for these sacrifices, and therefore a prayer, just as the עמידה is a surrogate for these sacrifices.

מעידני . . . בין גוי בין ישראל וכו׳—No one is unworthy to utter this prayer, and thus "to remind God"—the universalistic idea is a cliché, a kind of hyperbole for emphasis here, since a גוי would not ordinarily be expected to pray for Israel.

[3] זוכר . . . עקידת יצחק (8:)—There is no assurance other than that God "recalls," just as in prayer there is no assurance other than that God hears the prayer—no theurgy.

[4] זכות אבות—(52:1)—Deeds are those of the כנגד מעשה . . . ויעקב וכ׳ אבות but the reward is stored (צפונים, :1) for their descendants. This idea of זכות אבות was enlarged to include the righteous of past generations in general. The idea of corporate personality allows for expansion.

אברהם, . . . עמרם, ישנים . . . חדשים (:3)—The deeds of the חדשים are also treasured for Israel, the חדשים being no less worthy in their deeds than the אבות.

כשרים (:3)—Apparently it was not necessary to be צדיקים for their deeds to be treasured for their posterity. כשרים are below צדיקים evidently and only עמרם is a צדיק.

חבורתו של משה . . . ושל ר׳ מאיר (:4 f.)—Notice חבורתו in :4, 5: not occasional individuals but a "company," a society of men of virtue—reminiscent of rabbinic חבורות (Pharisees). Israel at its best, not just outstanding individual men.

The sense of corporate personality was very real to them, past *and* present, so to speak. Psychologically they could feel this way because the individuals and the groups in the past were looked upon as having an outlook, a manner of life, no different from that of the present.

II.12 (52:6 ff.)

[1] שלא יאמר . . . פנים (53:5)—Here the intention of a man is described (שלא יאמר). His *intention* is to commit sins: ד' מכוערים וד' שאינן ראויים (5:), (euphemism for sins) and to *propitiate* God by means of a costly sacrifice (בשר הרבה, 54:1).

אלא . . . מעשים טובים . . . בתשובה—Here God speaks (54:1-2); מעשים טובים are ethical deeds; no *propitiation*, evident again from the less costly sacrifice (איל)—simply the attitude of a pious, ethical God-fearing man.

[2] בתשובה (54:3)—עולה is a מתנה to atone for sins unknown to a man or when asking a favor from Him, lest such a sin prevent his request; תשובה here, then, is not repentance of actual sin. No real equivalent in English?

הקרבה באיל (3:)—To indicate that this is a heartfelt gift, not a propitiation. הקרבה = gift (מ"כ).

Chapter III

III.1 (54:5 ff.)

[1] . . . ר' יצחק פתח (5:)—The פתיחות end at 59:1 (אנן בחרנן לן); and with ד"א (59:1) there begins the דרשה on נפש כי תקריב, Lev. 2:1, the verse of the lection.

[2] טוב מלא כף . . . שני סדרים וכו' (5: f.)—Three applications of the verse to תלמוד תורה—all contrasting the תלמיד of integrity with "four-flushers" interested only in having a reputation (concept of גאוה, a sub-concept of דרך ארץ).

Perhaps כף נחת (58:2) in all these instances refers to the steady mood of study (satisfaction in study) in contrast to strain and hurry of sheer striving after more.

[3] טוב . . . מרי אוסיאן (55:4 ff.)—Three types of "four-flushers" in practical life; the concept of דרך ארץ (business). These teachings are folk wisdom, types characterized by the *folk* in popular apothegms, as can be recognized from their being in Aramaic, the language spoken by the folk.

פרגמטוטא (56:2)—It is no accident that a Greek word is used. The contact of Jews and Greco-Romans was in business.

בעל צדקה = (4:) מרי מצואתא. Notice that both in Hebrew and Aramaic צדקה = מצוה; this indicates that מצוה has an ethical connotation. All ethical acts are grasped at once by an ethical concept *and* by the concept of מצוה. מרי מצואתא—the term indicates that בעל צדקה was a real category of Jews. There was no philanthropy in Roman (and Hellenistic) life; gifts were given only to the state. Notice that צדקה = love = charity (*caritas*), i.e., help, money, clothing, etc., given to another out of love. Hence, acts of גזל, etc., can only mean that צדקה is given from another motive: self-aggrandizement. The modern idea that "charity is stealing in wholesale and giving in retail" is hardly related to the idea in this midrash.

[4] אמ' ר' ברכיה . . . לא היתה גאולה (57:3 f.)

מבת בכרות (5:)—בזה היתה גאולה to which Exod. 12:12 refers is the proximate cause of redemption. The concept of גאולה is usually redemption from servitude, never redemption from sin. There is hardly any point in saying God's deed is better than that of Moses and Aaron. But there is a point if we recognize that there is a contemporary warning here. The redemption from Roman servitude can come only by God, not by man.

[5] רעותיה . . . בהון (7:)—Men are not averse to working; more leisure would bore them. (Romans chided Jews for resting on שבת). Better: Jews need to work during the six days in order to make a living; they "want to do their work" because they have to.

תדע לך . . . תיושעון (7: f.)—Israel will be redeemed because of keeping שבת (בשבת, 58:1). This is "the proof"; not how important מנוחה is.

Medieval Jewish philosophy has a rational approach to שבת, e.g.:

1. Saadia says there are social benefits: study of Torah; they can make annoucements (in the synagogue?).

2. Maimonides says: By resting on that day, one proclaims the idea of חדוש העולם; one seventh of man's life is spent בהנאה ובמנוחה.

Occasionally the Rabbis themselves offer a similar rationalization for שבת (and for מצוות as well). See OT, p. 108–9 for other rationalizations of מצוות.

This rationalization-type of approach blots out the concept of קדושה; observing שבת is experiencing קדושה since שבת heads the hierarchy of קדושה of holy days—a psychological experience. Now, what of the concept of מנוחה? It is not a value concept in itself but it belongs to the first phase of דרך ארץ, being the opposite of מלאכה. It is associated with קדושה since מנוחה helps to make קדושה palpable—refraining from the 39 מלאכות. שבת is called מנוחה שלמה, complete מנוחה, since the קדושה of שבת is the highest in the hierarchy of holy days. The Festivals are not מנוחה שלמה.

This midrash represents pure rabbinic thought. It does not enlarge on מנוחה, for then it would have to rationalize; instead it combines שבת (58:1), which is קדושה, with another value concept, גאולה.

[6] כף נחת זה העוה"ב (58:2)—נחת = קורת רוח (5:), gratification.

רשעים (3:) . . . אלא . . . בעלמא הדין cause it to be otherwise for themselves in עוה"ב by deliberately doing bad deeds in עוה"ז—deliberately for רעותהון (3:), their desire.

[7] ר׳ יצחק . . . בחרון לן (6:ff.)

ממלא . . . בעבר הירדן (8:)—Since grazing requires far more land (cf. the ranchers vs. the nesters, in America).

רעותהון . . . בחרנן לן (9:)—The Aramaic here and throughout in explanation of רעות רוח (8:–9) is the result of rendering רעות as "desire." Perhaps this is an attempt to prevent emigration from the land of Israel by stressing its fruitfulness.

[8] קומץ מנחה נדבה (59:1-3)—it is נדבה (2:) and not a מנחה brought as a sin offering by the very poor (בדלי דלות) for here it is brought with שמן and לבונה (Lev. 2:1), and there, without them, specifically because it is a sin offering (Lev. 5:11).

נדבה (2:) is a value concept, having kinship with צדקה, and is also a sub-concept of קרבן (קדושה), as here.

מנחה (3:) is a value concept, subconcept of קרבן. קומץ (3:) is a cognitive concept, a measure of quantity. צבור (3 ,2:) is a cognitive concept of relationship ("heap") often associated with the value concept of Israel.

"כפרה (4:)—". . . שזו טעונה כפרה . . ." This carries with it כפרה—(מהרז"ו), that is, for sins (of the ציבור), whereas the מנחת עני *here* is not for sin but free will. In the case of the קטורת (3:) of the צבור, the value concepts embodied are: קדושה (Exod. 30:37); כונה, for every offering must be dedicated to God by כונה (intention); כפרה (4:), and of course חטא.

In the מנחה . . . שלענו (3:) the concepts of קרבן, קדושה (5, :) and כונה alone are embodied, and in the case of the עני (usually only an עני brings a מנחה) it is as though he offered up his life—it may be all he has. Only in the case of the מנחת עני, of all the sacrifices mentioned, is the word נפש (4:) used.

III.2   (60:1 f.)

[1] אילו יראי שמים . . . (2:)—"Fearers of Heaven" were semi-proselytes—they were Gentiles who acknowledged God and the moral laws, but remained uncircumcised. See Lieberman, *Greek in Jewish Palestine*, pp. 81 ff., on these and other types of semi-proselytes. Regarded here as individuals who praise God though not Jews—an emphasis on universalism. The concept of יראי שמים as standing for a category of גרים is itself universalistic.

באין . . . בא (3:)—Are technical terms for "come to be converted" (Lieberman, ibid., p. 80). The question is: "If converts (גרי צדק) will be accepted in the Days of the Messiah, then Antoninus will be accepted at the head of them." (Line 3 from "Whether they will be accepted" is a moot point.) This opinion implies that

Antoninus remained one of the יראי שמים (Lieberman, ibid., pp. 80 ff.).

[2] שָׁמֵעַ . . . בנוהג שבעולם (61:1 f.)—The parable is not a complete analogy, as usual, since God is just, but the point is made that He hears the prayer of the poor: ר' חגי . . . ענות עני (:3 f.); the concept of מדת רחמים is emphasized.

תפילה—(:5)כשם שלא . . . תקריב is equated here with קרבן. Not only the Amidah and תמידים, but prayer in general is equated with קרבן in general.

III.3

[1] חטא ;חטא, עון, פשע (62:2 f.)—Three concepts of sin: עון, פשע על כל עונותיי וכו' equals שגגה; עון and פשע are similar except that פשע may have the connotation of "rebellion" (פושעי ישראל).

    מחל and סלח are "forgiveness." כפר here is also "forgiveness" but elsewhere it means "atone." The terms are sometimes interchangeable, apparently.

[2] וישוב . . . זה בזה (:3 ff.)—מלחים (:4, 5) is greater emphasis on God's love than וירחמהו (:3), the word in the text, interpreted now as וילחמהו. No new concept but the idea of God's nearness, of close relationship, is added. Concepts are: מדת רחמים and תשובה both in the verse.

[3] Gen. 15:9 (63:1) is taken here to be God's answer to Abraham's question: במה אדע כי אירשנה (Gen. 15:8); Israel will inherit the land because they will make atonement for sins committed.

    The idea of corporate personality both in the Bible and in the midrash, except that in the midrash there is the concept of כפרה, implying, too, God's love, for He thus provides for Israel inheriting the land—also ירבה לסלוח (:5).

    Does not accord with רבנן. That opinion involves the idea of corporate personality, for עשירית האיפה was part of the answer to במה אדע כי אירשנה of Abraham; here (:5) it is divorced from that answer: היתיר לנו סליחה . . . משלו (:6) and not involved with corporate personality. In contrast with the "answer" it is a *new*

סליחה given לנו (6:), to the individual who brings the offering—an emphasis on the individual.

III.5 (65:4 ff.)

[1] ושסע . . . שלעני (4 f.:)

מזבח מהודר (66:1)—Concept of הדור מצוה applies to sacrifices (see Yoma 34b) both in regard to חובה and נדבה as well as to ס"ת, תפילין, etc.

בקורבנו שלעני (1:)—The poor man, in offering the fowl, gives more than he can afford and his intention (כונה) of הדור מצוה is therefore to be fully realized. Concept of הדור מצוה is a subconcept of כונה, also embodied in concept of מדת רחמים.

[2] שעשיתה . . . אגריפס (1 f.:)—Two examples (the other is at 67:4) of a poor man's small offering as more worthy than a rich man's large offering (יפ"ת).

אותה חותך פרנסתי (5:)—This idea is not compatible with true כונה—it is theurgy. In prayer, manifestation of God's love is only hoped for—here קרבן is literally *quid pro quo*—apparently a popular folklore view (the story is obviously a folk tale) of קרבן נדבה as efficacious for specific practical matters.

[3] שלעני קדמך . . . מעשה (67:4 f.)—Folk tales representing the poor as more virtuous apparently or perhaps as favored by God—but they lack the concept of כונה.

[4] . . . מעשה באשה (7 f.:)—United with the two preceding stories because the message here, too, is given in a dream. But now the "folk-tale" contains a true rabbinic idea—כאילו נפשה הקריבה (68:2). Furthermore, the folk motif, the dream, is used only as background for the rabbinic interpretation of that verse.

III.6 (68:5 ff.)

[1] וקמץ . . . כל שמנה (6:)—This is הלכה, but notice how it forms background for הגדה—integration of Halakah and Haggadah. Other

examples: 45:7; 48:2 f. (here, הלכה cannot be understood properly without awareness of the value concepts involved); 65:4 f. The integration is possible because Halakah and Haggadah are not two altogether distinct and separate categories since both are products of the same value concepts.

הרי שהביא . . . כמה וכמה (8 f.:)—The concept of כונה is involved. The man brings the מנחה from a long distance but with no *specific* purpose, in contrast to 66:5. Apparently he hopes for a manifestation of God's love in some manner. Notice that *others* reassure him. כונה here is almost like prayer.

[2] מישרים אהבוך . . . בריתי (70:5 ff.)—This baraita from the Sifra (ed. Weiss, 45d–46a) interprets Mal. 2:5–6 as referring to Aaron, and is an example of the rabbinic emphasis on the individual. None of the characteristics attributed to Aaron here are even hinted at in the biblical narratives. The acts and attitudes attributed to him here are all concretizations of rabbinic value concepts. The character of the individual depends on the value concepts he concretizes.

החיים . . . שלום בישראל (6:)—מ״כ quotes the famous passage in Abot deR. Nathan, Chapter XII, Version A, ed. Schechter, p. 25a, of how Aaron made peace between two who quarreled by first going to one and telling him how sorry and debased the other felt and then going to the other with a similar tale, the result being that the two became warm friends; a "modern" may object to Aaron's lying to both men. In an organismic complex *one concept may be stressed over another,* and here the concept of peace is stressed over truth (אמת). On the other hand, *truth* is stressed in כל המחליף בדבורו כאלו (Shab. 55a); and חותמו של הקב״ה אמת עובד ע״ז (Sanh. 92a), etc.

[3] The באימה ביראה וכו' (7:) describes here the attitude of the student (Aaron) to the teachings of the master (Moses)—in other words to a situation of תלמוד תורה. Elsewhere this attitude is enjoined upon the student in general but there it is based upon the idea that the very same emotions were experienced by Israel at מתן תורה. This was also the attitude required of Moses when he was taught the Torah by God—again מתן תורה.

This reflects an aspect of the normal mysticism of the Rabbis. Learning from the master was like מתן תורה—in other words תלמוד תורה was an experience akin to מתן תורה, as it were. That is why the same expression באימה ביראה וכו' (7:) could be used for both: מתן תורה was learning from God directly; תלמוד תורה was learning from God indirectly.

The presence of the word תורה in both concepts indicates that they are both subconcepts of Torah; as such they are akin to one another. In this case, the conceptual kinship requires the same emotional experience.

[4] מעילה . . . מה ת"ל (7: ff.)

מעילה (71:3)—A negative value concept with the connotation of "false dealing" (see Jastrow). Combined with the concept of קדושה, it has the specific meaning employed here (malapropriation of a holy thing; see מהרז"ו).

[5] כשמן . . . הוא יורד (71:3)—Anointing made Aaron holy, holier than the rest of Israel. (Holiness occurs in hierarchies—see WE, pp. 216 ff.). Aaron was thus made holier than Moses, but Moses rejoiced as though he himself had been made holy.

[6] With regard to טמא (7:, 8), the question is whether what he said is תורת אמת (7:); even if the decision was wrong, a person is permitted to eat and drink חולין that is טמא (see Maimonides, הלכות טומאת אוכלין, XVI.8; מורה נבוכים, Part III, Chapter XLVII). The concepts here are טומאה and טהרה.

[7] ורבים . . . לתלמוד תורה (10:)—What has ת"ת, study, to do with עון, acts? There is a conceptual phase of Torah, the efficacy of Torah, which teaches that knowledge of Torah has an immediate, though not inevitable effect on conduct (OT, pp. 68 ff.)—ת"ת already implies פושעים (10:) have changed their ways. Concepts are: ת"ת; השיב), תשובה ;פושע ;עון, 10:).

III.7 (72:4 ff.)

[1] ואמרו . . . המקום (6:)—Sacrifices are not propitiation: מעשיה קשין

(:6) a symbol for harsh deeds—ראויין . . . דברים (:7), euphemism for sins.

[2] שמן וגו' . . . אמר לו (73:1)—By means of symbolism, the sacrifice is moved from Temple ritual into the sphere of personal ethics—בללת מעשיך בדברי תורה (:1), knowledge of Torah is related to מעשים because of efficacy of Torah (see above 71:10).

שמן (:1-2) symbolizes both תורה and מעשים טובים (:2), the same symbol used for both because of efficacy of Torah—שמניך (:2), plural because it refers to תורה and מ״ט (יפ״ת).

As a reward (:3-4) for our desire to learn Torah, God (שמך, :4) teaches us Torah. A combination of concepts: God's love and His justice (as in אהבה רבה).

ואין קולו נשמע (:3)—A student does not become prideful (מהרז״ו); or perhaps: "Though His voice is not heard" in the oral teaching.

[3] בין כשהוא טוב וכו' (:5)—Sheer love of God, disinterested love. Emphasis on universality—some Gentiles come to this through *self*-effort: בחכמה ובבינה וכו' (:4). Also Torah is not irrational.

ד״א . . . אהבוך (:6 f.)—The essence of life, time itself, loves God—a poetic projection.

[4] Here עלמות (74:6) is taken as עַל מָוֶת, i.e., אפי' מת עליו (:5-6), even though slain. Again the idea that true knowledge of Torah brings with it love of God. Normal mysticism at its best comes only with true knowledge of Torah. Normal mysticism varies in intensity.

[5] יש (:7) . . . תורה . . . וחטא—An explicit instance of the *efficacy of Torah*. The מנחה of such a man is given out of love of God—sheer כונה, true מנחת נדבה. Symbolism of oil is not necessary for there is the presence of Torah in such a man already.

ויטמנו . . . (75:1)—Yet there is also reward: such a man will not forget his Torah—מים עמוקים (:2); מים = Torah.

Chapter IV

IV.1 (75:5 ff.)

[1] נפש . . . אוריה (:5 f.)—In the interpretation of Koh. 3:6, from here through 79:8 (בשטים), the emphasis is on God's punitive justice. It is entirely deserved even though at first it seems over harsh—an avowal of God's justice in history. On the other hand, the question *is* raised.

ורוח הקודש צווחת (76:1 and 77:3; etc.)—The כתובים, including קהלת, were regarded as given by God through the medium of human authors. Hence they can say here that the Holy Spirit cries out, but the first part of the verse is taken as a complaint addressed to God. Turning the verse into a dialogue is an aspect of indeterminacy of belief (RM, pp. 131 ff.), for it means inconsistency as to its authorship. For that reason, there is no need to be specific as to those who complain.

[2] מקום שצידקתים (77:4; 78:1; etc.)—"Where I acted *with love* toward them"—like the interpretation of מצדיקי הרבים (Dan. 12:3) in Sifre on Deut. 11:21, which interprets ומצדיקי as המאהיבים. For צדקה as love, see OT, p. 303.

[3] בדין (77:8)—The judgment after תחיית המתים; but there is also the view that there is דין for רשעים in גיהנם after death, and also גן עדן after death for the righteous (Abot V.19–20).

כתבתי (78:1; 7:)—Book of Job, written by רוח הקודש, but this "writing" means a manifestation of God's love in some definite manner.

מודה . . . נעבדנו כפירה (2:) ויאמרו לאל (see RM, pp. 341 ff. on and כופר)—rebellion against God is not denial of the existence of God, a philosophical principle. Notice that this idea is not only rabbinic but biblical as well (as here in Job).

[4] יד עני ואביון לא החזיקה (79:2)—Ezekiel here (Ezek. 16:49) refers to this as *the* sin of Sodom, not the sin of sodomy, and the midrash therefore accounts it as *another* sin of the Sodomites, a sin especially noteworthy in view of their fabulous prosperity.

[5] . . . במגפה . . . (5:)—In the explanation, the מגפה (Num. 25:9) is taken as punishment for the זנות (ibid, v. 1) and not this time for idolatry, and hence the double punishment. (In v. 5, punishment is for פנצמדים לבעל פעור.)

שצידקתים (6:)—is a manifestation of God's love; it is borne out here in כִּי אֲהֵבְךָ ד' אלהיך, which in Deut. 23:6 are the words which follow ויהפך ד' וגו'.

וצדקה (80:1–2)—Either צדקה is charity (love) or else it is "right-eousness"; the literal meaning is not lost for the Rabbis (CA, pp. 11 f., on צדקה).

[6] נפש (3:)—The rabbinic concept, נפש, is an amorphous concept, i.e., it has different meanings, practically independent of each other. On נפש 68:3 means "life"; נפש in אם נפשך לומר (Ḥul. 78b) means "desire," etc. (see Jastrow, נפש). The meaning of נפש is therefore dependent on the context, that is to say, the word נפש has to be mentioned, for the context without the word is not enough and in this respect it is like a cognitive concept. Yet it is not entirely a cognitive concept for it does not involve sensory perception nor is it a quasi-scientific concept. On the other hand, it is not a value concept either, for it is never imbedded in a statement.

But there is one usage of the word נפש which is related to value concepts. In the midrash here, it has relations with God's justice and with sin. It also has a vague implication of an entity: יוצאה ממקום וכו' (80:4) and (נתונה) במקום משפט but here, there is more emphasis on relations with value concepts. Because of its relation with value concepts, נפש is included in the ambience of the value complex, but only when it is thus related, i.e., when it is a permanent element in the category of significance. (On the category of significance, see RM, pp. 107 ff., 192–3).

במקום משפט (4:)—Refers to the law forbidding דם which is vio-lated, hence שמע הרשע (79:1).

וחוטאת . . . אני כתבתי (5:)—After הדם (6:) the verse continues with: כי הדם הוא הנפש, taken as indicating the special relevance of דם to נפש.

IV.2 (81:1 ff.)

[1] . . . היוצאין מן הוושט . . . (82:1-2)—The idea that the נפש is a bit "larger than its point of exit" indicates that נפש is regarded as an entity—the difficulty of egress implies, apparently, its being loath to leave the body.

[2] . . . לעצמה יְגִיעה . . . (83:1)—"Whatever it achieves by its labor, it achieves for itself." This idea is based on the relation of the נפש to the value concepts; its "subsistence" consists of מצוות ומע״ט (1 f.:) and hence it is never sated with מצוות ומע״ט. (We derived the notion of "subsistence" from שביעה (1:), it hungers for them.)

מלמעלה (4:)—Refers to the constitution of the נפש as being of the same character as that of the angels. See the same use of מלמעלה in Ber. R. 8:11, ed. Theodor, p. 64; also in reference to נפש see our comments on את מן העיליונים וכו' (90:7) below, IV.5[4].

[3] שלשה נוטלין . . . והמלכות (7:)—Reflects a favorable attitude to Rome, as the other instances seem to indicate; heavy taxes were spent by Rome for the public good.

[4] ר' יהושע . . . בשגגה (84:1)—Were it not for the creation of the נפש, all the other things of מעשה בראשית would not have been created. An emphasis on the individual rather than on society.

Apparently the nearest equivalent to נפש is the consciousness of the self, something not to be found in the rest of created things. (Yet I question my statement because it is not applicable to many other ideas here about נפש.)

את יוצאה . . . בשגגה (3:)—Instead of showing itself to be the purpose of creation, the נפש commits sins. No logical connection between not committing sins and being the purpose of creation. The latter is just a way of attaching high status to נפש. Not committing sins is a kind of *noblesse oblige,* an obligation to its high station.

IV.3 (84:4 ff.)

[1] גם . . . חוטא—Three interpretations of Prov. 19:2. In all of them בלא
ידע בלא טוב (84:6; 85:2, 5) means that the שוגג should have been
more careful, and that he is בלא טוב. Of course if he did know, he
is a מזיד, but that is regarded as על אחת כמה וכמה (84:6, etc.),
only an aggravated case.

[2] ר' יוחנן . . . ונדבות מותר (85:6 f.)

Another interpretation of Prov. 19:2—ר' יוחנן interprets גם בלא
דעת (86:2) as referring to חטאת ואשם, brought on שגגות which
are really לא טוב (2:), but not prohibited since he has to bring
them, and he interprets אץ ברגלים חוטא (2:) as referring to him
who always brings נדבות.

Such an attitude indicates a negative attitude to sacrifices, and
reflects the bond between the Rabbis and the prophets. In some
ways the Rabbis are more negative than the prophets, for even
heart-felt offerings make a man a חוטא according to ר' יוחנן. This
is in line with the passage above (73:1; 74:7) which takes the
מנחות as being symbolic.

[3] הה״ד . . . תחטא בשגגה (86:2)

שגגה עושה אותה חטאת . . . (3:)—This is the clearest statement
that שגגה amounts to a חטא. The emphasis on the individual is
here unmistakable: in the Bible, the שוגג brings a sacrifice and is
forgiven (ונסלח לו, Lev. 4:31), but the Rabbis in this passage
declare him to be לא טוב. The stigma remains—the individual is
responsible no matter what the circumstances.

IV.4 (86:4 f.)

[1] משמשין את הנפש (4:)—The purpose of all these things is either to
enable the body to function and thus to sustain the נפש or else to
serve as instruments of the נפש, in either case thus to serve the
נפש.

[2] למעלה מכולם (87:1)—The נפש is above them all, i.e., superior to all of
them, since they but serve the נפש; the נפש is the purpose of the

existence of these things. In all these interpretations of נפש, there is an emphasis on the individual person.

[3] (בשגגה) אמ' לה . . . תחטא (1:)—The superior status of נפש should have kept it from sinning through a kind of *noblesse oblige* as in 84:1. Here, too, as there, there is no logical connection between superior status and not sinning.

IV.5 (87:4 ff.)

[1] עימו . . . תני ר' ישמעאל (88:1 ff.)—According to this famous passage, the נפש and the גוף are equally guilty in sinning; one could not sin without the other. This is not implied in all the midrashim presented here so far.

[2] מחזיר נשמה לגוף וכו' (89:6)—This implies resurrection (תחיית המתים), and hence לעתיד לבא (2:) here refers to the judgment after תחיית המתים. (On תחיית המתים as a dogma, see RM, p. 361 f.)

נשמה (6, 7:)—An alternate for נפש (2, 5:) but only as the latter relates to value concepts.

[3] הה"ד . . . עימו (6 f.:)—The original home of נשמה is heaven (השמים, 7:) and the original home of גוף (90:1) is the earth (הארץ, 89:7).
     After death, apparently, נשמה returns to heaven as גוף does to earth, and hence they have to be brought together again for judgment, and that is implied also in ואחר כך (90:1), an indication of lapse of time.

עימו (1:)—The entire verse is made to refer to the individual, not as in the Bible to the people (עמו, 1:)—emphasis on the individual.

[4] לעתיד לבוא (90:5)—Here the term may refer to the time after the death of the individual for there is no mention of resurrection. The נפש alone is placed in judgment,

העילוונים . . . חוטאין (7:)—עיליונים are the angels dwelling in heaven where there is no sin, but the גוף is of the substance of the beings below on earth, and the earth is the place where there is sin. The very origin of the גוף renders it susceptible to sin and hence less to blame than the נפש—mitigating circumstance. By placing the primary blame on the נפש, the individual person is held responsible, whatever the circumstances. To all intents, the נפש, not the גוף, is the individual self.

IV.6 (91:2 ff.)

[1] 'תני חזקיה . . . יחטא וגו (2:)—Israel is regarded as a corporate entity, so that if one sins, all of them are punished.

'יחטא וגו . . . (3:)—The rest of the words of Num. 16:22 read: ועל כל העדה תקצף, that is to say, all the people are punished; it is not taken as a question. This verse (Num. 16:22) is the proof text, and hence the comment is not an interpretation of נפש כי תֶחֱטָא.

[2] תני ר' שמעון . . . עוונותיך (4:f.)

'משל לבני אדם וכו (4:f.)—The parable is applied here to Job and his friends, the situation makes of them, for the time being, a corporate entity.

מספיק (92:3)—We are partners in your sinning, for we hear you blaspheme and do not refute; when Job sins it is not, as he argues, that he alone sins.

[3] לעבודה זרה (92:5)—עבודה זרה refers both to idol worship and to the idol itself. Its biblical antecedent is אלהים אחרים, but the rabbinic term is distinctly pejorative.

דחיתה בקנה (93:2)—"You pushed him away with a reed." Used frequently by the students who hear the reply of the master to a question by a גוי (e.g., Tan. Ḥukkat, par. 8; Num. R., 19:4). Here, however, the master's reply to the Gentile is in harmony with the one to the students: How can we agree with you when there is no agreement among yourselves? You yourselves differ with regard to your gods.

[4] Because (על ידי, 6:) Esau worshipped אלהות הרבה (6:), his household (נפשות ביתו, 4:) is described as נפשות הרבה (6:) though its members were much fewer than Jacob's, each person apparently worshipping a different deity among the deities of Esau. But

because Jacob did not worship אלהות הרבה his household is described as נפש אחת (7:). Though consisting of 70 members— שבעים נפש (5, 7:)—the 70 are נפש אחת, that is, a single corporate entity.

אלהות הרבה is the equivalent of ע"ז and hence the singular אלוה is not used here as a generic term, a term including God. That is also why the singular cannot be used here to describe what Jacob *did* worship, for that would imply that Jacob worshipped one among many possible gods (see RM, p. 198 f. on generic terms for God). "Monotheism" is not a rabbinic term.

Obviously implied here is that it is the worship of God which makes Israel a corporate entity, a people. Today the idea is advanced that the unity of Israel gave rise to the idea of monotheism; but of course there were so many other peoples who had a sense of unity and were at the same time polytheists.

IV.7 (94:1 f.)

[1] ברכי נפשי את ד' (95:1)—There is an affinity between the נפש and the חומש. Perhaps: the manner in which the נפש praises God is by reciting חומש—ברכי נפשי את ד'. Or: נפש thanks God for the five books of the חומש.

[2] ר' יהושע . . . עוד וגו' (94:2 f.)

כנגד חמשה עולמות . . . (3:)—The נפש ought to praise God on the five occasions when a man "sees" a new stage of his life, a new "world," implying that it is the נפש which is *aware* that there *is* a new stage.

קרבי (4:)—Not really his own but his mother's. Even in the mother's womb, the נפש itself already exists as complete, not a matter of birth and growth.

לעתיד לבוא (95:3)—In which there will be no חטאים and רשעים.

שראה במפלתן של רשעים . . . (5, 6:)—One of the great boons—a reflection of their own oppression.

IV.8 (96:1 ff.)

Related again to נפש in Lev. 4:2. We describe as "related" a midrash which is not an actual interpretation of a word in the סדר but is merely associated with such a word. This form of association is only a little stronger than the association exemplified in פתיחות, each midrash in the latter being completely independent.

[1] These words, מה ראתה נפשו של דוד לקלס להקב״ה, begin a passage frequently regarded as containing the Stoic idea that God is the soul of the world. This view of the passage is not correct. The Stoic idea is pantheism, that is, the world and God are co-existent; here, however, it is stated that הקב״ה מבלה את עולמו (97:2, 4). "God outlives (survives) His world"—the world and God are not co-existent. There is a decided implication, also, that God is beyond the world even when the world exists. In the Stoic outlook a man's soul and the world's Soul or Reason are not two distinct matters, but a man's soul or reason is itself a part of God, a shrine of God. Here, however, the נפש is regarded only as analogous to God and as *distinct* from God, e.g., נפש זו ממלא את הגוף והקב״ה ממלא את כל העולם (96:1, 2); were the נפש a part of God it could not be regarded as analogous to God. But the entire analogy is only an idea in the service of the main idea in this midrash. The main idea involves a value concept, קלוס, found in every analogy given here—why the soul is peculiarly fit to praise God. If the value concept of praise is ignored and the analogy alone considered, the real point of the midrash is lost and the midrash as a whole is misunderstood. Only when the value concepts are reckoned with can we comprehend a midrash.

[2] טהורה בגוף (97:8)—It is the גוף which becomes levitically unclean. Also, the idea that the נפש itself does not become sullied though the man does evil.

Chapter V

V.1 (98:8 ff.)

[1] אם הכהן . . . דייך מאיר (8 f.:)—A statement that God is indifferent and hence a rebuke by the חכמים. But it is curious—no love, no justice!

[2] הולין (99:1)—When the curtain, *velum*, was drawn, the judge no longer saw what went on outside (Lieberman, here, p. 872).

[3] ד״א והוא . . . אחת (99:3–102:4)

The fabulous circumstances and security of the דור המבול (3:) are presented as justifying God's punishment all the more—there was no cause for their sinning; God's justice.

לשלשה ימים . . . ליום אחד . . . (99:5 f.)—Rabbinic folklore. An example of indeterminacy of belief. Notice the differences among the various descriptions.

אמרו . . . מודע לך (100:4 f.)—Like Paul Bunyan stories, obviously folk tales and hence soon lapses into Aramaic, the folk language. The Rabbis' interaction with the folk is expressed, among other ways, in their use of folk tales and, even more strongly, in justifying these tales by means of support from biblical verses. Interaction with the folk, just as is the case with indeterminacy of belief produces a type of thought entirely different from discursive philosophic thought.

[4] כשורה (102:1)—Relates to ישורנו (101:6) (מ״כ). God's justice.

יחד . . . אחת (3:)—יחד (3:) is taken as אחד. גוי is here taken as "nation," i.e., the biblical meaning is not lost for the Rabbis.

V.3 (103:6 ff.)

In the two preceding sections, the Rabbis, by their utilization of extravagant folk tales, reflected the integration of the Rabbis and the folk. The present section reflects their character as, in addition, a distinct group within the people as a whole, an academic, intellectual, educational group of spiritual leaders: they take pains to identify biblical cities; they emphasize God's justice with regard to Israel's position in their own day by a midrashic interpretation from a prophet; they implicitly warn against license and luxurious living; they make a point of emphasizing the individual.

[1] נקובי . . . ומשם ומעבר (104:3)—The Rabbis taught that Israel was among the most ancient peoples.

[2] אומות העולם . . . עשיר (4:)—As against Israel, all the other nations constituted a single collective personality (אוה"ע); *they* could thus boast with men from different nations. Israel counters with its own boast, "Ahitophel was not a wise man?" etc., descends thus to תפלות (5:), frivolity. In this boast, men of poor character are doubtless named deliberately.

[3] עברו . . . מגבולכם (7: f.)—This attempt to identify the biblical cities with those of their own day is a prelude to the Rabbis' interpretation of the next verse as referring to their own day.

[4] המנדים . . . חמס (105:2)—God's justice as prophesied by Amos.

גלות (3:)—A value concept. Often גלות is characterized as "night." Here it refers to the Jewish communities in the Roman Empire, as indicated in the following entry.

ותגישון . . . תכסך (3:)—The present גלות is the result of Israel's past deeds.

[5] השוכבים . . . גולים וגו' (4:-108:1)—License and luxury were the basic cause of גלות; an implicit warning for their own day.

רב . . . זרבוביות (106:3)—Three opinions of scholars—not only descriptions of play and luxury but reflect academic interest in the meaning of מזרק (3:).

מהיכן . . . אנטכטן (5: f.)—These statements are ethical in purpose rather than academic.

נתפתו וגלו (107:1)—This and the preceding "etymology" are midrashic interpretations of names, and notice, not biblical names. This is a kind of "excess function" of midrashic interpretation, but this type, too, has moral bearings.

לכן עתה יגלו . . . (108:1)—The punishment is to be exile, measure for measure, the exile of Rome. A good illustration of how a biblical verse is itself part of the midrash.

[6] נעשה מהן . . . מהו מרזח מהו מרזח (2:)—The luxury indulged in included licentiousness (תיעוב, 4:)—all of one piece. Hence exile was God's justice.

[7] This פתיחה leads directly to verses in the סדר.

God shows favor equally to a צבור (109:6) which has sinned and to an individual (יחיד, 6:) who has sinned, unlike man who shows favor to the צבור but not to the individual. Both the High Priest and the צבור bring the same kind of sacrifice for an unwitting sin—a פר (7, 8:).

Here is a decided emphasis on the individual by the Rabbis. True, the Bible texts themselves prescribe the same kind of sacrifice for the High Priest and the community *but* the Rabbis point this out and hence supply an emphasis *and* the rank of the High Priest is "lost," as it were, when he is spoken of as a יחיד. It is not his preëminence which is the factor in the rabbinic teaching but his being an individual.

The concepts here are: God's love (forgiveness) and justice combined; חטא; קרבן (קדושה).

V.4 (110:1 ff.)

[1] לפי מתנתך מרחיבין לך (3:)—"In accordance with thy gifts, thy (borders) will be enlarged," but the omission of "borders" indicates that the midrashic rendering is directed to the individual everywhere.

לפי מתנתך (3:)—The idea in the verses is generalized and made to refer to צדקה in general, not just to the לוי.

מרחיבין לך (3:)—You will prosper according to the size or amount of your gifts to the needy (צדקה, מתנה). The concepts are צדקה; God's justice.

(3:) ר' הונא . . . מעשה [2]

עבד קודם לרבו (4:)—The larger offering (פר, 3:) of the עבד is sacrificed first. עבד is thus honored by being given precedence over his master—מתנתך מרחיבין לך (3:).

The concept here is כונה. The circumstances of a person indicate how intense is the כונה in bringing the offering. Compare, on the offering by the woman, at 68:1 f. There is no need to reconcile the various rabbinic ideas on כונה, e.g., אחד המרבה ואחד הממעיט ובלבד שיכון לבו לשמים (Men. 110a, Ber. 17a)—circumstances differ.

דתנן . . . מעשה (4:)—Because the sacrifices are equal, that of the High Priest precedes, but if not, the inference is that the larger sacrifice of the עבד precedes.

(6 ff.:) מתן אדם . . . רמויה . . . לו [3]

מתן . . . טומוס . . . לו (6:-113:2)—The concept of God's justice was always in need of concretizations and this was done in stories approaching folk tales, as here.

מצוה (111:1)—צדקה is also a מצוה, i.e., the act is interpreted by both concepts, but so frequent were such acts and so highly esteemed that צדקה was regarded as a מצוה par excellence, and thus מצוה was used in place of צדקה. An ethical act is always grasped by at least two concepts, an ethical concept and the concept of מצוה.

המקום ימלא חסרונך (5:)—Said to a person at loss of property (Ber. 16b; Y.D. 377).

ר' חייה . . . לו וגו' [4]

ולפני גדולים ינחנו (113:2 f.)-וגו' (4:) i.e.,—The Rabbis were aware of their spiritual status. Evidently it was deliberately omitted in 113:2 for there the point is made of divine compensation to אבא יודן, yet he was also honored, והושיבוהו אצלם (1:).

רמאי (114:1)—Two concepts are involved: רמאי חס ושלום לא היה רמוי and צדקה, but רמאי is negated as not really applicable here.

ירחיב לו (3:)—Without וגו' (see [4] above) here, too, man's affluence is regarded as compensation for his frequent generosity.

V.5 (114:4 ff.)

גופא—Interpretation of the סדר directly; no פתיחה.

[1] זה שבנא (4:)—The verse אם הכהן המשיח יחטא (4:) relates only to a solitary instance. It was hardly thinkable to them, apparently, that it could refer to High Priests in general. Why? Because כהנים are קדושים in a higher degree than Israelites and קדושה implies observance of the מצוות; the כהן גדול, by his rank, has the further obligation of *noblesse oblige*. Moreover, יחטא here is taken as sinning not occasionally but steadily, i.e., as characterizing a sinful person, if we are to judge from שבנא.

[2] כהן גדול (5:)-אמרכל' (6:)—An official in charge of the treasuries in the Temple. In either case, the concept of מעילה (diversion of holy things to his own use) could be applied, and is so applied in 117:3 f., below.

[3] וחזקיה וישעיה . . . ר' ברכיה (117:6)—Add treachery (בגידה) to his evil acts.

ויואח (7:)—מהרז"ו calls attention to II Kings 19:2 which mentions שבנא but not יואח, whereas in 18:18 both are mentioned, something which may "indicate" that יואח had defected in the brief interval.

V.6 (118:4 ff.)

[1] דכת' (5:)—דתנן in most manuscripts, referring to Yoma I.1. We shall see in V.7 that the כהן משיח ought properly to be a צדיק. If, instead, he commits sins, as the Bible indicates here, then he should, by bringing a חטאת, at least be free of sin when he is מכפר for the sin of the ציבור.

[2] אם הכהן . . . נפשן (6:)

וכהן משיח חטא (6:)—Said in astonishment. Obviously, it is

assumed that he is, in general, a צַדִּיק—notice how Aaron is characterized as צדיק (Abot deR. Nathan I, ed. Schechter, p. 25) and
there in the well-known description of the High Priest שמעון
הצדיק in Ben Sira. The concept of צדיק is imbedded in the midrash
whereas it is in no way implied in the Bible text.

אמ' ר' לוי . . . נפשן (6:)—Analogies suggest that the ציבור suffers
seriously when the כהן משיח is not a צדיק. The entire function of
the High Priest is impaired.

[3] אש . . . כך אמ' (119:2, 3)—An example of indeterminacy of belief. It
says here that הקב"ה (3:) not only had שבנא (3:) specifically in
mind but that, in this verse, He also stated the manner of his
punishment. All this amounts to saying that this verse is a
prophecy, but was it indeed regarded as a prophecy?

ההקדשות (3:)—But the word קרבנות is used at 117:3. Both parable
and נמשל contain the idea of מדה כנגד מדה.

[4] אכלין . . . אמ' ר' איבו (120:4-3:)—Associated with [3] because of מדה
כנגד מדה (he prevented the dogs from getting the meat that was
theirs). Again a case of trust and the exploitation of that trust.

[5] והביא . . . הפר וגו' (120:5)—Another example of indeterminacy of
belief.

דורון (6:)—a gift, refers to the sacrifice, and קילוסין refers to the
accompanying וידוי, confession of sin. But the sacrifice is a חטאת
and the וידוי, being a confession, is not praise of God. The
midrash, however, changes, as it were, the חטאת into a נדבה, a
gift to God, and the וידוי into קילוסין.
In view of the explicit biblical character of sacrifice as לחטאת
(Lev. 4:3, the preceding verse) the meaning given it in the midrash
must represent indeterminacy of belief.
The midrash is informed by an emphasis on God's love. The
High Priest who has commited a sin is now characterized as a
"lover of God" (אוהבו, 6:) and the new, midrashic view of the
sacrifice as a whole embodies the concept of God's love.

V.7 (120:8 ff.)

[1] סומכין (9:)—וסמכו (8:)—ידיהם . . . וסמכו are supporters, leaders who sustain them.

וסמכו זקני העדה (121:1)—The זקני העדה are the spirtual leaders; סמיכה (i.e., סנהדרין) המיוחדין שבעדה (Sanh. 13b). The actual סמיכה here is done by the three זקנים (ibid.); they are few but sustain the people of Israel. Israel is regarded as having a corporate character in which the virtues of the spiritual leaders endow the people as a whole with virtue. Notice that the midrash does not use the biblical text literally; according to the verse (Lev. 4:15), the סמיכה is על ראש הפר, but the idea of "supporting" as is to be seen from ונפלו סומכי מצרים (120:9) implies bracing from below.

[2] אוה"ע . . . עדה . . . ישראל . . . עדה (2 f.:)—Begins a series in which the same terms are employed as designations of both אוה"ע and Israel, but in dispraise of אוה"ע and in praise of Israel. The effect of the same designations is to make the contrasts all the sharper.

וסמכו זקני העדה (3:)—This is used in the same sense as in [1] above. The virtue with which עדה is endowed, in contrast to חנף (2:) characterizing the עדה of the Nations.

אבירי לב . . . (5:)—It seems to me that אבירי לב is taken as controlling their יצר (לב) in contrast to אבירים which are like cattle.

ואנשים צדיקים (122:2)—There are some individuals also who are צדיקים among the אוה"ע, but the entire people of Israel are צדיקים, i.e., עמך כולם צדיקים (3:).

גבורי כח עושי דברו (5:)—Those who perform מצוות, i.e., Israel. In all such comparisons, it ought to be recognized that any individual member of the אוה"ע can become affiliated with Israel, and so change his "character" completely, through conversion.

V.8 (122:6 ff.)

[1] מה נגדין . . . בוראן (6:)—Only analogies follow this statement—how the people of Israel show that they know how to make themselves

acceptable to God is not told. However, it seems obvious that the statement refers to the תפלה, which begins with praise of God (the first three ברכות), and only then goes on with בקשות. Integration of Haggadah and Halakah.

נגדין (6:) = נַגְרִין (in printed edition)—Artisans, "clever" (מ"כ). Here is another quality of Israel, and thus associated with the preceding passage although no verse is given, and neither is there a comparison with אוה"ע.

[2] ושתי . . . אמ' ר' יודן (7: f.)—This analogy and the subsequent ones as well give instances of cleverness in asking, but they do not throw light on [1] above. Their purpose is to entertain rather than to instruct; they describe amusing situations with which the hearers were familiar and hence would arouse and hold their interest. Because of that, however, they call attention to the point made in [1]. In contrast to [1], however, the "stories" are in Aramaic—reflect folk experience—examples of how the Rabbis were integrated with the folk.

[3] לאו . . . אמ' ר' אחא (123:3 f.)

אית איתתא וכו' (3:)—Must have been intended to catch the interest of the women, speaking as it does of the housewife's experience. As for the application to [1] above, women are also obliged to say the תפלה.

גבך . . . אמ' ר' הוניא (124:2 f.)—This authority addressed himself to the probably large number of tenant farmers in his audience.

[4] עבירות . . . אמ' ר' הוניא דוד (125:6 f.)—This passage on David bears out, we think, what we said about [1] above. Ps. XIX is interpreted as a prayer beginning with praise of God (משרי בקילוס, 6:), and finally going on to בקשות. And it is introduced with a reference to "the good tenant," a story first supplied by the same author who apparently told it after quoting [1].

אמ' . . . השמים . . . הרקיע . . . אתה (7:)—Perhaps: God said to him, "Have you indeed been in the heavens . . . in the firmament?" Else how did David know that they tell of His glory and His handiwork. מספרים is taken to mean actual speech and אין אומר וגו' (v. 4) to refer only to day and night.

שגיאות . . . עבירות (126:2)—David's "cleverness" is expressed not only in first singing praises but extends also to his בקשות—he begins with light sins and ends with grievous ones.

הא שרי והא שביק לך (3, 4:)—A formula indicating forgiveness (compare סלח לנו . . . מחל לנו in the Amidah). So certain are the Rabbis that God always forgives when appealed to for forgiveness that *here* there is interpolated in the text of the Psalm a response by God expressed in the formula for forgiveness. The concepts are: God's love; forgiveness; sin. All this, the pleas and the response are given in Aramaic for the benefit of the folk at large.

[5] ונקיתי . . . רב הוא (5:)—An independent midrash—a different authority ר׳ לוי (6:).

. . . אלֹה (6, 7:)—A generic term which, therefore, includes anything accepted as a deity, as well as God. The Rabbis usually employ appellatives, e.g., הקב״ה, not this generic term, except in discussions with Gentiles. See RM, p. 206 f. Here, evidently to negate the generic quality of the term, two appellatives for God immediately precede: (6:) הקב״ה, רבונו של עולם.

Chapter VI

VI.1 (127:2 ff.)

[1] אילו ישראל (3:)—They are עד חינם (2:).

[2] ואתם עדי וגו׳ (3:)—From the sequel, עדי here means that Israel's function is to acknowledge מלכות שמים.

רֵעַ . . . זה הקב״ה (3:)—רֵעֲךָ בְּ is a term of normal relationship and here it expresses a relationship to God. Other such terms are: "Father," "King," and "Brother." The relationship to God cannot be expressed otherwise than through *various* terms of human relationship—a mystical experience struggling for expression through different terms of normal relationships—normal mysticism. (See RM, pp. 270 f.).

רֵעֲךָ . . . תעזב (4:)—Identifies הקב״ה as רֵעֲךָ.

לסוף . . . לעגל אֵלֶה אלהיך וגו' (5:)—By worshipping ז״ע, Israel is ת״יפ—עד שקר), false to its function as עד. Con-)(2:) עד חנם cept of מלכות שמים negates ע״ז. Concepts embodied are: מלכות שמים; עבודה זרה; ישראל; שקר.

[3] אעשה לו . . . אמ' ר' אחא (6:)—Frequently, as here, refers to divine inspiration of Proverbs and other Books of the Ketubim. Here, however, it is in a context where it speaks to God and is thus distinct, in a manner, from God. This is made possible by virtue of רוה״ק being a concept in itself and thus permitting personifica- tion. That is also true occasionally of מדת הדין and of מדת רחמים. Again, this is possible because of the wide latitude of indetermi- nacy of belief.

[4] ולא איש . . . אמ' ר' פינחס (8:)—This statement is also found below at 139:8 where the phrase עברו ברית (Hos. 6:7) refers, in the rabbinic context there, to the transgression of the covenant at Sinai. Here, however, no such reference is actually given. We take it, therefore, as an interpolation here by the editor who was unhappy at the idea of the preceding statement that God needs to be reminded, as it were, to forgive.

עד חנם (Prov. 24:28) is implied, for ראובן (128:2) is such an עד. First assenting and then refusing to give testimony, he amounts to a "false witness."

VI.2 (128:8 ff.)

הקבלנין (129:1)—Buyers of stolen goods. These were killed where- as the thieves themselves were only flogged.

הרי מן המלכות (130:1)—This is not said in definite approval, but only to indicate that חולק עם גנב שונא נפשו (128:8)—incurs his own death.

שמע קול מכריז (3:)—This impressed the man with the sin he intended to commit.

VI.3 (130:5 ff.)

[1] גופא . . . אמות (5 f.:)—גופא, meaning, the passage interprets the text directly, i.e., no פתיחה. But here, apparently the idea of עד in Lev. 5:1 gives rise to the related matter of שבועת שוא (5:), and שבועה in general (ר' אסי . . . על אמת, 132:1).

[2] אמ' ר' סימון . . . על אמת (131:5)

כך המשביע וכו' (132:1)—He who causes someone to swear in a trumped-up case (לשקר, 1:) will be thus punished. But this is introduced by a statement regarding the swearing in of a person.

[3] דברייתא . . . לא תיעול (135:3)—A folk adage, and there is a Greek equivalent (Lieberman, *Greek in Jewish Palestine*, p. 124). But the entire story is a folk tale and indicates how deeply the folk felt on not swearing, even to the truth.

[4] מלאכי חבלה (5:)—Punitive angels—apparently a group of angels assigned only to the execution of God's justice. Instead of the abstract אָלָה, the midrash has the man punished by the more concrete מלאכי חבלה, a conception familiar to the folk.

אין להן קפיצין (5:)—"They have no joints." "Angels" is a cognitive concept, since the idea involves cognitive concepts as here (joints). *But* it is a cognitive concept employed only as background for, or in behalf of, value concepts—in this case, in behalf of God's justice.

Not having joints, they are always mobile, apparently an indication that they perform their function without tarrying. But when it comes to punishing for a false oath, they not only tarry but stay in the house, implying continuous punishment.

VI.4 (136:4 f.)

[1] והוא עד (6:)—Refers to God. No other עד was there. So also או ראה (7:), and או ידע (7:) refer to God (יפ"ת). Obviously here the idea of God's omniscience is implied but such ideas are not crystalliza-

tions of a person's experience, and hence are not crystallized in a rabbinic conceptual term. These are always tied to what *is* a crystallization of experience, a value concept. Here the idea of God's omniscience is tied to the concept of sin (שחטאה, 5:). See RM, pp. 55, 220.

VI.5 (137:3 ff.)

[1] נפש כי תחטא (3:)—Lev. 5:1 relates in its literal sense to the individual, yet it is interpreted to refer to Israel, in the plural. The verses adduced as prooftexts have plural verbs. No explanation is given for this, nor need there be. This is an indication that the biblical text serves basically as only a stimulus for the rabbinic interpretation—something which, of course, is even more clearly indicated by the fact that the context of Lev. 5:1 is entirely different from the meaning given the verse by the interpretation.

[2] אלה (4:)—According to מהרז״ו, this word acts as a peg for the midrashim which now follow. It is associated with ובאלתו (139:4) of Deut. 29:11, and it relates to the oath regarding the covenant between God and Israel. This association is sufficient to permit a number of midrashim on the covenant to be given here. It seems to me that ואת קולו שמענו (4:) is the prooftext for קול אלה, meaning that what they heard was an אלה, an oath, which made Israel committed to act as witness for God. This idea is made more explicit at 142:1 ff., which continues with the midrash broken off here. What follows now are other midrashim concerning commitment of God to Israel and of Israel to God. Israel's commitment consists in the acknowledgment of מלכות שמים.

[3] אמ׳ ר׳ יצחק . . . צוארו (6:f.)

בסייף (138:1)—The sword acts as a symbol of the punishment of soldiers who break their oath; they will die by the sword. In precisely this way, the blood of the covenant at Sinai acts as a symbol of the punishment of those who break this covenant. This is not stated explicitly but is implied in the analogy of the sword.

[4] ויקח משה . . . ובחלקו (138:2)—A new midrash obviously associated

with [3] above. The blood was divided *exactly* in half. This is
emphasized by all the opinions here, apparently implying that
the responsibility for the covenant was to be on both parties
equally.

מעשה ניסים (3:)—But most of the solu-
tions were likewise ניסים. This one is described as מעשה ניסים
because it was visible, whereas others were not. נס here is what we
call "supernatural," miraculous.

בת קול (4:)—The בת קול often pronounces a decision. It is not
רוח הקודש, for it is seldom reckoned with in Halakah (see RM,
p. 261 f.) מלאך (5:)—The angel's function here is that of a
messenger of God, as always. In other words, the division of the
blood was a נס in this opinion too, an angel used in connection
with a value concept.

בקי היה משה (6:)—See רד"ל. This is to indicate that it was *not* a
נס. Moses is ח"ת.

[5] אמ' לפניו וכו' (7:)—The midrash insists that the covenant was an iron
clad, perfect commitment on both sides, hence the need for the
perfect division of the blood. That is why באגנת (7:) is interpreted
so as to convey the idea of a perfect division. The notion of the
covenant is, of course, biblical but it has been made more pointed
in the midrash.

[6] ר' ברכיה . . . האלה (139:2)

הוא נשבע להן והן נשבעו לו וכו' (3 f.:)—In Exodus 24, which tells
of the ברית at Sinai, there is no mention of oaths; still, the association of oath and covenant is not in itself solely rabbinic. The
midrash refers here to Ezek. 16:8 (4:) and Deut. 29:11 although, as
the midrash recognizes, the former refers only to an oath by God,
and the latter, to one by Israel. What the midrash does is not only
to present the idea of a blood covenant at Sinai, as does Exodus 24,
but as a covenant accompanied by oaths, an ironclad covenant.

אמ' ר' פינחס . . . ולא איש (8:)—The contrast is made between
Israel who are men and therefore prone to break the covenant, and
God who nevertheless did not reject them. God will not break His

covenant entirely. ברם הכא (8:) evidently relates, therefore, to this retention of the covenant by God. The concepts here are: God's love and forgiveness.

In view of the fact that the Bible itself thus declares that God will retain His covenant despite Israel's defection, what is the Rabbis' contribution to the idea? They here make the Covenant at Sinai a central matter, adding the idea that the covenant was reinforced by oaths and identifying it as the covenant which God retains. Perhaps there is here a polemical element, for the Covenant at Sinai was never repudiated by God despite Israel's defections. There is all the more reason to regard this construction by the Rabbis as polemical since, in·the prayers, other covenants are invoked, e.g., ברית אבות and ברית י״ג מידות.

[7] ביצע אמרתו (140:2)—Compare Lam. 2:7, ביצע אמרתו, the literal meaning of which is כלה גזרתו (according to Rashi and Ibn Ezra). But here it is taken to imply "compromise, not full punishment," and thus altogether softened, reflecting the Rabbis' emphasis on God's love.

[8] ר' יעקב . . . פרפריה (140:3)—God tore His purple robe. Another interpretation, saying that when He carried out His decree, He mourned like an אבל. An even stronger emphasis on God's love, though combined with His justice.

[9] כיון דאתו . . . ואין קובר (141:4 f.)—Associated with the previous midrashim. These men did not break the Covenant at Sinai and were ready to die to maintain it. Also mentions הדם שבסיני (8:).

אמ' להון . . . מבור (7:)—God tells these men that He recalls the Covenant at Sinai and will now redeem the exiles in Babylon. The act of the three men apparently recalled the covenant to God, and thus brought about the redemption from the exile. The redemption was a manifestation of God's love; the saving of the three men was an act of God's justice and love combined.

[10] אלהותי (142:4)—My Godhood = My Kingship, if our interpretation is correct. But how can מלכות שמים be told to others? When Israel, during the exile, is challenged by being told to worship pagan deities by the אומות, then they (Israel) accept upon themselves

instead מ"ש, in the hearing of the אומות. Notice that here the
אומות themselves do not make an acknowledgement of any kind
on their part; that is done only when there is קדוש השם in relation
to an individual Gentile (see e.g., WE, p. 133).

VI.6 (142:6 ff.).

[1] אמ' ר' סימון . . . וחבירו (6:)—Why were those two verses attributed, in
this midrash, to בארי or בארה? In I Chron. 5:6 it is said that בארה
was exiled by תלגת פלנאסר, King of Assyria. His message, therefore, is relevant to Israel in exile (see Rashi to Isa. 8:19).

רבנן אמרין בין . . . אבי נביא (143:6 f.)—Even if the father's name
is not mentioned, he was also a prophet. Prophecy was not an
ephemeral phenomenon in Israel—always a matter of two generations, almost a matter of inheritance, inherent in Israel.

[2] כל אומה (144:3)—Let each nation worship its own god. The pagan
nations will worship idols, dead, inert things. Only Israel worships a living God.

אמ' ר' לוי . . . ולא ישמעו (4:f.)—The helplessness, the futility of
the idols is emphasized by a parable, in contrast to the everliving
God.

עולם (145:2)—Refers as in the פשט to time, since the statement
preceding it is חי וקיים לעולמי עולמים. But העולם (3:) and שבעולם
(144:6) refer to "world."

מתים . . . למתים (4:)—A direct answer to the nations. Since
the idols are worshipped, the Rabbis feel that the pagans themselves regard them as deities—the same view as that of the
prophets; see Y. Kaufmann.

[3] The word התורה (5:) indicates that the warning refers to a statement
in the Pentateuch.

שחר (7:)—The גאולה. Israel will not be redeemed if it will not
fulfill its function (to be a witness for God).

שלרומי (146:4)—Rome and Egypt are often related. Here Rome
will be punished more severely than Egypt.

רבנן . . . יִזְרַח ה' (5:)—Evidently refers to the ימות המש׳, regarded here as reward for practicing Torah.

Chapter VII

VII.1 (147:2 ff.)

[1] כבושה (5:)—Suppressed. Not spoken of until Ezekiel. Israel worshipped idols in Egypt and did not give them up even at God's
command (Ezek. 20:7-8). שנאה (5:) means an "estrangement"
rather than hate. When Israel worshipped idols, they and God
were estranged, and this estrangement was hidden from later
generations.

שלא יתחלל . . . בתוכם (148:1)—The reason Israel was not destroyed is plainly given: it would be חלול השם (Ezek. 20:8-9). It
was not due to God's love.

תכסה אהבה (2:)—God's love "covered," i.e., hid, the sin of idolatry. It was not mentioned for close to 900 years (see also מהרז״ו).
Ezekiel's exposure of a grave sin by Israel in the past is made the
occasion to emphasize God's love. The sin was hidden until
Ezekiel exposed it.

[2] ממש . . . אמ' ר' אסי (5:)—After ממש (6:) add the statement found in
the printed editions (Margulies, in his apparatus): מוטב היה להן
שידונו שוגגין ואל ידונו מזידים.

מזידים . . . שוגגין—Better for them to have been judged as שוגגין,
inadvertent sinners. The worship of the Golden Calf was עבודה
זרה, and the statement implies that those who regard an idol as
having efficacy are only inadvertent sinners (שוגגין). The Nations
who worship ע״ז are thus only שוגגין, in line with the opinion of
ר' יוחנן (Ḥul. 13b) that the Gentiles outside of the land of Israel
are not idol worshippers, for they only follow the practice of their
fathers. By reckoning with the concept of ע״ז involved in our text,
we become aware of the implications of the text.

מי אשר חטא (6:)—Refers to an individual, Aaron (see מ"כ), whereas in the Bible it refers to the sinners of the people. The change from the biblical to the rabbinic is made possible by the greater emphasis on the individual in rabbinic literature.

[3] תפילה שהתפלל משה (149:3)—If this can be generalized, praying for another person is an evidence of love—אהבה (3:).

[4] מתחילת . . . באר . . . לאמר (4:f.)—If the sons of Aaron are found worthy to officiate, how can their father be rejected? An application of זכות בנים.

כדתנן . . . גפן (7:f.)—The olive and the vine are not to be used for the מערכה, not burned. The reason given here is that oil and wine are offered on the altar, an analogy of זכות בנים. In Tamid 29b the reason given is ישוב ארץ ישראל. The concept here is דרך ארץ, a phase of which is practical wisdom, and it is combined with the concept of קדושה (ארץ ישראל). This is an example of how there may be different opinions even though in both the law is the same, the opinions differing with respect to the concepts embodied in the law.

שבתפילתך (150:2)—The תפילה of Moses had efficacy beyond the argument embodying the idea of זכות בנים. Aaron was to be primary and his children secondary. The plea in the תפילה is larger than the content.

VII.2 (150:4 ff.)

[1] זבחי . . . שלתורה . . . נשברה (4:f.).

בתשובה (5:)—There is no תשובה for a past misdeed without רוח נשברה (151:1). The sin was his misconduct with Bathsheba to which Ps. 51:2 alludes.

אם מקבלני וכו' (5:)—David hopes that his רוח נשברה will be accepted as a sacrifice. If he becomes aware that it is accepted, and hence his תשובה is accepted, then he will know that his son Solomon will build the Temple and offer sacrifices. All this is derived from Ps. 51:19–21, although only verse 19 is quoted. The awareness that his תשובה is accepted is not a kind of omen. What we have here is the idea of corporate personality; David and Solomon are not two separate entities but a single corporate personality. David's reconciliation with God enables that personality to be worthy to build the Temple and engage in the sacrificial offerings.

But the connection between David's תשובה and Solomon's building the Temple and offering the sacrifices in it is not an arbitrary one in another respect as well: a רוח נשברה is itself a sacrifice, as indicated in Ps. 51:19 and hence David's תשובה is of a piece with what was achieved by Solomon (see [2] below here).

[2] אוחרן ... נשברה (151:1)—The connection between תשובה and Temple sacrifice becomes more evident when it is not a matter of corporate personality but of any individual. A person who does תשובה is regarded as though he had offered up all the sacrifices. That is, רוח נשברה is, as it were, the sum of all the offerings, and this implies that the offerings involve, just like the רוח נשברה, the person himself. This idea is already adumbrated in the biblical text itself, Ps. 51:19. The rabbinic interpretation, however, identifies רוח נשברה with תשובה.

ורבנן ... נשברה (4 f.:)—Only in the old Palestinian version does the ברכה itself suggest that after the עבודה there is "bowing" (לשוח, 5:).

[3] אמ׳ ר׳ אבא . . . תבזה (152:1)—In this midrash a demarcation is made between a man himself and a sacrifice, whereas in the other passages the connection between them is implied. That is why only the second half of Ps. 51:19 is given as proof here.

כלי תשמישיו שבורין (4:)—The "vessel" that God uses is the person in regard to whom God's love is especially evident. Were these persons not broken-hearted, etc., they would not be in this crucial need of Him.

[4] וכליל . . . אמ׳ ר׳ אבא (7 f.:)—שכיבדו (7:); כיבדתי (8:); מכבדך (153:1)— emphasizing that the sacrifices are to honor God and not that God needs them.

VII.3 (153:5 ff.)

[1] הרהור הלב (5:)—A sinful thought. Interpreting: זאת תורת העולה היא העולה (Lev. 6:12) which is taken to mean that the "law of העולה" concerns the sacrifice which is to atone for an unexpressed wrong or sinful thought (יפ״ת). To be sure, no sin has actually been committed, and hence an עולה is not actually a sin-offering, but it amounts to a sin-offering. A man is held responsible even for unuttered thoughts—הרהור הלב.

הרהור הלב (5:)—Is a value concept for it takes on meaning as it combines with value concepts, e.g., blasphemy *in the heart*, as in the possibility that Job's sons did so (155:2).

The rabbinic value complex has a much greater range than the biblical antecedents; it interprets matters the Bible leaves uninterpreted, as in the case of some sacrifices. The Bible, for example, does not say what is the function of the עולה, but the midrash here does give it a function. (Elsewhere the Rabbis give a different function to the daily communal עולה). Similarly, the components of the meal-offering are interpreted symbolically, whereas the offering is not given a "meaning" in the Bible.

[2] והלכו . . . ר' תנחום . . . מאיר (154:1)—The משתה (1:) was an innocent occasion, according to both authorities, not licentious (ידי משה). Apparently to emphasize the point that it was not for actual misconduct that Job offered up עולות.

. . . מהו ויקדשם (3:)—Notice that התקדשו למחר (Num. 11:18) (5:), the verse in support of the opinion of ר' מאיר, is not given a rabbinic interpretation but is in consonance with the פשט (comp. the new J.P.S. translation). The literal meaning is not lost for the Rabbis (see CA, pp. 9 f.). On the other hand, no verse at all is given for the opinion of ר' תנחום—the phrase שקידשו להן נשים (6:) is a purely rabbinic use of קדש (betrothed). Where a rabbinic idea can be conveyed by a word in the biblical text, there is hardly any use for another supporting verse.

[3] ר' אחא . . . אתם (155:3 f.)—Study here is a surrogate for the actual offering of the sacrifices—כאילו אתם מקריבין אותם (5:). It implies that study and experience in this case are not two separate things;

תלמוד תורה is often the mind-set which is present also when the things studied are practical. A kindred idea is the efficacy of Torah, a phase of the study of Torah, teaching that study has an immediate, but not an inevitable effect on conduct (see OT, pp. 68 ff.). An element of universality is contained in this midrash. The actual observance of the laws of the sacrifices is possible only in the Temple in Jerusalem, whereas the study of the laws, which is the surrogate, can take place anywhere in the world.

[4] בבבל . . . וכי יש קמיצה (156:3)—The contrast between the particular locality which characterizes observance of these laws and the universality characteristic of their study is most noticeable here. In these midrashim תלמוד תורה emerges as a concept with a universalistic connotation.

[5] בטהורין . . . איסי ר' אמ' (6:)—Once more, study of the laws of the sacrifices is tantamount to practicing them but the sacrifices are "pure," קרבנות טהורין (7:), that is, require observance of the laws of ritual purity. Since the children are pure, their study of the laws of the sacrifices is thus tantamount to practicing them. Hence in the absence of the Temple, sacrifices are still offered, in a sense, and properly offered.

But טהורין (7:) in the case of children refers to ethical purity, whereas in regard to the sacrifices, it refers to ritual purity. In this midrash, therefore, there is a link between the ethical and the ritual. Indeed, the assumption of a demarcation between the ceremonial and the external on the one hand, and the ethical and the inward on the other is not justified. He who brings any kind of sacrifice for a sin must first have repented and he utters a confession at the sacrifice in which he acknowledges the specific sin and avows he had repented (see Maimonides, Hilkot Ma'aseh ha-Ḳorbanot III:14–15; see also OT, pp. 102 ff.)

VII.4 (157:1 ff.)

[1] יותר . . . אלא . . . ברכיה ר' (1:)—We have pointed out a number of times that a parable is never a complete analogy. This is, obviously, also the case here where the point made is simply that

while God was pleased with the offering of Noah, He is still more pleased with Israel's offerings. Still, the analogy of the king who so enjoyed especially the dish prepared by the second of the cooks more than implies that the offerings are given, in some sense, for God's enjoyment. This runs counter to a number of passages which emphasize that the offerings are pleasing to God only indirectly, that He really has no need of them, that they are for man's sake. Such passages teach the idea of God's otherness, an idea found in many different contexts as well. (See the entire section in RM on "The Otherness of God," pp. 303 ff.)

[2] עבודה זרה בעולם (158:5)—As in the days of both Noah and Abel, all offerings will be brought only to God (see מ"כ). So long as there is ע"ז in the world, not even Israel's offerings are completely pleasing to God; בעולם, "in the world," is the rabbinic usage of עולם; apparently עולם (3:) in Isa. 54:9 is also taken as "world," the new world of Noah (see מהרז"ו). The new rabbinic usage of the word is indicative of the rabbinic emphasis on universalism; the biblical meaning refers to time only. עולם in rabbinic usage is a noun (note בעולם), not a modifier.

VII.5 (159:4 f.)

[1] ואש . . . באש (4:)—The מזבח itself was on fire, and it was this fire of the מזבח which consumed the offering, so that the consumption of the offering was a נס.

The מזבח is קדושה, belonging to God. What looked like a human institution—the offering of the sacrifices on the altar—was only apparently so.

[2] תנא . . . היה בו (5: f.)—The wooden altar with its very thin layer of copper could not have remained entirely intact for so long without a נס.

VII.6 (161:1 ff.)

[1] Those who are arrogant, exalt themselves, are punished by fire. This is followed by examples—מי שמתגאה וכ' (1:). The concepts are מדת הדין and גאוה.

[2] סדומיים (161:5)—שנתגאו (162:1) here means a feeling of superiority to the rest of mankind and thus brutal on principle, as it were.

מלכות הרשעה (163:2)—Rome; Ps. 73:25 taken in a negative manner.

[3] בתוכה . . . אבל ישראל (4:)—

נבזין (5:)—by others, ושפלים (5:)—in their own eyes, do not exalt themselves. Otherwise, no contrast is made between them and those who do.

Chapter VIII

VIII.1 (164:2 ff.).

[1] לזו . . . זה קרבן (164:2-167:1)—The פתיחה begins with the different answer given the Roman lady, according to ר' ברכיה (167:1) and [1] is thus associated with that answer.

יפה תורתכם (166:2)—Apparently only a semi-proselyte, for she (the Roman lady) says תורתכם, even though she speaks of God as הקב"ה (165:1). She has recognized that God indeed completed creation in six days as the Torah says and that, after the appearance of man on the sixth day, God's work has been that of ומזויג זיווגים (165:3).

קשה . . . (3:)—The כקריעת ים סוף (166:3 f.)- אם קלה . . . זה לזו joining of couples in marriage is a נס, as difficult a one as splitting the Red Sea; that is why it can be done only by God.

דכתיב . . . (4:)—Ps. 68:7 is rendered to mean: God takes a single man and a single woman (יחידים, 4:) and settles them in a home *volens nolens* (that is the force of מוציא אסירים, 4:).

בכושרות (5:)—Rendered as בכו and שירות; some weeping (unhappy) and some singing (happy). This refers to before the marriage, probably as מה . . . זו לזו (5: f.) seems to indicate.

[2] ירים . . . אמ' ר' ברכיה (167:1)—God's occupation now is to dispense justice to every man (אלהים שופט, 3:). This is made vivid by the figure that He is engaged in making ladders so that one man is made to go down and another to rise. An emphasis on the individual which is already found in the verse itself (זה ישפיל וזה ירים, 3:), but now is made more vivid by the figure.

[3] זה בלשון (4:)—The word זה indicates a relationship between two matters. It is used in connection with the sin of the golden calf and it is used in connection with the half-shekel (Exod. 30:13) which was כפרה, atonement for sin. Hence, in the one case the word זה refers to the occasion when Israel descended to a low state (הושפלו, 4:) and in the other, to their being lifted up from that state (הוגבהו, 5:).

זה יתנו . . . הפקודים (Exod. 30:13) (5:)—The מצוה of the half-shekel atoned for the sin of the golden calf. The idea that the half-shekel was a כפרה for the עגל is rabbinic. It is an example of the rabbinic emphasis on God's love, for it is only the Rabbis who thus teach that Israel is permitted to atone for that grave sin. The concept of כפרה is, then, combined here with the concept of מדת רחמים. But this midrash is also an example of indeterminacy of belief since the biblical reason for the half-shekel is plainly given as ונתנו איש כפר נפשו לה' בפקד אתם ולא יהיה בהם נגף בפקד אתם (Exod. 30:12). In the face of this statement, the divergent application of the idea of כפרה in the midrash can only be characterized as an example of indeterminacy of belief. The conceptual term itself, כפרה, is rabbinic and the concept is thus of wider range than its biblical antecedents, even applied to human beings, e.g., Nega'im II.1 (בני ישראל אני כפרתן).

[4] זה קרבן אהרון וגו' (168:1)—Aaron's קרבן is כפרה for his making the calf. This is purely rabbinic and once more an example of the rabbinic emphasis on God's love, for no hint of any such statement is in the Bible. It is also another example of the Rabbis giving a function to a sacrifice to which no explicit purpose has been assigned in the Bible.

VIII.2 (168:2 f.)

[1] אשתאל . . . ר' יהודה (5:) - רוח הקדש (6:)—All three interpretations of
רוח ה' (4:) teach that רוח הקדש inspires Samson with physical
prowess, a singular use of the term, and this is also true, obviously,
of רוח ה'. But the rabbinic interpretations make of Samson a
figure of utter fantasy, implying a being of unimaginable dimen-
sions, whereas רוח ה' (see verses quoted in 169:3, 4, 5) endows him
only with marvelous strength. In the rabbinic interpretations רוח
הקדש is itself the power, and Samson, no more than a figure
exemplifying that power. The emphasis is entirely on the concept;
Samson is less than incidental.

[2] ובניו . . . כך אהרון (169:10)—This statement relates to the demarcation
between the priests and the people. This demarcation was challenged by a contrary tradition in which there was an attempt to
extend the holiness of the priests to all Israel, a tradition which
had its roots in the Bible. (See WE, p. 222 f. and the notes.) The
statement here does not refer to that tradition, but it does recognize
that the demarcation between the priests and the people is not
complete. Here, however, the awareness is that there is a point
where priests are like the people rather than the other way around.
This point itself is a biblical datum and the midrash only elicits
the implication of that datum.

VIII.3 (170:1 ff.)

[1] גופה (1:)—This word usually indicates, in Leviticus Rabbah, that the
rabbinic interpretation deals directly, i.e., without a פתיחה, with
a verse in the lection read. Here, however, that verse is interpreted
only in the midrash beginning at 170:7 which closes a passage in
the offerings of the נשיאים. Apparently, that passage was originally a series of interpretations on Num. 7:17, for the word כן
(= כאן) "here," in lines 5 and 7, refers to that verse. That series
constituted a unit, and it is to the last interpretation of the series
that the word גופה refers.

[2] אהרן . . . אמ' ר' אידי (1:)

מתאוה (1:)—Should read מתאוה היה. But why did David desire to bring the same sort of offering as the נשיאים brought (לקרבן נשיאים, 1:)? Because the offering of the נשיאים was made on the occasion of the dedication of the altar of the Tabernacle, i.e., on the occasion of the dedication of the Tabernacle, and it was David's great desire to build the Temple, as we know from II Sam. 7:25. To be allowed to bring that offering implied therefore that he was to be allowed to build the Temple. Two different hierarchies of קדושה are here implicated in each other—the hierarchy of sacrifices and the hierarchy of areas (the משכן), hierarchies that in general are related to each other. The concepts here are: הודאה (4:); נשיאים ישראל (4:); ישראל (4:); קרבן, קדושה (4:); ישראל (שריה, 4:). No concept is emphasized above the others.

קרבנן, קדושה (6:)—The concepts here are: ר' נחמיה א' . . . קרבן (6:); ישראל (נשיאים, 6:); and the concept of Torah concretized in כשני לוחות הברית (6:). Here (7:f.) the concept of קדושה is embodied both in קרבן אהרן (8:) and in של נשיאים (8:). What distinguishes them is that the former also embodies the concept of כהונה and the latter, the concept of Israel. On the surface, then, this is an instance in which the concept of כהונה (אהרן, 8:) and the concept of Israel (של נשיאים, 8:) are equally emphasized, but this is only apparently so.

Why should the midrash have said that Aaron's sacrifice was as precious as that of the נשיאים? Why not the other way around? In both, the common factor is the offering brought, but that of the נשיאים was very costly and Aaron's, the offering of a poor man, מנחה. In this midrash, therefore, כהונה is really emphasized above the concept of Israel. What is offered by Aaron is as precious as that of the נשיאים, even though not comparable in cost, only because he embodies the concept of כהונה.

VIII.4 (171:4)

[1] . . . כמה חס המקום על ממונם (172:1)—God has consideration for the property of Israel. An individual is not to bring a voluntary sacrifice beyond his means.

Two concepts are involved here. It is the concept of נדבה that prompts an individual to bring a voluntary sacrifice but מדת רחמים (חס המקום, 1:) assures him (by means of biblical verses) that the נדבה is completely fulfilled through less costly offerings if these alone are within his means.

This idea is not contradicted by the concept of הדור מצוה, a subconcept of כונה. The concept of הדור מצוה teaches that a man should make a lovely סוכה, get a lovely לולב, lovely תפלין, etc., though they cost considerably more than others which are less beautiful. But these objects remain the property of the individual, whereas any sacrifice represents monetary loss.

לא מצא . . . (172:2, 3, 4)—If he cannot afford the more costly sacrifice (see ת״פי). This idea is not expressed in the texts quoted, but is injected by the midrash. It makes of the biblical verse thus introduced an example of how God has consideration for the property of Israel, and the verse in this rabbinic interpretation is now indicative of God's love. Because this idea is added to the verse, we have a rabbinic emphasis on God's love. But the idea is adumbrated, perhaps more so, in the mandatory sacrifice described in Lev. 5:7, 11. There, the idea is undoubtedly the basis for the midrash here.

בערב . . . ולא עוד (5:)—The כהן גדול brought half an עשרון in the morning and half in the evening (Menaḥot IV.5). This offering, too, is seen as an example of God's consideration for the property of Israel, for He accepts even half an עשרון (ת״יפ).

The daily offering of the כהן גדול is accounted to him as though it were the daily offering of the whole world, an acknowledgment and exaltation of God's name by the Nations everywhere. The idea here is an example of the rabbinic emphasis on universalism (Simon Greenberg). Furthermore, this is another example of how the Rabbis seek to find reasons for the offerings, some of which we noticed before.

Chapter IX

IX.1 (173:2 ff.)

[1] ר' הונא . . . יכבדני (3:)—It is the one who brings a תודה, a thanks offering who honors God, not one who brings a חטאת or an אשם, both of which are mandatory and brought for sins. This is not only a characterization of תודה, but what amounts to an explanation of the rabbinic ברכה, except that a ברכה mentions the specific occasion of gratitude. Rabbinic worship consists largely of ברכות and hence it may be said that Rabbinic worship is a development out of the biblical תודה.

It is a development because the rabbinic concept of ברכה is of much wider range than the biblical תודה and is therefore far more applicable. The תודה was brought, apparently, for a spectacular act of goodness by God, as can be seen from Ps. 107:22. ברכות, however, are said out of gratitude not only for the rare or spectacular benefits but for the many daily occasions felt to be manifestations of מדת רחמים, such as the eating of a morsel of bread and numerous other "commonplace" matters, the commonplace now made significant by a ברכה.

[2] ר' יודן . . . עולם הבא (4:)

. . . יכבדני (4:)—The addition of another נ implies not only בעוה"ז (5:) but also העוה"ב (5:). Apparently the reading should be יכבדני בעוה"ב, as in two Mss., "he will also honor Me in עוה"ב," for nothing but a תודה will be offered in the future (ידי משה). Perhaps, however, יכבדני בעוה"ב does not refer to a sacrifice at all but simply indicates that he who offered a תודה בעוה"ז will be present in עוה"ב. Cf. p. 185, lines 6 f.

[3] זבח יצרו (6:)—יצר with a genitive as here usually stands for יצר הרע. עכן with his confession, involving as it did repentance, "killed" his יצר הרע, the impulse that had prompted his evil acts.

כתודה (6:)—Should read as in the variants: בתודה, and תודה = ודוי, "confession."

שים נא כבוד (6:)—Hence יכבדנני (6:). By his confession, he gave glory to God. תודה in Josh. 7:17 is confession, הודאה, as in the Targum.

ושם דרך . . . לשבים (174:1)—He showed the way to repentant sinners by confessing (see Sanh. VI.2). שבים in the sense of repentant sinner is rabbinic, and so is the noun form, תשובה, as meaning repentance. All this indicates that the idea played a much larger role in rabbinic life and literature than in the Bible. In fact, repentance was actually institutionalized in the עשרת ימי תשובה. Confession is an expression of the emotion of repentance.

[4] . . . עכן אלא מלמד שאף . . . (175:1)—By including עכן in a list containing Abraham, Joseph and Moses, the purifying power of תשובה is demonstrated; עכן is now as worthy as they are.

אראנו . . . לעולם הבא (2:)—This is a remarkable instance of the rabbinic emphasis on God's love. The words יעכרך ה' ביום הזה (Josh. 7:25) express in their literal meaning unmitigated condemnation, but the midrash (and other sources) interpret them to convey an assurance of life in the עוה"ב.

IX.2 (175:4 ff.)

[1] דרכים . . . ד"א (4:)—The מסקלי דרכים (4:) remove the stones from the roads and hence they "make" the roads (ושם דרך, 4:). אראנו בישע אלהים, the words in Ps. 50:23 which follow (but are not quoted here) indicate that these public benefactors will inherit עוה"ב. Though the clause is not quoted, it is implied here and in the other midrashim in this section.

מ"כ characterizes this act as גמילות חסד לרבים. The concept גמילות חסדים refers to an act of kindness done by one person to another and here it is likewise personal kindness to each traveller on the road. The concept of God's justice is implied in the sequel of the verse quoted here and in other midrashim.

[2] באמונה . . . ד"א (4:)—The commentators explan that these teachers of children open "the way of life" for the children. But it seems to us that the midrash may be explained in another fashion. Perhaps

the words ושם דרך (4:) are taken as ותם דרך (cf. Prov. 13:6), "the upright in the way." The teachers of children, who teach באמונה (5:) are thus characterized as "upright." The concept of אמונה here connotes faithfulness, honesty.

ד"א . . . לרבים (5:)—Here as well ושם דרך (5:) may have been taken as ותם דרך. The storekeepers (not wholesalers) who are careful to sell only products that are tithed are characterized as "upright." The concepts are: מצוה and אמונה.

[3] אמ' ר' שמעון . . . לרבים (176:1)—The concept here is זכות אבות. Saul was rewarded by being made king for acts done by his grandfather. Involved is the idea of corporate personality. (Cf. CA, pp. 47, 101, 225.)

אמרו . . . לרבים (2:)—Not only is גמילות חסדים embodied here but there is also the concept of תפלה (לבית הכנסת, 2:).

IX.3 (176:6 ff.)

[1] מעשה בר' ינייי . . . שוי (176:6–179:1)

בדקו . . . ולא מצאו (177:2)—He did not know any תורה. The concept of תלמוד תורה.

בריך . . . בבייתיה (4:)—He did not know ברכת המזון. The concept of ברכה.

[2] דרך ארץ . . . סגי שוי (178:5)—דרך ארץ here is obviously ethical conduct and refers specifically to no לשון הרע and to שלום. דרך ארץ is set off against תלמוד תורה and ברכה and is here regarded as at least of equal worth, since it gives a man great worth (סגי שוי, 179:1).

[3] עשרים וששה דורות (179:1)—From Adam to Moses, the world existed by means of ד"א alone. (For a discussion of דרך ארץ, see WE, pp. 39 ff.)

קדמה (1:)—Implied is not that ד"א is more important than Torah, but that a necessary basis for Torah is ד"א. Nevertheless, it is an emphasis on ד"א for it is conceived as existing without Torah.

[4] לנו . . . אראנו (3:)—The idea here can be understood only in the light of the idea that God shares, as it were, the afflictions and exile of Israel, and hence when He redeems them, He also redeems Himself. The emphasis is on God's love.

IX.4 (179:5 f.)

[1] ביתו לכבדו . . . (5:)—The parable, as usual, is not entirely in accord with the application. The king's attendants and servitors wish to honor him, whereas that is not the reason for those who bring a חטאת or אשם. These are prescribed duties.

כך חטאת . . . חטא (180:3)—Preceding the laws of the תודה are the laws governing the חטאת and the אשם.

[2] אם על תודה יקריבנו (3:)—God's nearness is an experience that is basic to normal mysticism, mystical experience which expresses itself through the concepts of תלמוד תורה, תשובה, ברכה, תפלה. In itself, however, God's nearness remains unconceptualized in normal mysticism, although it is conceptualized in the Haggadah in the concept of גלוי שכינה. This midrash indicates that God's nearness was regarded as a gift from God and thus an expression of God's love. To be sure, here it is described as a reward, but notice that this reward comes when a man offers a תודה, an offering, which already implies a vivid sense of a relationship to God. יקריבנו (4:), in this rabbinic interpretation, *may* therefore refer to the reward of גלוי שכינה, but in any case, the experience of normal mysticism involved in an ardent apprehension of God's love was there at the beginning.

The change in יקריבנו from its literal meaning of simply "bringing an offering" to its rabbinic meaning involving God's nearness is indicative of the emphasis on the inward life in rabbinic thought. On the other hand, the very presence of a concept like תודה indicates also that this inward life was certainly foreshadowed in the Bible. The radical change in the meaning of יקריבנו as referring to God and not to man indicates that a rabbinic concept has been called into play; that concept is גלוי שכינה. In the case of a חטאת or אשם, since they are brought for a sin, there is no גלוי שכינה, whereas there is ג"ש when a תודה is brought and

a man then has a visual experience of God's nearness to him
(יקריבנו). As in all rabbinic concepts, the roots are biblical (see
RM, pp. 259 f.). Indeed, while the conceptual term ג"ש is not
biblical, what the Bible refers to are really instances of ג"ש.

גלוי שכינה is not really a *reward* for a תודה; the very idea of a
תודה is that of a free will offering not undertaken for a reward.
Rather, ג"ש is the assurance that the תודה has been accepted by
God. Such acceptance is not experienced in the case of a sin
offering. In normal mysticism, where there is no ג"ש—and this
takes in practically all of rabbinic experience—the experience of
God's nearness is not conceptualized in itself. Nevertheless, it is
basic in normal mysticism where it is an experience involving
other concepts. Thus, whereas ג"ש, though vivid, is at best occasional, in normal mysticism the experience of God's nearness is
steady and, so to say, constant.

IX.5 (180:5 f.)

IX.6 (182:1 ff.)

[1] בני נח (:1) is a term for all mankind, including Israel before there was
מתן תורה, through the giving of the Ten Commandments.

שלמים (:1)—Part of the שלמים was eaten by the one who brought
the sacrifice. The קרבן was holy, and for a man to eat of the קרבן
would mean that he was holy too, and this was not true of the
בני נח. The view of ר' אלעזר here, therefore, represents an extreme
universalism. It is a decided emphasis on God's love above the
concept of קדושה. יפ"ת says that in שלמים both God and man
participate, as it were, and that could be only after Shekinah was
present in the Tabernacle (in a comment to Ber. R. XXII.5).

עולות הקריבו (:2)—Here there is a trend to universalism, but no
more (comp. above at 48:3). It does not involve eating of any part
of the sacrifice and there is no participation in the sacrifice. There
is no "negation" or "contradiction" of the concept of קדושה.

שחלבו קרב (:3)—This seems to be the פשט (see Luzzatto, also
Cassuto on the verse). In the verse here (Gen. 4:4), and in the
one on Jethro (Exod. 18:12), there is certainly, in their literal

meanings, a universalistic note (see Luzzatto, and also Cassuto, on Exod. 18:12 as well). The difference between the literal meaning and the opinion of ר׳ אלעזר is in the concept of בני נח which is not crystallized in the Bible, and it is this concept which makes the universalistic emphasis an emphasis at all.

נערי בני ישראל (5:)—This was before מתן תורה (see Rashi to Exod. 24:1). Everybody before מתן תורה was regarded as בני נח. The giving of the Ten Commandments marks the occasion when Israel ceased to be regarded as בני נח and became simply Israel. The concept of Israel is here determined by the concept of מתן תורה, but notice (183:1) that Jethro could be converted before מ״ת, i.e., became an Israelite and not just a בן נח. In one statement there is an emphasis on מ״ת, in the other, an emphasis on Israel. Conversion before מ״ת apparently meant acknowledgment of God and מילה (cf. Sanh. 94a).

[5] היה יָשֵׁן ונתעורר (183:6)—The practice was quiescent but was "awakened" again when the Tabernacle was built.

[6] . . . המלך המשיח (184:7)—They conceive of the משיח as living now (i.e., in the rabbinic period) in Rome. All three interpretations of ר׳ אלעזר on the same verse (Song of Songs 4:16) refer to ימות המשיח, describing successive stages (see also יפ״ת).

[7] דרך ארץ (185:3)—Refers to manners here, but such manners have ethical bearings.

IX.7 (185:6 f.)

[1] וקרבן תודה . . . לעתיד לבא (185:6–186:4)

. . . הקורבנות בטילין (7:)—Since the sacrifices are brought by individuals for sins, and לעת״ל people will not sin, but תמידין ומוספין, etc., will still be brought (יפ״ת)—לעת״ל is before עוה״ב and hence is in part like עוה״ז.

תודה אינו בטל (7:)—Sacrifices of gratitude. Notice that here there is no aversion to sacrifices as such.

הודאה אינה בטילה (7:)—In contrast to התפילות (7:), which are petitions and hence in לעת״ל unnecessary, הודאה is gratitude expressed through words and the perfect conditions of life will give rise to such הודאות.

Basicaly this attitude is an extension of rabbinic practice. The ברכות are a form of הודאה, and the occasions for them are many. Even the תפלה has its petitions closing with ברכות, while the first three are praises. Even the petitions of the individual were inserted in the תפלה or added at the end. The people were nurtured, trained to make of life a constant occasion for הודאה, while leaving room for the spontaneous expression of personal petition. (See RM, pp. 207 ff.)

[2] מביאים תודה and זה קרבן תודה (186:2)—In this midrash and in the following one (:3), הודאה and קרבן תודה are parallel forms of expression of gratitude. The קרבן is not displaced by verbal acts, nor is the verbal expression by קרבן. This is the ideal state, as it were.

וכך דוד . . . וקרבן תודה (:3)—This refers to the future when the only sacrifice will be the תודה (יפ״ת).

IX.8 (186:5 f.)

[1] . . . התעסקו בתורה (187:1)—Study of Torah is in place of the sacrifices.

[2] שלמים . . . ר׳ שמעון (:5)—He is שלם when his mind is at rest, and not when he is אוֹנֵן (a mourner before burial) (Rashi to M.Ḳ. 15b).

IX.9 (187:6 ff.)

[1] —This entire section is given a place because of the statement at the end of R. Mani (194:3) which contains a comment on Lev. 7:37, a comment which tells why שלמים are placed at the end and which adduces also related verses (יפ״ת). The section is a unit on the theme of שלום but is, of course, composed of independent statements, as in this very case of the statement of R. Mani. Notice the *various* authorities throughout.

[2] בשלום . . . אמ' ר' שמעון (‎.6 f:)—גדול שלום (6:) here and in the rest is an emphasis on this concept.

כלולות (6:)—Because יברך (188:1) includes all the ברכות.

[3] אחר . . . אמ' חזקיה (188:1)—The seeking after שלום is a מצוה. Whereas in other מצוות the מצוה is obligatory only when there is an occasion for it, in the case of שלום, "pursue it."

[4] לבניי . . . כיון שבאו (6:)—The point here is: They did not achieve unity *because* they were about to receive the Torah; rather, because of their new unity, concord, as indicated by ויחן (7:) (in the singular), God decided to give them the Torah.

[5] זקנתי . . . בר קפרא (‎.8 f:)—In this midrash and in the following one at 189:4 (also by the same author), and in the one at 190:1 (by a different author), the concept of שלום is emphasized above the concept of אמת (truth). This is possible because these concepts are organismic and one concept may be emphasized above another. In science, truth is the only value concept. See our disccussion also above at 70:6 on רודף שלום.

שדיברו הכתובים דברי בדיי (189:1)—Evidently a congealed expression, for it is used also in the other two passages just mentioned. בדיי = "fiction" and no attempt is made to mitigate this expression, obviously to emphasize שלום, i.e., בשביל להטיל שלום (2:).

[6] וכמה . . . בר קפרא (7:)—Even absence of cause preventing שלום does not in itself make for שלום. שלום needs conscious, positive effort.

שדברו הכתובים (190:1)—For the verse to report what was not true is tantamount to their saying the untruth themselves. They have thus assumed the responsibility for the untruth, but this was done for a purpose, namely to make for שלום. Unlike the other two examples of the כתובים telling a "fiction," this was not for שלום בית where relations between man and wife are involved.

לאשתו . . . תני ר' ישמעאל (6:)—How important is שלום בית! What in the Bible is ritualistic, perhaps even a kind of charm consisting of drinking the written words (see Greenstone, *Book of Numbers*, p. 54) is here interpreted as embodying an ethical concept.

[7] צפה ברוח הקודש (192:1)—Evidently the folk believed that the חכמים possessed רוח הקודש which made them aware of what they would otherwise not know. This expression is in the Hebrew probably because רוח הקודש being a value concept, was not translated into Aramaic. (See RM on the term בראשית.)

למילחש לעיינא (2:)—Another folklore element. These charms were largely in the possession of women everywhere. Notice that the word "witch" usually refers to a woman, but the pupils of ר' מאיר also knew (and used?) them. Did ר' מאיר, too, actually believe in these charms? They were regarded as medicine.

לא דיו למאיר וכו' (193:1)—An example of how haggadic midrash affected the conduct of a scholar. The concept of שלום as a drive is given additional force.

[8] אמ' ר' שמעון . . . העיליונים (3: f.)—In the creation of the world, consisting of עיליונים and תחתונים (4:), the numerical balance between the two was for the purpose of שלום. Man is composed of both so as to maintain that balance. His very composition is thus the thrust of the principle of שלום in the universe. שלום is a cosmic principle and is not only a value concept relating to man.

[9] נשמת חיים (194:2)—This is taken to be the נשמה and as referring to an element of the עיליונים. The implication is that the נשמה has a prior existence above, and from there it enters man at birth.

[10] שכל הברכות . . . חותמיהן בשלום (3:)—The חתימה of a ברכה summarizes the character of the ברכה; hence, the final חתימה involves the character of all the ברכות. Thus the ברכה of שלום is, so to speak, an element of them all; and so with טובות ונחמות.

בקרית שמע . . . שלום (4:)—Apparently was said also on weekdays in Palestine. Also indicates that . . . ברוך ה' לעולם was not said there and is of later Babylonian origin.

בקורבנות . . . ולמנחה (6:)—It is not only a matter of bringing sacrifices, but of reading in the Torah about sacrifices. In the reading, the rest of the sacrifices are seen to partake of the nature of שלמים, of peace offerings. Notice that they interpret שלמים as stemming from שלום, peace.

שלום . . . רבנין (195:4)—Here משיח is a מבשר, apparently of עוה״ב.

Chapter X

X.1 (195:8 ff.)

[1] The first three paragraphs constitute a composite פתיחה on Lev. 8:2, in which Aaron is placed last since קח את אהרן is the verse of the lection. The first application of Ps. 45 is to Abraham—אברהם אבינו (:9).

סדומיים (196:1)—Instead of סדום (biblical). Emphasis on the individual.

[2] הַשֹּׁפֵט כל הארץ (4:)—Interpreted as הַשּׁוֹפֵט—with the definite article (רד״ל, מ״כ)—must not do justice (לא יעשה משפט), but mercy (מ״כ). Change here from biblical concept of God's justice to rabbinic emphasis on God's love. "The judge of the whole world" must not act with strict justice.

[3] אמ׳ לו . . . דבר ה׳ (7 f.:)

אהבת לְצֶדֶק (197:1)—Here לְצֶדֶק is used as the opposite of לחייבן (1:), and yet the note of love is not absent. It is not "to justify," and especially so in view of what Abraham said, according to this midrash.

X.2 (197:5 ff.)

[1] לאשראה שכינתיה (198:1)—שכינה here refers to prophecy, an aspect of גלוי שכינה. God does not need men of oratory or charisma as prophets.

ואיני כדיי . . . (6:)—Isaiah refuses to regard Israel's certain mistreatment as derogatory to their high worth.

לצדק (199:1)—לצדק את בניי certainly does not mean "to justify" but it means to relate to "my sons" with love (as צדקה in rabbinic literature so often means "love"). Isaiah, in his words, איני כדיי וכו', reveals his love for Israel.

ששנאת לחייבן (1:)—He refused to condemn them, again referring to the implication of איני כדיי.

על כן . . . נחמו עמי (1:) [2]

שמן ששון מחביריך . . . אותי (2:)—This indubitably indicates that שמן ששון refers to prophecy. Notice the term נביאות (3:) as referring to prophecy in general. נבואה is a single prophecy and its plural is נבואות (5:).

נבואות . . . כפולות (5:)—It is a reward for a prophet to prophecy נחמות (6:). The very utterance of each word is a נחמה, so that doubling a word of נחמה is another נחמה. The concepts involved are: ישראל, נחמה, נבואה.

X.3 (199:8 ff.)

ואחרכך . . . מיד הן גולין (200:3)—As we shall see, Aaron is regarded here as a צדיק. In the Bible, he is without a sharply defined character, giving in to the crowd, and his explanation (Exod. 32:22 ff.) testifies to his weakness. Here, however, his character is not only strong but in the interpretation in [3] below, actually heroic. Emphasis here is on the individual.

מיד הן גולין (7:)—"Will be in perpetual exile" (Lam. 2:20) is taken as Israel's sin and regarded as the reason for exile. Aaron's fear was not for himself (נתיירא, 4:) but for Israel.

לעבודה זרה (201:2) refers apparently both to the idol and its worship. [2]

מתוך שאני . . . מחר (2:)—A new idea, again referring to the altar. Aaron wants to redeem what is possible from the situation and this indicates he is not to be associated with the idolaters. This midrash obviously assumes that the עגל was not regarded as merely a symbol. (See the contrary opinion in Luzzatto on Exod. 32:4 and the many medieval authorities he cites.)

[3] אתו . . . מה ראה . . . ד"א (4 ff.:)—Another interpretation of Exod. 32:5. Here Aaron emerges as a true צדיק and as a heroic personality.

ולא בישראל (5:)—Concerned for Israel above all, as in [1] above, but in an even stronger degree, for this comes close to כפרה, vicarious atonement (מוטב שיתלה הסירחון בי, 5:).

אהבת צדק (202:6)—לצדק certainly does not mean "to justify" here; rather, it means "to relate to them with love."

X.4 (203:3 f.)

[1] וקם ליה (204:1)—No actual נס is involved in this version, though רד"ל attempts to make it a kind of נס (נזדעזע from זיעה, sweated with fever).

[2] שנים . . . מתו שנים (4:)—The statement of ר' חנן does not seem to apply to the sons at all, but only to Aaron. Also it does not refer to prayer. Moses saves Aaron from death because of the עגל when he "takes" (קח, 4:) Aaron and his sons.

X.5 (204:6 ff.)

A complex passage in which the midrash at the end (6 f.:) is made to apply to Lev. 8:2, the verse in the lection. It is composed of midrashim, apparently originally independent, for they are found elsewhere in different versions.

[1] יהודה . . . ותפילה עשה . . . מחצה (6 f.:)—The statements of both יהודה and ר' יהושע illustrate certain characteristics of organismic thought: one value concept may be stressed above another; also, two authorities may contradict each other, and no attempt is made at resolving the contradiction. In Haggadah each statement is independent.

ותפילה עשה את הכל (205:1)—Whereas there תשובה remits but half the punishment, here תפילה is stressed above תשובה.

ור' יהושע . . . עשה מחצה (1:)—ר' יהודה has precisely the opposite view.

[2] וכיון שעשה תשובה (3:)—Apparently the correct text is in the printed editions which contain this statement after the word גזירה (4:) in the quotation of Gen. 4:13. עון in the verse means "punishment," the consequence of sin, according to Ibn Ezra and Luzzatto. The rabbinic interpretation here, however, takes the verse to say that Cain thus acknowledged and confessed his sin as being beyond forgiveness. תשובה (4:) is hence a characteristic of man almost from the beginning, and, indeed, as we shall see, Adam himself extols תשובה when he becomes aware of its potency. The Rabbis assume that the inward life is a characteristic of man as such, a universalistic idea. Yet see Cassuto (מאדם עד נח, p. 127) who, quoting רמב"ן takes the literal meaning of: גדול עוני מנשוא to be עווני גדול מלסלוח. But even so he does employ the concept of תשובה.

גזירה (4:)—Decree, here a subconcept of מדת הדין. (For its other meaning, see WE, pp. 210 f..)

[3] מהיכן יצא (5:)—For it could not mean מלפני ה' (Gen. 4:16) literally, since God is everywhere (see מהרז"ו). The rabbinic idea of the otherness of God: He is not like man and hence, in the comments to follow, ויצא means he went out of the encounter with God.

יצא כגונב דעת העילֿיונה (6:)—"He went forth from the encounter with God as though he deceived God." דעת העיליונה refers to God Who was not deceived, of course. Cain's repentance was only make-believe.

ר' חונא . . . לקראתך (7:f.)—This does accord with the view of יהודה. His תשובה was genuine.

יצא שמח (206:1)—He went forth from the encounter with God happy. The word יצא is used in the verse which concludes ושמח בלבו (Exod. 4:14).

אדם הראשון—(2:) כיון שיצא . . . אדם הראשון . . . אמרו This term specifies a person, the first Adam. Emphasis on universalism, for Adam is thus not a name but a concept: man.

. . . (3:) . . . כל כך . . . כוחה של תשובה—Adam did know of תשובה, but did not know its efficacy (לא הייתי יודע, 4:). When he became aware of its efficacy, he said: מזמור שיר ליום השבת [טוב להודות לה'] (4:), "it is good to confess to God" (להודות לה'). Concept of תשובה and hence the inward life ascribed to man as such; universalism.

[4] מצליח . . . על דעת' דר' יהושע (9 ff.:)—In both instances here the doing of תשובה is something inferred from the apparent retraction to some form of the decreed punishment. Neither instance is by רבי יהושע himself.

[5] לא יצלח בימיו (208:2)—Jer. 22:30 continues by saying that no one from his seed will be a ruler in Judah.

בימי בנו מצליח (3:)—Stresses בימיו, "in *his* days," but there will be a ruler in his son's days, namely, his son's son, זרובבל. From this the inference is that יכניה must have done תשובה.

גדולה תשובה וכו' (4:)—In the organic complex one concept may be stressed above another, here above two other concepts (cf. X.5 [1] above).

[6] נדרו . . . אמ' ר' תנחומא (209:2)—The idea that God was absolved from His oath when He applied לבית דין שלמעלה (3:) can only be a case of indeterminacy of belief. It posits a heavenly court of beings at least on a parity with God. It is in stark contrast with the otherness of God as expressed in such a phrase as מהיכן יצא (205:5), in this very section. See our comment on the phrase there.

[7] אתו . . . על דעת' (4:)—This last statement of what is evidently a composition on תשובה (which begins at 204:6) relates to Lev. 8:2, the text of the lection.

תפילה עשה מחצה (4:)—This prayer is by one person in behalf of another, whereas in the case of Hezekiah (at 206:8) it is by Hezekiah himself.

כיון שהתפלל (7:)—Referring to Moses in behalf of Aaron (Deut. 9:20).

X.6 (210:1 ff.)

[1] וציץ . . . ואת הבגדים (1:)

כשם שהקרבנות מכפרין כך הבגדים מכפרין (1:)—The comment
connects the בגדים of the כהן גדול in Lev. 8:2 with the קרבנות
which are named in a few verses previous (in 7:37). It teaches that
just as the קרבנות affect atonement, so the בגדים affect atonement
(Rashi to the version in Zeb. 88b, s.v. למה נסמכה).

The רא"ש declares that the בגדים have no atoning efficacy unless
a person who committed the sin had first done תשובה. He says:
וכי בגדי כהונה מכפרין שלא יענשו אף מי שאינו שב בתשובה א"כ
למה גלו ישראל והלא נתכפר להם על עבודה זרה שעבדו ועל גלוי
עריות ושפיכות דמים (שיטה מקובצת) #9 to the version in 'Ar. 16a).
See also RM, p. 182, on the atoning power of יום כפור.

X.7 (213:1 ff.)

X.8 (213:7 ff.) סוף . . . ואת שמן המשחה (7:).

[1] מעשה ניסין (8:)—In the anointing of Aaron, his sons and the Temple
objects, there is embedded not only the concept of נס, but also the
concept of קדושה. The holiness of all these is not the result of the
efficacy of the oil but of a series of נסים, i.e., it was done by God.
קדושה connotes belonging to God in a special sense, and the ניסין
tell that this was here declared, so to speak, by God himself.

מתחילה ועד סוף (8:)—As we shall see, מתחילה refers to the נס of
the small amount of oil used, and the סוף to the נס when it was
not diminished. Notice that by bringing to light the combination
of the concepts of קדושה and נס, a conceptual approach, we were
able to recognize once more that holiness is not a matter of efficacy
or theurgy (see RM, pp. 178 ff.).

אפילו כהן גדול . . . שתי שנים (214:5 f.)—In the case of neither of
these is the anointing a matter of קדושה, but of public ceremony.
The person chosen as High Priest in Temple days was already
holy since he was a כהן. Anointing him indicated new status but
not more holiness. The blessing of the priests reads: אשר קדשנו

בקדושתו של אהרון (Soṭ. 39a), implying that all priests are equal
to the High Priest in holiness.

אין מושחין מלך בן מלך (6:)—Kingship is inherited, hence no
anointing of a בן מלך is required, but כהונה גדולה is not inherited
and therefore the High Priest is anointed. Of course, the anointing
of a king did make him holier than his son who was not anointed.

מפני מה . . . שתי שנים (6 f.:)—Here is a clear indication that
anointing of the king was a matter of public ceremony, of giving
prestige, not of conferring holiness. We thus have further indication that the oil as a physical entity did not impart holiness; there
is no magical efficacy.

[2] לי . . . וכלו קַיָם (215:1)—The entire amount of oil remained after all
this use, the final נס. In the days of the Messiah (לעתיד לבוא, 1:),
the oil would again be used for the משיח (note the name!) and the
High Priest.

הה״ד . . . יהיה זה לי (1:)—In this verse (Exod. 30:31) the word לי,
when taken together with the same word in other verses, teaches
that the matter referred to will endure both in this world and in
the next world.

X.9 (215:6 ff.)

[1] עשה כמין גבעה (7:)—A hill, to indicate that Aaron and his sons are
exalted above the people so that the latter would give them honor
(יפ״ת). The concept of holiness is conveyed by means of the symbol of a hill; see also the suggestion of רד״ל.

[2] ואת כל העדה . . . חי בקרבכם (8 ff.:)—All these are נסים characterized
by אחד מן המקומות שהחזיק מועט במרובה (216:1), a small space
which was made by a נס to contain what would otherwise have
been much too large for it. Here נס means supernatural miracle.
They posited or "expected" such miracles because they were
accustomed to regard daily events such as sustenance, recovery
from illness, etc., also as נסים, even though they were non-
supernatural. (See RM, pp. 159 ff.)

דכוותה (216:2)—"Similarly" (also 5:, et al.), the very multiplication of the instances indicates that there was an entire type of miracle, a type that could be characterized by a common principle (אחד מן המקומות, 1:). This common principle suggests that to them it was almost an expected "order of things."

ממה שההחזיק . . . חי בקרבכם (218:1)—The direct implication is that it was not Joshua who really performed the נס but God and that Joshua was only the agent. Every נס is the work of God, even if it appears to be performed by a human being.

[3] אף בירושלם כן (1:)—An instance of the principle of: אחד מן המקומות (216:1) in the period of the Rabbis, though early in the period—an indication that they regarded supernatural miracles as in the expected order of things even in their own days, not only occurring in biblical times.

תפילתו של חבירו . . . (4:)—The purpose of the נס in this comment was to make possible purely private prayer rather than only to perform a ritual. The concept of תפילה is emphasized.

[4] אף לעתיד לבוא כן (4:)—The final instance of אחד מן המקומות will be לעת"ל, apparently, in the days of the Messiah.

כל הגוים (5:)—The universalism is expressed in the verse; they will come to worship God (רד"ק on Jer. 3:17). גוים is probably taken as Gentiles by the comment.

Chapter XI

XI.1 (219:2 f.) ויהי ביום . . . תשוב

[1] בחכמה . . . (4:)—The purpose of creation was man; all the various stages of creation therefore indicate God's חכמה, each being preparatory for man. העולם (4:) is a universalistic rabbinic value concept, and the contexts here imply that it was not just Adam, but man in general, אדם as embodying a universalistic concept, who was the purpose of creation.

טבחה . . . חיה למינה (6:)—Unless this contradicts the statement in Sanh. 59b, Adam was not permitted to eat animal food. (On this prohibition, see also Cassuto, מאדם עד נח, p. 30, on Gen. 1:29.) The interpretation here has in mind mankind, not Adam, apparently.

XI.2 (220:7 f.)   ר' יונה . . . השדה

[1] בגוג לעתיד לבוא (7:)—This definitely indicates that לעתיד לבוא is the stage before עוה"ב—a rabbinic dogma. On rabbinic dogmas, see RM, p. 340 f.

זה בית המקדש (8:)—It will be built by God, for חכמות (7:) stands for God as in the preceding midrash (219:3).

שלצדיקים לעתיד לבוא (221:3)—Only the צדיקים will be living לעת"ל. "The seven years" are the prelude to that age, the implication being that the others who are not צדיקים wll die during this prelude. Since the צדיקים are people who are among those living in the prelude, this means that תחיית המתים has not yet taken place, and that the entire period of לעת"ל is before the resurrection. לעת"ל is thus to be a period of a kind of bliss before עוה"ב. This idea seems to indicate that rabbinic dogmas leave room for an individual's opinion, since this entire description is that of ר' אבא (220:9). Moreover, no mention at all is made here of the destruction of Rome by God before ימות המשיח.

וסימנא דאכיל וכו' (4:)—The phrase is taken from J.T. Shebu. IV.8. The passage there contains an idea similar to that of the midrash but does not mention צדיקים, an absence of the concept which leaves the passage with only a negative idea.

שלחה נערותיה (6:) is made to apply to Ezekiel by יפ"ת through comparison with נער in Exod. 33:11. It is noteworthy that the prophet is designated as שליח, a matter developed by Y. Kaufmann, though not on the basis of any midrash.

XI.3 (222:1 ff.)

[1] חכמות . . . רשאית דרכו (1:)—Prov. 8:22 (quoted here to prove that חכמות בנתה ביתה refers to the Torah) is the prooftext also for the

idea in Ber. R. I.1 (edit. Theodor, p. 2; cf. ibid., 4, edit. Theodor, p. 6), that the world was created by God using the Torah as His plan. One midrash here seems to contain the same idea. ביתה (:1) would thus refer to the world. Another explanation is given in הוספות לחדושי הרש״ש.

[2] . . . וקרא אותן אלהות . . . (:7)—When God gave the Torah to Israel, it was on condition that Israel was to be immortal (אלהות, like God or angels ובני עליון, :7). But when they sinned with the Golden Calf, He decreed that they be mortal. See 'Abodah Zarah 5a, and Rashi on Ps. 82:6–7; similarly, above at 77:4.)

אדם הראשון (223:2)—Like כאדם.

XI.4 (223:4)

XI.5 (223:9)

[1] זרעך . . . עם חסיד (:9 ff.)—The midrash tells of Abraham's encounters with God. The character of every encounter depends on what Abraham says and does, so that what God says or does in each instance constitutes a response which can be described as מדה כנגד מדה.

[2] תמים, חסיד, בחסידות . . . בתמימות וכו׳ (224:1)—In II Sam. 22:26–27, etc., are each of them different individuals, each characterized by a different quality. In the Midrash, Abraham combines all these qualities in himself, and so does Moses. These spiritual heroes have rich, complex characters, they are not ordinary men. This does not mean, however, that they are treated differently from ordinary men. In their very encounters with God, an exhibit of a good aspect of their characters is rewarded, and an exhibit of an unworthy aspect is punished.

בחסידות (:3)—With kindness, for he was engaged in הכנסת אורחים, which is גמילות חסדים.

אל נא תעבר מעל עבדך (:3)—He asks God to wait until he has taken care of the אורחים, and see Shab. 127a.

ואברהם עודנו עומד לפני ה' (4:)—On the "corrections of the סופרים," see Lieberman, Hellenism in Jewish Palestine, pp. 28–37, and also RM, p. 336, n.47.

[3] בתמימות (5:)—He actually believed that there were a number of righteous men in Sodom, and God did not contradict him (אמרי יושר). Here תמימות is not a value concept as is חסידות but a trait of man (see re the first phase of דרך ארץ in WE, p. 39), "simplicity." עקמנות (7:) is likewise such a trait of man.

ויירשך זה (8:)—This is a clarification of the future, not a reproach, for the next verse amplifies the statement.

נתברר על עסקיו (8 f.:)—Should read: בעקמנות (as in 7: above). The meaning here is "indirection," i.e., by saying: במה אדע וגו' (225:1), Abram expresses lack of trust by indirection.

[4] מדוע לא יבער הסנה (225:5) (Exod. 3:3)—תמימות, for he expressed simple curiousity. The response is likewise direct, in the language of the folk, Aramaic, and not in a verse, apparently to indicate simplicity, directness.

הראני נא את כבודך (6:) (Exod. 33:18)—Moses asks for knowledge of God's ways so he can follow them (יפ"ת). This attitude is חסידות, piety.

(ד)יקרי (6:)—A term used for גלוי שכינה.

נתברר על עסקיו (226:3)—But the verses ought to be Exod. 3:13–14. Moses wants to know how to refer to God when talking to the people. Moses' reply angered God (Exod. 4:14) for it was בעקמנות, an indirect refusal, even after God reassured him. Moses will speak to the people only indirectly, בעקמנות.

XI.6 (226:5 ff.)   ר' יודן . . . הלוי (5 f.:)

[1] . . . מלשמש בכהונה גדולה (6:)—According to this statement Moses and Aaron served together as כהנים גדולים for the forty years in the wilderness. This implies that Moses embodied קדושה in the same sense that Aaron did, the single exception of a זר embodying the holiness of a כהן.

לא נמנע (6:)—Suggests that Moses had the option of doing so. It was not a complete, even if solitary, extension of קדושה, even in the case of Moses. (On the hierarchies of קדושה, and this one in particular, see WE, p. 222.) On the other hand, the idea that Moses, a זר, did embody the same קדושה as Aaron seems to relate to the attempt of the חבורות to have non-priests, too, live על טהרת הקודש. (See WE, p. 222, the quotation from ספר אליהו, "לא לכהנים בלבד נתנה קדושה", an instance of interrelation of Halakah and Haggadah.)

ומשה איש האלהים (227:1)—The interpretation is that Moses, unlike his sons who were לויים, was, in a special sense God's own since the connotation of קדושה is belonging to God in a special sense, and thus implying that he was like Aaron, who was קדש קדשים (226:8).

אבל (1:)—Not in the verse, of course, but for the midrashic purpose of stressing the difference between Moses and his sons with respect to קדושה.

[2] ר' תנחום . . . על פניהם (3:)

בכהונה גדולה (4:)—Here the point is made that during the seven days Moses did embody קדושה, and yet that it was not like that of Aaron.

ולא שרת שכינה עליו . . . (4:)—In the Tabernacle there was גלוי שכינה, but only after Aaron officiated (Lev. 9:23), not during the preceding period of Moses' ministration. וירא כל העם וגו' (4:) refers to the fire from God that consumed the offerings of Aaron, something that did not take place after the offerings of Moses. Apparently Moses' קדושה was of a lower grade than the hierarchical קדושה of Aaron, for it was not a matter of the worthiness of Aaron as against that of Moses.

[3] כל שבעת . . . למצרים (5:)—The encounter at the סנה lasted seven days and during all that time God attempted to persuade Moses to undertake his commission to Egypt.

ר' לוי אמ' . . . את הידרן הזה (228:2)—An instance of מדה כנגד מדה. Moses prayed and pleaded all the seven days of Adar corresponding to the seven days of the plea by God. His prayer to be

allowed to enter the land was of no avail, and thus he was punished for his own earlier obstinancy. Here is a striking case of
indeterminacy of belief. In Num. 20:12 an entirely different reason
for Moses not being allowed to enter the land is given. Furthermore, in contrast to this midrash of מדה כנגד מדה where the
culpability was purely personal, the Bible places blame on Israel:
Deut. 1:37—ויתעבר ה' בי; ibid., 3:26—גם בי התאנף ה' בגללכם וגו';
ויקציפו על מי מריבה וירע למשה בעבורם—Ps. 106:32—למענכם וגו'.
These statements in the Bible could not be set aside, of course, and
hence the midrash here can only be regarded as subject to belief
which was indeterminate. (For another similar case, see CA,
p. 212 f.)

[4] אמ' לו לא שלך היא אלא וכ' (5:)—Moses' punishment was his dis-
appointment when told that the כהונה גדולה was not his (וכסבור
שלו היא, 5:), that it belonged to Aaron always. God did not give it
to Moses and then take it away from him. The seven days in
which Moses served בכהונה גדולה were, so far as his expectation
was concerned, in vain, just as were the seven days of God's plea,
and hence מדה כנגד מדה.

XI.7 (228:7 ff.)

[1] ויהי צרה (8:)—This is the correct reading (Margulies). The printed
editions read:ויהי בימי צרה—צרה is the opposite of שמחה at 234:6
and thus has overtones of sadness, sorrow. Just as שמחה is a
human characteristic, so is צרה, and both belong to the first phase
of דרך ארץ.

[2] ונברכו בך (229:6)—Interpreted to say that the whole world was blessed
because of him, as can be seen from: ובשבילו היה הקב״ה ניזק לכל
העולם כולו (6:). The concepts here are: אבות, עולם, ברכה and
מדת רחמים, but the statement also embodies the idea of corporate
personality, all of mankind benefiting because of Abraham's
presence among them.

אלא לגלגל . . . עין שעשתה מידת הדין . . . לסמותה (9-10:)—This
is very difficult and the commentaries struggled with it. It says
something, apparently about Abraham's softening or restricting

God's justice (מדת הדין, 10:) in the world, but what is the relation to עין (10:)?

הוא שקידש . . . האש (230:1)—The first instance of קידוש השם.

[3] . . . משרה שכינתו (9-10:)—The midrash teaches that the בתי כנסיות ובמ"ד (9:) are the abode of the Shekinah since they are devoted to תלמוד תורה and to תפילה. (Compare OT, p. 39 and p. 275, n. 134.) עולם(ב) refers to Israel (in the parallel in J.T. Sanh. X.2, the reading is על ישראל), as is often the case but משרה שכינתו (9-10:) here can only refer to normal mysticism, since אחז had defiled the Temple where there was גלוי שכינה.

וחכיתי . . . מפי זרעו (231:1 f.)—Which implies loss of knowledge of תורה, since a few verses later there is the promise כי לא תשכח מפי זרעו (3:), and this can only relate to Torah.

מה הועיל וכ' (3:)—The deed of Ahaz did not avail him, for Isaiah raised up students of Torah, and thus the trust in the promise was vindicated, שתלמידו שלאדם נקרא בנו (5:), for by teaching a child Torah, a man is the means for giving him חיי עולם, just as the parent is the means for giving him physical life.

[4] The parallel in Tanḥuma, שמיני IX contains a later addition which attempts to apply the parable at 231:8 f. in its entirety, but it gives an altogether different turn to this parable. Usually a parable is not completely analogous to the application, as we have often pointed out, and here what is applied is only the disrespect toward the rescripts of the king when they were read in his own city.

[5] שמעון . . . תבנה הבית (234:5 ff.)

ועבדה פלגא (7:)—Divided the idea into two separate ideas, assigning to צרה the word ויהי and to שמחה, the word והיה.

אדם (10:)—Refers to אדם הראשון, and שראה (11:) apparently means "foresaw."

שכל מה שנברא בששת ימי בראשית (235:6)—In contrast, apparently, to the new world, the עולם הבא, where the creation will be complete and there will be no need for man's work (עשייה, 6:) at all. The concept of עוה"ב is thus imbedded here.

זה יאיר ששקול כרובה שלסנהדרין . . . (236:4)—The concepts here are: חכם; scholar; and God's justice, that is, the phase of corporate justice. The sin was committed by another person, עכן, but the idea of corporate justice involves the people as a whole in the punishment. The death of such a scholar as יאיר was a grievous loss to the people as a whole. The idea of corporate justice is already present in the literal meaning of Joshua 7:5, though on a different plane, the loss being כשלשים וששה איש, warriors.

[6] על עוונותיהם (237:4)—When Jerusalem was captured, the people of Israel were requited for their sins; hence it was not altogether a צרה.

דאמ' . . . להגלותך (4:)—This statement is apparently only indirect support for the statement immediately preceding. Lam. 4:21-22 are regarded as a prophecy by Jeremiah that Rome (Edom) would destroy the Second Temple and that this would be אפכה שלמה (5:) for Israel's sins, so that no exile would follow the exile by Rome: לא יוסיף להגלותך, 6:. (See Rashi on these verses and cf. Lam. R. on 4:22.) Thus, the day on which Jerusalem was captured by Babylon was likewise איפכי (4:) for Israel's sins (in the days of the First Temple).

XI.8 (237:7 ff.)

[1] חוץ מזקניהם (238:1)—זקניהם here is in accordance with the rabbinic meaning, namely, חכמים, scholars. Were it to mean "chiefs," there would be no point to the statement, and were it to mean "their old men," then it could not refer to ולזקני ישראל (see Rashi, l.c. Exod. 3:16). The concept embodied is תורה. There is undoubtedly a reflection here of the Rabbis' own day when the חכמים were the judges, the teachers, even the communal leaders. (See RM, "The Integration of the Rabbis and the Folk," pp. 84 ff.)

[2] חביבין הן . . . (2:)—If they are old men, their longevity indicates they are beloved by God. In Exod. R. V.12 the phrase reads חביבין לפני הקב״ה.

ואם נערים הם (2:)—This refers to זקנים in the sense of young men who are חכמים—a rabbinic meaning noted above in [1], זקן being a notarikon for זקן מי שקנה חכמה (Kid. 32b).

[3] ונגד זקיניו כבוד (239:3)—כבוד is a term for גלוי שכינה, but the concept of גלוי שכינה was largely merely a haggadic concept, that is, seldom concretized in daily life, and as a haggadic concept subject especially to indeterminacy of belief (RM, p. 238f.). The other concepts embodied are Torah and עוה"ב.

וצדיקים (4:)—But the text has זקניו (חכמים). Here is another instance where צדיקים and חכמים are overlapping concepts.

לפניו (4:)—All of the זקנים will see God, being seated with Him in a semicircle: כחצי גורן עגולה וכו' (240:1), an interpretation of ונגד זקניו כבוד (Isa. 24:23). כבוד is again taken as גלוי שכינה. Embodied here also is the concept of Torah since the צדיקים (4:) are זקיניו, scholars.

XI.9 (240:4 f.)

[1] תופפות . . . ר' ברכיה (4 f.:)

עוה"ב in גלוי שכינה Again—(5:) להיות ראש חולא לצדיקים, but now the concept of Torah is not embodied. There is thus no relation at all to the daily experience of תלמוד תורה, and indeterminacy of belief characterizes this statement all the more.

[2] מות . . . עלמות (241:3 f.)—Another and totally different interpretation, with עלמות = אַלְמָוֶת, immortatlity. God will guide us in a world where there is no death (עוה"ב).

[3] הבא . . . עלמות (242:1)—עלמות is now taken as עוֹלָמוֹת (pl.), "in two worlds": He guides us in עוה"ז and will guide us in עוה"ב.

PART TWO

Chapter XII

XII.1 (243:2 ff.)

[1] This contains a theme, the evils of drunkenness, although it is composed of discrete, separate statements. The connection with the biblical text in :2 (Lev. 10:9) is at 256:4. Teachings about the bad effects of excessive drinking belong to the second phase of דרך ארץ, the phase of practical wisdom and a sub-concept of Torah.

כי יתאו דם וכו' (3:)—Wine incites to זנות and even involves נדה or זבה (יפ"ת); concepts of זנות and טומאה.

בלשון נקי (4:)—Avoiding indecency in speech. Concept of דרך ארץ (proper behavior).

[2] א"ר איסי . . . הטמא (244:1)—A new interpretation of יתהלך במישרים (3:) in Prov. 23:31. A scholar accustomed to drink will eventually declare what is impure to be pure and vice versa, since everything will seem plain to him (מ"כ).

[3] ודאי מסמיק ליה (2:)—ודאי is used here in the sense of כמשמעו, literally: he will redden with shame.

[4] א"ר אחא . . . יומיה (245:2 ff.)—A story introduced by repeating part of the first statement (above, 244:4), and thus an elaboration of it. The kind of humor here and the "happy" ending seem to indicate that it contains elements of several folk stories. The ending is in its own way a sort of כבוד אב, but even this derides the toper.

[5] כך השותה . . . עליו (248:3)—Makes explicit what the פשט implies, but the Aramaic comparisons indicate that the elaboration of פשט was intended for the folk.

[6] בדברי תורה . . . למי אוי (249:5)—This does not refer to the toper but is a saying of רב הונא (6:) regarding him who neglects study of Torah (see also מ"כ). An independent wordplay in Hebrew which was apparently attached to an interpretation of Prov. 23:29 in Aramaic, the latter telling about the toper. Notice that after this Aramaic interpretation of v. 29, the passage reverts to v. 32 at 252:4, from which point on the interpretations are of an entirely different character and in Hebrew.

דעיינין . . . עובדא (250:1 f.)—A story in Aramaic, again characteristic of the folk and its rather "slapstick humor," which contains an apt application of the same verse. An illustration, like the preceding material, of the integration of the Rabbis and the folk.

[7] אל תשת . . . אחריתו (252:4 ff.)—The passage goes back to Prov. 23:32 and hence originally followed the interpretations of the preceding verse (v. 31). These interpetations of Prov. 23:32 deal not with the toper but with events narrated in the Bible which, according to the interpretations, resulted from drinking wine in any form. They are concretizations of God's justice and are in Hebrew, and are thus directed, apparently, to the people at large. That is, they consist of edifying Haggadah.

לעולם . . . דא"ר יהודה (5: f.)—This statement, given as authority for what has been said about Adam and Eve, tells that the fruit eaten by Adam consisted of grapes and concludes with: האוי שענבים הביאו מרורות לעולם (253:2). It tells that grapes brought bitterness into the world, the bitterness of death. The statement preceding, therefore, can only mean that wine was the cause of the death of Adam and Eve. The reading in one of the manuscripts has וחוה, not לחוה. On wine rather than just grapes, see Ber. R. XIX.5.

There are other views which identify the forbidden fruit with the fig, etrog, wheat, and nut, and grounds are given for each of these views (see Ginzberg, *Legends*, V, pp. 97–98). On the basis of our passages here, the grape was forbidden because wine may lead, as the other examples indicate, to drunkenness and misconduct; it was thus forbidden out of God's love.

בקהל ה' . . . מתוך כן (254:2)—According to this statement, they are excluded because of ממזרות (253:9), but the Bible gives a different reason (Deut. 23:4-5). Hence we have here an example of indeterminacy of belief. The prohibition of incest is among the 'ז מצוות בני נח.

אנו יודעי' שלא (255:5-6), and כך הפריש יין בין אהרן לבניו למיתה מתו אלא מפני היין (256:3)—Indeterminacy of belief here is the only ground on which this idea can be accounted for. Lev. 10:1 plainly gives the biblical reason, namely: ויקריבו לפני ה' אש זרה אשר לא צוה אֹתם. Then ibid., v. 2 tells of their punishment. Yet the passage here actually quotes v. 2 but continues by saying: אין אנו יודעי' מפני מה מתו (256:2). Other haggadot do take Lev. 10:1 into account (see Ginzberg, *Legends*, III, 188) but the present passage does not.

וייחד עליו הדיבור (256:4)—The דבור was specifically directed to him. בפני עצמו (4:). That is, only to Aaron was the דבור directed and not to both Moses and Aaron. The reason is made more explicit in the parallel at 258:1.

XII.2 (256:5 ff.)

[1] Two concepts are involved here, קדוש השם and קדושה. Both relate to the same event, the death of Nadab and Abihu in punishment for offering אש זרה אשר לא צוה אֹתם (Lev. 10:1). God Himself sanctifies His Name when there is a manifestation of God's justice as here, and this idea is connoted by קדושת שמו של הקב״ה (257:4); ולהתקדש בהן אני . . . עתיד אני וכ' (256:7). (See CA, p. 114 for other examples; see ibid. on p. 245 f., 247 and 248 f.) On the other hand, the קדושה of the משכן is referred to also: בית זה מתקדש (257:2 and 8:); אני מקדשו (257:8). And the idea now seems to be that the holiness of the Tabernacle was made evident through the punishment of Nadab and Abihu for its violation. The Tabernacle itself was not made holy by their death for it was made holy by God's "resting" or "dwelling in it," as stated in Exod. 23:43 (see Rashi there), and the פשט here is retained by the Rabbis even when the verse is also interpreted. The ideas embodying the two concepts are intermingled here and this makes the passage a difficult one. (The passage as given in the printed editions embodies the concept of קדושה and not that of קדוש השם, but is also much briefer.)

There is also another difficulty involving God's foreknowledge, as we shall see. The great number of variant readings indicates that the passage is one which early scribes and editors struggled with.

[2] בכבודי . . . עתיד אני (256:7 f.)—להתקדש (7:) relates to ק״השם, but ונקדש בכבודי (8:) seems to embody the concept of קדושה and hence to relate to the משכן; the two ideas are intermingled. Involved in both is another idea, that of God's foreknowledge. Not possessing a conceptual term, it is tied here to both the concepts of קדושה and ק״השם. We have described such ideas as auxiliary ideas (see RM, pp. 58 ff. and 220). But here the foreknowledge of God is only apparently tied to the concepts of ק״השם and קדושה. Nothing whatever indicates that the subject of God's foreknowledge was the specific sin committed by Nadab and Abihu, and yet it is the punishment for that sin which embodies the concept of ק״השם or of קדושה.

וירא . . . פניהם (257:1)—On the eighth day both what is referred to by ונועדתי שמה (256:8), and the death of Nadab and Abihu took place. וירא כל העם וכו׳ (257:1) concludes the prooftext beginning with וַיֵּרָא כבוד ד׳ אל כל העם (Lev. 9:23) and it is this to which ונועדתי שמה points, i.e., it points to the גלוי שכינה which the whole people experienced, as described in Lev. 9:23 f.

[3] ומאהרן אחי . . . מי חביב (2:)—Concepts of God's love and צדיק.

שבהן בית זה מתקדש . . . בשביל קדושת שמו של הקב״ה (2: f.)—Begins with concept of קדושה of the משכן and concludes with the concept of קדוש השם. Intermingling of the concepts makes it difficult to tell what is meant.

הוא אשר . . . אקדש (4:)—This prooftext embodies the concept of קדוש השם, since it refers to the immediately preceding statement. The other prooftext, concluding with ונקדש בכבודי at 256:8 refers apparently to the קדושה of the משכן.

ידועי שמים הם (9:)—Seems to be equivalent to חביבין (9:), beloved of God.

XII.3 (258:4 ff.)

[1] דברי תורה (5:)—A concept which often implies תלמוד תורה, as here, but which may also refer simply to תורה.

מלוגמי . . . מרפא (7 f.:)—Are these healing properties of תלמוד תורה taken literally? The very mention of specific remedies indicates these remedies were resorted to. The study of Torah was not engaged in for physical well-being. Apparently this is simply exuberant praise of דברי תורה even though more literal than the prooftexts employed.

XII.4 (259:6 ff.)

[1] א״ר תנחומא . . . מן פלחיה חֲמֹר (6:)—If he drinks his proper portion (פלחיה) he becomes flushed (i.e., handsome) but if more, he becomes like an ass (play on חמר). The concept here is דרך ארץ as referring to the phase of practical wisdom (see WE, p. 40 f.). Most of the warnings here against excessive drinking belong to this phase of דרך ארץ which is also a subconcept of Torah.

[2] א״ר תנחומא . . . למיקם (261:1)—When the vine is laden with grapes it cannot stand without support, and this is used as a symbol to draw attention to the fact that he who drinks to excess cannot stand up by himself. The symbol is forceful because so widely prevalent.

אימיה (1:)—To emphasize the lesson. If the "mother" herself is overpowered, you are all the more likely to be overpowered.

[3] א״ר סימון לקרבנות . . . סיקסים (2:)—Here is another instance where offerings are regarded as a symbol for the individual's behavior. The various definite measures for the offerings of wine on the altar contain the lesson that an individual, too, is not to drink without measure or restriction. The concepts are: Torah, קרבן (holiness) and, implied, דרך ארץ (the phase of practical wisdom).

As can be seen, there is no one type of symbol employed by the Rabbis. The main characteristic of rabbinic symbols is simply analogy of any kind. The symbols adduced in II.12 (52:6 ff.) and III.7 (72:4 ff.) relate to voluntary sacrifices. Here, the symbolism in the wine offerings consists in the *amount* as being ordained and hence contains the notion of an imperative, of a command.

בר קפרא . . . סוד (:4-5)—The analogy consists in the same numerical value of the letters in יין as in סוד, again practical wisdom characterizes the lesson.

ר' אבין אמ' תרת' . . . מחקק כת' (:5 f.)—Much drinking causes total forgetting, "forgetting in all of the 248 members of his body."

XII.5 (262:7 ff.)

[1] שתה יין . . . לא שתה (:7-8)—Abstaining from wine during the building of the Temple was in keeping with the spirit of יין ושכר אל תשתה (Lev. 10:9). Engaging in the holy task may also have removed him from the temptation to drink.

שתה יין (:8)—This made for the hilarity marking the celebration of the marriage with בת פרעה, an event that caused the destruction of the Temple.

של מי אקביל . . . של אילו (263:2)—From what follows immediately, it is obvious that this is only a rhetorical question. Underlying it is the idea of corporate responsibility which involved the people as a whole in punishment, not only those at the ball of בת פרעה. There is a shift from the individual (Solomon) to the people.

ועוקם את חוטמו (:4)—As several commentators point out, this interprets על אפי (:3); reflection of a desire not to allow the loss of Jerusalem to be overwhelming. The destruction of Jerusalem and the Temple was a manifestation of God's justice not only in this legend—it is even more emphasized in the supportng text (Jer. 32:31). In both, the decision by God goes back to the "beginning"; there is no inevitable association of God with the Temple and Jerusalem.

[2] פירושו כמפרס, כלומר כמפרס: כמן פרס (264:2)—Lieberman, here p. 873 השמים (see also his references). The marriage with בת פרעה almost prevented the proper functioning of the Temple from the

start since the next morning represented the first occasion to offer
the תמיד של שחר (1:).

[3] וימת . . . נכנסה אמו (4:)

. . . וכינס שמונים אלף (5:)—Indeterminacy of belief, of course.
Here it is practically a way of indicating what we call a legend.

חייך . . . קימעה . . . וימת (8 f.:)—"Power corrupts."

[4] של אל . . . אין נותנין (266:2)—An ideal rather than an observation.

[5] השטים . . . הזה שבעולם לפי —(268:1)שמחה . . . היין תקלה (1:)—
The period of לעת"ל (1:) is usually ימות המשיח; that period is an
extension of עולם הזה (1:), but without the evil in it. Wine is a
תקלה and שמחה in עה"ז but in לעת"ל it will be productive only
of שמחה.

השטים . . . עסיס . . . והיה ההה"ד —(2:)לעתיד לבא is a purely
rabbinic term, yet the concept is rooted in the Bible, as always.
What we have here, however, is not only a biblical antecedent, but
what amounts to a concretization of the concept. It has both
characters because the concept depends upon antecedents which
are poetic products of the imagination and hence given to vivid
concrete details.

Chapter XIII

XIII.1 (268:6 ff.)

[1] דרש דרש משה וכו' (269:2)—Had Moses not become angry, he would
himself have known and taught the הלכה concerning אונן not
eating קדשים. But he immediately became angry (ויקצף, 4: . . .)
with the sons of Aaron.

[2] נתעלמה—(4-5:) וכיון שכעס נתעלמה הלכה ממנו means that Moses
had known the law, but that he forgot it temporarily. The

"forgetting," it would seem, was not the psychological result of having become angry, but a punishment for having become angry. The concepts are: God's justice and דרך ארץ, and, of course, Torah.

[3] אני טעיתי (272:3)—"I had forgotten" (Jastrow). A rabbinic instance of Moses' humility.

[4] ידע את ההלכה . . . (:3, :4)—The sons of Aaron are characterized as scholars, not only Moses and Aaron. Concept here is: חכם. Biblical characters are interpreted by rabbinic concepts.

ושתק (:3, :4)—Because of the honor of Moses.

זכו שנתייחד . . . ולאיתמר (:4)—They merited that at one time in their lives (בחייהן, :5, interpreting חיים, 268:7), the דיבור was addressed to them and to their father and to their uncle. Concepts are: God's justice and דיבור.

XIII.2 (272:7 ff.)

[1] מדד הקב"ה בכל האומות . . . המדבר (273:1)—Israel alone was fit to receive the Torah, and God's choice of Israel was really God's justice. It was not a matter of favoritism. We have pointed out there is no conceptual term for the "election of Israel," although the idea is found as an auxiliary idea (RM, pp. 54 ff.). Here, however, that idea is not present.

אלא דור המדבר (:2)—Here, too, it is a matter of worth, ראוי (:2). In contrast to the biblical view, the דור המדבר is regarded here as more meritorious than the other generations.

[2] ראה ויתר . . . במתניהם (274:2)—Negative statements about Gentiles such as these are no doubt a reaction to the severe persecutions of the Jews by the Romans and the hostility of the Hellenistic world. But the very concept of צדיקי אומות העולם is a necessary, indispensable element of the rabbinic value-complex. (See RM, pp. 27–28.)

שבע מצוות (275:3)—Universal ethics.

ופרקום על ישראל (4:)—"Unloaded them on Israel," i.e., so that now Israel alone observes these מצוות.

[3] א"ר תנחום . . . על הארץ (276:1)

לרופא . . . הבו ליה (1:)—The parable teaches that, in the case of the first patient, he will continue to live only on condition that he maintains a proper diet.

אומות העולם . . . כל (3:) - כך . . . על הארץ—The law in Gen. 9:3 is directed to the בני נח, but they are designated here as אומות העולם (3:). Strictly speaking, בני נח includes Israel too, until the giving of Torah. By observing these laws regarding permitted and prohibited animals, etc., Israel helped to secure for itself עוה"ב. The עוה"ב was, apparently, to some extent conditioned upon Israel's observance of these laws now; this is the idea to which the parable points. In this statement combining the concepts of אומות העולם, ישראל, מצוות and עוה"ב, the parable thus serves to stress the concept of עוה"ב.

XIII.3 (277:1 ff.)

[1] The teaching here is that the מצוות have the function of testing men as to whether they can obey God's commands, and that if they do so, they will be protected by God (מגן הוא לחוסים בו, 2:). This is the function of the מצוות, for it makes no difference to God as to מי ששוחט מן הצואר ומי ששוחט מן העורף. This teaching certainly does not represent a consensus; if it is just a matter of performing a מצוה and that alone is sufficient, then there need be no כונה in the act, but of course there are those who say that מצוות צריכות כונה. Furthermore, despite the example given, the fact that the term מצוות is used implies that this applies to all מצוות, the ethical as well (notice כל אמרת, 1:), and the Books of the Prophets and the legislation in the Bible surely teach that this does make a difference to God.

    There is no rabbinic term which designates what we call ritualistic מצוות or what is known today as מצוות מעשיות. This means that no demarcation really exists between the ethical and the ritualistic. Indeed, the ritualistic may involve the ethical, and the very ritual of שחיטה involves the concept of צער בעלי חיים.

Even if the midrash here is limited to the ritualistic, the ethical aspects involved do make them of concern to God, if we take into account Jewish tradition as a whole.

[2] לעולם הבא (4:)—Should read לעתיד לבוא to be consistent with that term in the line above (שלצדיקים לעתיד לבוא, 3:), and as can be seen from the readings in several MSS. לעת״ל is an extension of עוה״ז but without the element of evil (cf. our remarks at 268:1). The hunt or chase (קניגין, 3:–4:) indulged in by the Nations of the World is a source of keen pleasure to them, but it is a cruel sport. The element of cruelty is removed here, for there is no hunt but a battle between two "prehistoric," and presumably evil animals—a sort of moral equivalent of the chase.

כיצד הן נשחטין (4:)—It is not sport for both will be food for צדיקים (3:). זו שחיטה כשירה (278:2) is a question, and this question indicates that the laws of עוה״ז are expected to apply in the period of לעת״ל.

[3] מלמד שהיה . . . ומראה להן לישראל וכו׳ (279:5)—Teaching by the direct method overcomes the difficulties of accurate, concrete description. The concept of תלמוד תורה (see CA, p. 65 on integration of Haggadah and Halakah).

XIII.4 (280:3 ff.)

[1] אמ׳ ר׳ אבהו . . . פסולה . . . לאו תאכלו (3:)—Both are instances of the concept of תלמוד תורה as applied to הלכה.

אמ׳ ר׳ אבהו . . . פסולה (3:)—Again, teaching by direct method. An interpretation of: זאת החיה אשר תאכלו (Lev. 11:12) (מהרז״ו). But now the teacher is God and the pupil is Moses; integration of Haggadah and Halakah.

[2] אם זכיתם . . . (6:)—It is not predetermined that the מלכיות will oppress you. If you will be worthy, you will destroy them; not predestination but מדת הדין.

עבד תתובא (281:1)—Poverty is a stimulus to תשובה; apparently a popular apothegm.

(2:)—כי ערקתא סומקתא וכו' The aesthetic criterion of "fitting," "suitable," but see how רד"ל interpreted it valuationally—evidently aesthetic interest was lost.

XIII.5 (281:3 ff.)

[1] The four successive world empires are named here, empires which oppressed Israel. But only the fourth, Rome, is completely evil, the first three having some redeeming features. Rome, which oppressed Israel in the rabbinic period, is therefore to be the last of these empires, and after that only God alone will rule. The tradition about the four Empires goes back at least to the passage in Daniel, here interpreted at 286:1 and probably even earlier. The connection with Lev. 11:4, the text in the lection, is at 292:4.

When מלכות is the singular of מלכיות (3-4:) it refers to a single nation having dominion over the entire world, not just an empire. מלכות שמים means the sovereignty of God, שמים in this term being an epithet for God, and this refers to "above and below and the four directions." The מלכיות are subject to this sovereignty and sometimes they even acknowledge it by praising God (see at 292:2 f., 293:4 and 6:), i.e., all but Rome (293:7). But they are all essentially evil for they oppress Israel. Israel alone, including converts, acknowledges מלכות שמים daily. When Rome will be destroyed לעת"ל, history will have run its course, for the changes that represent history only take place in עוה"ז; in עוה"ב there is no change, only bliss.

מלכות שמים is a value concept which gives significance to the world as a whole. The opposite to the Kingship of Heaven (מלכות שמים) are the human מלכיות, especially מלכות הרשעה, Rome, and hence ד' מלכיות (282:1) has a negative valuation (see our comment at 292:2).

[2] כל הנביאים (3:)—A rabbinic usage meaning a "a number." Since the prophets "saw" (ראו, 3:) the four מלכיות before these existed, the implication is that they were preordained by God, and that their downfall, including that of Rome, was likewise preordained, but their evil power was not inevitable (see at 280:6, 286:3, 289:3).

[3] אדם הראשון (3:)—Notice that אדם here is a concept, not a name, made

specific by the modifier, הראשון. An emphasis on universalism. Man is a universalistic concept. The preordained character of the empires is emphasized by these empires having been "seen" already by Adam.

[4] פושכא . . . ופשו . . . פישון (282:1-2)—In proof that פישון (:1) refers to Babylon whose emperor was פושכא (:2), referring to the tiny Nebuchadnezer. Of course there is an implied derision.

שמיחלת (:4)—A mystical idea regarding a relation between ארץ ישראל and God. הוחילי (:4) is brought in proof that החוילה (:3), with almost the same consonants, means "hopes for."

מלמד שאין תורה וכו' (:6)—The superiority of תורה developed in Palestine as against that of Babylon, due to the mystical relation between the Land and God. חכמה (:6) refers to the logical deductions (see Rashi to Ḳid. 49b, s.v. דברי חכמה), and bespeaks superiority of the mind.

מתאשרים מישראל וכו' (283:3)—Became strong through Israel (but how?). In the case of נינוה and מצרים, the names indicate that the מלכיות oppressed Israel.

[5] שלזקן (:6)—Refers to the ברכה of Isaac. An indication that the ברכה of a human being was regarded by the Rabbis as a תפלה.

לעולמו (284:1)—Although עולם often refers to Israel, here it probably refers to the world, for לבנו (:1) refers to Israel.

אימה . . . חמה (:4)—Apparently א, too (not only ע), was pronounced somewhat like ח.

[6] דניאל . . . ותכפל (286:1-290:2)

ממכיא . . . דכואתא . . . אם זכיתם (286:3 f.)—Here the force of the preordained character of the מלכיות is blunted; their effectiveness for evil depends on Israel's conduct. If Israel merits it, the מלכיות will be powerless. There is thus no real predestination.

שנין . . . מן הכל (287:2)—שנין is taken as "hating" (with ש). Israel was hated in greater degree by each succeeding מלכות, and was hated and oppressed more than any other people. Israel is the special object of hatred and oppresion of the מלכיות.

אדעתא . . . עצמו משובותיהם (289:1)—An interpretation of Jer. 5:6 which takes the verse to allude to the ד' מלכיות, and brought here to confirm that ר' יוחנן interprets זאב as מדי. Jeremiah is thus another prophet who "saw" the four מלכיות, but his symbols are the same as Daniel's.

[7] צדיק ורשע (290:5)—Margulies points to כורש as צדיק and אחשורוש as רשע. Notice that the term צדיק is applied to a Gentile, and that the term is thus not limited to Israel (see RM, p. 27 f.). Also that a מלכות, in the case of מדי, may have good qualities as well as bad.

מה חזיר הזה . . . בימה (291:5)—The hypocrisy of Rome; it appears to be executing justice but actually robs and despoils.

אותו האיש (292:2)—That is, "I myself."

ד"א את הגמל . . . בארץ (:2 f.)—Each of the מלכיות, except Rome, on a specific occasion, praises God. In other words all but Rome do at times acknowledge מלכות שמים. The opposite to מלכות שמים is, then, chiefly Rome, called מלכות הרשעה (291:6).

אותו הרשע (:4), Nebuchanezzer is called רשע מקלסת לקב"ה (:3)—despite his praise of God, inclusive as it was. The acknowledgment did not redeem his character, nor does it redeem בבל, it would seem.

בריך אלהיה (293:7) . . . —A formula of a ברכה involving קדוש השם, but not actual acknowledgment of God.

ולא דייה . . . מחרפת (:8) . . . —Rome blasphemes and opposes מלכות שמים.

[8] ד"א (:9 f.) . . . זו בבל . . . וחביריו—Again a virtue present in every one of the מלכיות except Rome—exalting הצדיקים (:10 etc.).

שמגדלת את הצדיקים (:10 etc.)—Here צדיקים refers to Jews, since the term does most frequently refer to Jews.

קאים על ריגליה (294:3)—No ברכה formula here as at 293:7, for what he did was to show respect to man.

ולא דייה . . . אלא הורגת (:6)—Not just the absence of the virtue characterizes Rome but the slaying of צדיקים. The prooftext (Isa. 47:6) has as its context Babylon and not Rome, but מהרז"ו

explains that גברת ממלכות there is taken to refer to Rome and he
points to Yalkut on Isaiah, ch. 47.

שמחזרת עטרה לבעלה (295:2)—לבעלה refers to God, and not to
Israel, for the prooftext (Obad. 1:21) definitely states והיתה לה'
המלוכה (3:). Rome will return the "crown" to God, its proper
owner, but of course, not voluntarily. The presence of the ד'
מלכיות, even though there is מלכות שמים, represents a paradox,
and this paradox will disappear when Rome will be destroyed by
God and God alone will then exercise sovereignty, מלכות.

Chapter XIV

XIV.1 (295:6 ff.)—אחור וקדם . . . הרחק.

[1] כפיך . . . אם זכה (6 f.:)—The עוה"ב is not intended for the select few,
but for every man. If a man does not merit it, he will be held to
account. Every man is created with the possibility of inheriting
שני עולמות (7:), the two worlds. Apparently here it includes the
Gentiles since it speaks of אדם (7:).

[2] מיכן . . . אמ' ר' ישמעאל (296:2)—אחור וקדם (295:6) means, in this
interpretation, that "back and front" are singled out so as to
describe the creation of man, and so also in the following
entry (4:), here. In both statements, woman is made coeval with
man, a suggestion of equality on the sheerly human plane.

דו פרצופין (4:)—Has perhaps more of the idea of equality than the
preceding idea.

[3] כפיך . . . ר' יהודה . . . ר' ברכיה (6 f.:)—The concept of אדם is sometimes interchangeable with that of עולם. For example, מקיים נפש
אחת . . . כאילו קיים עולם מלא (San. IV.5). (On this idea, and for
more examples, see RM, p. 150 f.)—an emphasis on universalism.
This idea is reflected in the two midrashim here where אדם is
practically identified with עולם, since he fills it, as is explicitly
said in the second midrash.

גולמי ראו עיניך (297:2)—Since God sees everywhere, גולמי was everywhere in the world.

[4] נפש חיה . . . רוחו של אדם הראשון (298:1)—נפש, here equated with רוח, is regarded as being Adam himself, although the body had not yet been created. The soul exists before the body, this statement says. The emphasis is on the interpretation of וקדם (297:6), for this is a new and entirely rabbinic idea. What precedes in creation is regarded as having a higher status; here the creation of cattle and (other) animals means that man's status is higher. The Bible itself does not have this criterion for status and the higher status of man is stated in a direct and explicit manner in Gen. 1:26.

קדמתה למעשה בראשית (:5)—Apparently וקדם (:2) is interpreted as before יום ראשון. The status of man is thus higher than all the rest of creation if he shows himself worthy; and if he is not worthy, he is lower than even a worm.

[5] וקדם לכל העונשים (:5)—Refers to Adam, the first to sin.

[6] וכל לאומים . . . ר' נחמיה (:6 f.)—Although this statement is connected with the idea that even a שילשול (worm) was created on the sixth day before man, it is really an independent statement for it does relate to a judgment regarding a man's merit. In one respect, it says, man's status is inferior to that of cattle, etc., for the latter's praise of God (קילוסו, :6) precedes that of man. Apparently this teaches the need to be humble since in one respect the animals are always above man.

[7] זכר . . . אמ' ר' שמלאי (299:2)—Associated with the previous statement through having a similar idea. Not only was the creation of man (שצורתו, :2) later, but תורתו (:3) is after that of the cattle, etc. Again a lesson in humility for man.

XIV.2 (299:5 ff.)

[1] ואמר על הרחוקים שנתקרבו (300:1)—Refers to sinners (רחוקים) who repented. An interpretation of למרחוק (299:5) which is taken as two words, לא מרחוק, i.e., they had been far away from God but are now near Him (מהרז"ו and cf. הוספות לחדושי רש"ש).

[2] אתן צדק (300:1)—צדק is taken here throughout as שבח, praise, as can
be seen from 302:1 and :5. It is, however, not interchangeable with
שבח, being limited, as all the instances in the passage indicated,
to praise for God's love. This accords with the rabbinic meaning
of צדקה as love. The concepts in this midrash are: צדקה, תשובה
and שבח, with the concepts of צדקה and שבח coalescing and
taking on a combined meaning. This coalescence is possible
because the concepts in an organic complex are not discrete but
part of an organic whole. תשובה is made possible, the midrash
implies, because of God's love.

[3] שבח שבחים . . . ר' שמואל (301:2)—שבח שבחים means, apparently,
that the verse refers to most extraordinary matters, not only to the
daily things which also call for praise of God.

[4] צדק . . . ר' לוי . . . ר' לוי (:4 f.)—All three statements (תלת, :4) are
interpretations of ולפעלי אתן צדק, and now ולפעלי "to Him that
made me" relates to birth; all three matters embody the concepts
of God's love, man and נס. Although not daily, commonplace
things, these נסים are not "miracles" in the sense that they con-
travene the natural order, סדרי בראשית, but are extraordinary
events within סדרי בראשית. Herein the concept of נס is not the
same as the philosophic concept of "miracle," the latter always
referring to something which contravenes the natural order (see
RM, p. 159 ff.).

XIV.3 (303:1 ff.)

[1] The connection with Lev. 12:2 is at the end. All the midrashim here,
likewise, embody the concepts of God's love, man and נס, the
latter again in the sense of extraordinary occurrences within סדרי
בראשית. But in the instances here, the idea of נס is emphasized by
contrasting most instances with a situation everybody recognizes
as not a נס, but normal.

XIV.4 (306:1 f.)

[1] לפי שהולד וכו' (307:4-5)—An infant is greeted with every evidence of warm love despite its filthy appearance. That is a נס.

XIV.5 (308:1 ff.)

[1] The conception of a child is a נס.

[2] צד אחד (:2)—Since the parents had in mind primarily their own gratification, conception is a manifestation of God's love and is a נס. It is assumed that the act of the parents in itself does not result in conception because at best that is not their whole intention.

[3] כי אבי ואמי . . . יאספני (:5)—Not his parents but God is the creator of every child.

ובחטא . . . וילדה זכר (309:1)—Conception of a child is a reward for טבילה of a woman, not just a natural matter.

ובחטא (מ"כ) ואין חטא אלא לשון טהרה (:1). The midrash, by interpreting חטא as "purification" instead of "sin" (which is here the literal meaning), gives ובחטא יחמתני (:1) this meaning: Because of the purification (through טבילה), my mother conceived me. A negative concept is here apparently replaced by a positive concept. (On negative concepts, see WE, p. 25.) Even so, however, the concept of חטא, in the Bible too, sometimes has the meaning of "purify," as in וחטא את הבית (Lev. 14:52) and תחטאני באזוב ואטהר (Ps. 51:9). Cf. also מהרז"ו. It remains true that every rabbinic concept has its roots in the Bible. The concepts here are God's justice, man and נס.

XIV.6 (309:4 f.)

[1] שללבינות (:5) = של לבנית (see Lieberman, p. 873 here). Man is created from only the best, the whitest drop.

XIV.7 (310:4 f.)

XIV.8 (311:2 f.)

The text (Lev. 12:2) is interpreted directly (גופה, :2) at :5. The point of this midrash is that the entire change from embryo to child is a נס, including the egress from the womb when what has been open (the umbilicus) is now closed, and what has been closed (the mouth) is now open (314:4).

XIV.9 (314:5 ff.)

[1] לעתיד לבוא (315:1)—Refers to תחיית המתים as is to be recognized from the prooftext (Ezek. 37:8). This indicates that the correct text is לעתיד לבוא and not לעוה"ב as in Ber. R., for עוה"ב was believed to be after תחיית המתים.

[2] בעולם הבא (316:1)—Should read, as in a number of MSS: לעתיד לבוא, for as the thought continues, the text reads לעתיד לבוא (:2), which bears out our remark above on this term. לעת"ל is usually the stage *before* עוה"ב.

Chapter XV

XV.1 (318:6 ff.)

[1] א' ר' יהושע . . . שאני עשיתי (:7 f.)—The wind is tempered, weakened, so that it will not harm men (נשמות, 319:4)—God's love.

[2] תן דעתך וכו' (319:1)—The wind is here and elsewhere, often regarded as having personality. Being an element in a statement embodying God's love, a value concept, it is, like a value concept, solely characterized by the category of significance; other categories, then, are now irrelevant. A kind of valuational poetry. (On the category of significance, see RM, p. 107 ff.)

קוזמיקון (320:5)—Only in the case of אליהו did the wind relate to the whole world, but there is no mention of a desire "to destroy the world." Wind is not a factor in the life of אליהו as it is in the case of the other two (איוב and יונה), but it is a precursor of גלוי שכינה.

ומים . . . מערכך (321:1)—Rain, too, given by measure so as not to harm man (see יפ"ת)—God's love. No personality is attached to rain as was attached to the wind.

XV.2 (321:4 ff.)

[1] . . . ומים (322:3)—מים is a symbol for Torah. There are also other symbols for Torah: דגן, מלחמה, לחם. Their great emphasis on Torah made the Rabbis see allusions to it in the Bible everywhere but the major symbols are "water" and "bread" because they are life-sustaining. A symbol is more than an allegory, for it is often used almost habitually as here where no reference is made to the idea that מים is a symbol.

[2] דברי תורה שניתנו מלמעלה (4:)—Not only מקרא (4:) but the divisions of Torah, recognized by the Rabbis as produced by the Rabbis themselves, are regarded as divine (מלמעלה, 4:) (see RM, pp. 353 f.).

מידה (4:)—אלא במידה refers to the fact that דברי תורה (4:) are divided into "quantities": מקרא, משנה וכו' (4:4 f.). זוכה (5-6:) implies that in each case what is acquired is a reward of merit.

[3] רוחו רחבה וכו' (323:1)—רוח רחבה is used here in our sense of large-spirited, generous. Does all this mean that there is pre-determinism? Characterized here as a folk idea and hence perhaps not actually a rabbinic thought.

XV.3 (324:3 ff.)

[1] מעשה בחסיד . . . ליה בורייה (4:4 f.)—Here the man changes his mind as a result of the teaching of this haggadah. Haggadah may sometimes have direct effect on behavior and not be merely edifying.

[2] אמרה לו אשתו (325:1)—The role of the pious wife is often alluded to

in Haggadah (see also, e.g., 36:1; 111:3). Combination of God's love and His justice.

[3] העולם . . . קצטרא . . . ודרך (5:)—Their view of nature was teleological, of course, as was also the case among the Greeks, even that of Aristotle, but it was for the Rabbis more than that. It supplied instances of God's love in accord with rabbinic emphasis on God's love, and it also emphasized universalism at the same time, referring to העולם (326:1-6:). On the other hand, the Greek view, as expressed by Anaximander and others, insisted that this teleology was a matter of justice (see Cornford, "From Religion to Philosophy," on Anaximander; and Bertrand Russell, "A History of Western Philosophy," p. 27).

זוכה אדם (326:2)—The healing or the worsening is not chance but God's justice; if the man merits it, he is healed.

XV.4 (326:5 ff.–328:2)   בור בשרו . . . נכונו ללצים (5:)

[1] שפטים . . . הכא . . . נכונו (5:)—As given here, it is a question whether this statement refers to נגעים only or to punishments in general. In either case, misfortunes are regarded as punishments, i.e., God's justice, and the statement has in mind Israel.

כסילים (326:5) and מכת מות—(327:1) מחה למות refer to the nations. They are characterized as כסילים presumably because they are addicted to עבודה זרה. The inference is that if they abandon עבודה זרה they will no longer be subject to נגעים. It was, of course, obvious that there were Israelites who were afflicted with נגעים (3:), but these were regarded as sinners, as indicated in [1] above.

[2] משיח י"י (329:2)—The verse continues with נלכד בשחיתותם and is here taken to mean that Rabbi suffered because of "their," the generation's, sins. The concept here is כפרה, vicarious atonement which has numerous concretizations, e.g., הריני כפרת משכבו (Ḳid.31b) says a son, referring to his deceased father (see also Neg. II.1). When this concept contracted to a single concretization, it was no longer a true value concept, but a dogma (RM, p. 318n.). יפ"ת accounts for the passage being given here by pointing out

that it explains כאובים (328:3) of the צדיק which are not punishments as in the case of the רשע but are vicarious atonement for
the sins of his generation, as is taught in this passage.

ר' אליעזר . . . יסובבנו (330:3)—Another interpretation of Ps. 32:10,
saying that the רשע, if he repents, will be healed (חסד יסובבנו, 4:),
this רשע having suffered from מכאובים (328:3). This interpretation apparently refers to the person who suffers from נגעים because
of his sins. The concepts here: God's love, חטא, רשע, תשובה,
טומאה (נגעים).

XV.5 (331:1 ff.)

[1] כך מי . . . את נידתה (3:)—There it is not מצורע (4:) who has done
wrong but the mother, an aspect of corporate justice in which
parents and children are regarded as a single corporate personality.
(See CA, pp. 47, 101, 225).

XV.6 (332:4 f.)   ר' אבין . . . הכהן

[1] חייך שאני מצריכך וכו' (6:)—Concepts of God's justice, sin and טומאה.
But they must have been aware that the conjuncture of the two
matters was not inevitable. We take this statement, therefore, to be
an instance of indeterminacy of belief.

[2] כילו (כאילו) . . . כאילו (333:1–2)—Means "as though," indicating that
the idea here is an exhortation, and yet one which manages
to associate observance and non-observance with, respectively,
destruction and worship of idols.
    In observing מצות חלה (1:), a person achieves an embodiment
of קדושה, whereas עבודה זרה embodies טומאה (see WE, pp. 217 ff.,
on hierarchies of קדושה; also p. 231 on עבודה זרה). That is why
they may be placed in contrast.

אמ' ר' לעזר . . . לחם (2:)—Connected with the preceding midrash
through association of ideas; here non-observance of מעשרות,
also an aspect of קדושה. This is not a clear instance of ritual sin
"causing" (גרם, 3:) moral sin. מעשרות belong to the כהן, and by
not observing the ritual law, a person also steals from a priest, a

moral trespass. (On the difficulty of making a demarcation
between the ritualistic and the moral, see OT, pp. 102 f.)

[3] אל הכהן . . . אמ' ר' שמעון (4:)—Another midrash employing the
principle וכי מה עיניין זה לזה (5:), a form of סמוכין. Here, as in [1]
above, they must have been aware that the conjunction of the two
matters was not inevitable, and hence also here we have indeterminacy of belief.

XV.7 (334:1 f.)

[1] ברכות מברכות את בעליהן (1:)—The word יהיה (2:) in Deut. 25:15 is
taken as a blessing by God upon him who acts in the manner
prescribed by that verse, a blessing fulfilled. Concepts are: God's
justice and מצוה (the verse), and ברכה. The concept ברכה has
three phases: a ברכה by God, as above here; a ברכה by man—this
is a form of תפלה, a petition (see CA, p. 141 on וברכתם גם אותי,
Exod. 12:32); and a ברכה which is an expression of gratitude in
which the stimulus and expression form a unitary whole.

XV.8 (335:3 ff.)

[1] תנא . . . לתגלחתו (3: f.)—Concretizations in law of the concept of
טומאה. Value concepts are concretized both in Halakah and
Haggadah.

[2] תנא כל הנגעין . . . קרוביו (336:3)—A halakic introduction to the haggadah which follows. An instance of the interrelation of Halakah
and Haggadah.

[3] מי ראה . . . עד האסף מרים (3: f.)

אני כהנא וכו' (5:)—This statement is an instance of indeterminacy
of belief. It is assumed here that, as in all cases of צרעת, it was
necesary for a כהן to declare to Miriam that she was טהורה, and
hence it must have been God who acted as a כהן (אני מטהרה, 5:);
it was a manifestation of God's love (מדת רחמים). In the biblical
narrative (Num. 12:9 ff.) Miriam's returning to the camp after 7
days is part of the original decree by God (Num. 12:14), and no

particular act permitting her to do so was necessary. The biblical
narrative is characterized by a manifestation of God's justice.

עם השכינה (337:1)—Implies some form of גלוי שכינה. [4]

XV.9 (338:1 ff.)

אבל לעתיד לבוא (339:4)—There will be נגעים, apparently, in the
period of לעת״ל, but it will be God who will purify, not the
priests. Again it is obvious that the לעת״ל is not עוה״ב. This
seems to be in accord with the idea (ר׳ יוחנן; RM, pp. 362 f.) that
the prophets prophesied concerning ימות המ׳ (or לעת״ל) only,
not עוה״ב. Here, it is יחזקאל.

Chapter XVI

XVI.1 (340:2 ff.)

This section is an interpretation of Prov. 6:16–19, an interpretation consisting of comments on the successive phrases of the
verses. The last comment leads to Lev. 14:2, the verse in the lection.
The comments are not independent entities but are united by the
concept of רשע, each comment enlarging on a wicked trait or act
described in one of the phrases. The basis for this unitary entity is
thus the biblical text itself. (See also רד״ל.)

The ethical sphere applies to all men, not only to Israel. פרעה
is punished for being guilty of one of the matters enumerated here
(see 347:9 f.; cf. also our remarks on 374:3.)

שש הנה . . . בין אחים (2:)—[1]

שש הנה . . . נפשו (2:)—Only רשעים can be characterized in this
manner. This characterization makes it unnecessary to use the
word רשע as label.

משלח מדנים בין) לשון הרע . . . ושבע (4:)—The seventh, אחים

אחים, (5:) is as wicked a thing as all the rest together (כנגד כולם, 4:). But it does not say here that it brings about all the rest.

[2] סירון . . . אמ' ר' יוחנן (346:2–7:)

וכולם לקו בצרעת (7:)—God's justice. The same punishment for each one is another unifying principle of the section.

גסות רוח (341:1)—A negative value concept (see WE, p. 25).

זרע קודש וכו' (345:3)—See Ezra 9:2. זרע קודש does not imply a virtue possessed by the women for they are described as כזונות (344:2). It refers to the קדושה inherent in Israel; but this mystic quality is something that must be achieved by the people through observance of the מצוות (אשר קדשנו במצוותיו). In a sense, therefore, the קדושה inherent in the people is a potential quality which only deeds can make an actual quality. It is this potential quality that is lost when there is assimilation, an idea expressed in: שלא יתערב זרע קודש בעמי הארצות (3:).

בעמי הארצות (3:)—The biblical meaning of the term as it is used in Ezra 9:2 and referring to the non-Jews, not the rabbinic usage where it refers to the ignorant Jews in contrast to תלמידי חכמים. Another instance indicating that the biblical meaning was not lost for the Rabbis.

[3] המוציא רע (348:5)—A wordplay on המצורע (5:). It refers to speaking לשון הרע, as is to be recognized from the same wordplay on נצר לשונך מרע . . . שומר מצ' נפשו . . . המוציא רע 350:4 f.:

XVI.2   (349:1 ff.)

[1] מי האיש . . . נצר . . . ורדפהו (350:3)—The rabbinic setting here brings into even stronger relief the emphasis on the ethical contained in the biblical text itself. There is another matter involved: נצר לשונך מרע (4:) is taken to refer to the negative rabbinic concept of לשון הרע which stands for scandal mongering not only when this is false but also when true. This rabbinic concept is brought out in what follows here, but what need is there for these individual ethical concepts when all is included in: סור מרע ועשה טוב (5:)? But טוב and רע are not specifically ethical matters,

e.g., there can be good and bad apples. New rabbinic ethical concepts such as לשון הרע make the ethical life richer and more sensitive. They represent a remarkable development in ethics.

[2] אמ' ר' חגי . . . שומר פיו ולשונו שומר נפשו מצרעת (351:2)—That is, he who guards himself against speaking לשון הרע guards himself thereby from being afflicted with צרעת.

תורת המצורע תורת המוציא רע (4:)--Conversely, the מצורע is thus afflicted because he brought forth (המוציא), spoke, לשן הרע—the word play embodies the concept of God's justice.

XVI.3 (351:5 ff.)   אם יעלה . . . הכירוהו (5 f.:)

In this midrash, the punishment of the מצורע is inflicted because of גסות הרוח (רד"ל). There is no word play here on מצורע.

[1] אם יעלה . . . לעננא (5:)—They take the biblical phrase as a figurative characterization of גסות הרוח.

[2] ר' יוחנן (352:3) . . . מאה אמות . . . להלך—Halakah on topic of מצורע, the danger of what we would say is infection.

[3] על שום . . . המוציא רע (353:5)—Refers to the emphasis here on separating the מצורע from the rest of the community, regarding it as punishment for לשון הרע. Just as he caused people to be separated through המוציא רע) לשון הרע, 5:), so he is now separated from people (מ"כ and רד"ל), and hence מדה כנגד מדה—integration of Halakah and Haggadah.

XVI.4 (354:1 ff.)

[1] אני מחריז דברי תורה וכו' (4:)—He makes this "string" by showing that the idea he found in a text in דברי תורה is also contained in the text he adduces from the נביאים and from the כתובים. This procedure is similar to the one described in the next midrash, and hence the two statements are associated.

ודברי תורה שמחין . . . לב השמים (5:)—Through the repetition of

the idea in the נביאים, and then again in the כתובים, the דברי
תורה are, so to speak, given again; hence their rejoicing as when
they were given at Sinai. Rabbinic interpretation is here described
as having a background of מתן תורה, a dramatic expression of the
idea that what the Rabbis regarded as their own teaching is also
divinely inspired (RM, p. 356).

[2] בקילוסו שלרשע . . . (355:2)—A רשע, too, may have experience of God
and hence will utter praise of Him. What makes him a רשע is his
conduct, including לשון הרע, and since his conduct is offensive to
God, He does not want that praise. Apparently, in the case of a
רשע, his experience of God is not a steady experience—were it
steady, it would be involved with מצוות and מעשים טובים.

[3] המוציא רע . . . ר' לעזר (356:2)—This statement is apparently a comment on ולשונך תצמיד מרמה (Ps. 50:19), telling how dangerous is
the לשון (:4).

XVI.5 (356:8 ff.)

This section is placed here because two of its interpretations deal
with לשון הרע, the punishment for which is צרעת—the subject of
the next section and thus related to that section. Essentially, XVI.5
consists of different interpretations of Koh. 5:5 and thus consists
of independent entities united or organized through and around
that verse. Each interpretation is different but does not negate the
ideas in the others. They are different because the rabbinic concepts emphasized or concretized are different.

[1] שפוסקין צדקה ברבים (357:1)—The concept concretized is, of course,
צדקה (:1), but the phrase indicates something more. The rabbinic
concept is here concretized in an institution, the pledging of a
specific amount in an assembly (see RM, p. 79 for other institutions which are concretizations of צדקה; such institutions constitute types of concretization of the concept).

המלאך (:3)—In its literal sense of "agent," שליח, through whom
the announcement is made; not the biblical meaning here.

[2] ערבוביה . . . ר' בנימן פתר (:6 f.)—"Pretenders of scholarship" (Jastrow). A compound term composed of the components of Torah and חנופה, a subconcept of שקר. In such compound value concepts the first component indicates whether the concept has a positive or a negative character, and here the character is negative. Similarly, in a compound wherein the first concept is a cognitive one, it is this cognitive concept which gives the compound its character (see RM, p. 151 f.).

המלאך זה הרב (358:2)—The חכמים are sometimes spoken of as מלאכים (Ned. 20b, and cf. Ḳid. 72a).

זה מלאך הגוף (:7)—Apparently this posits an angel assigned to each individual to report on his deeds, akin to "guardian angels."

אפילו מעט איברים וכו' (:9)—According to the Rabbis, the body has 248 איברים (356:3), and not just a few. But the style here parallels that of the other interpretations and is not meant literally. This conformity suggests an editor.

[3] המלאך זה זקן (359:2)—See above, at 358:2. זקן = חכם. The resort to היתר נדרים (Ḥag. I.8) is provided for in the Halakah, and so we have here another instance of the integration of Halakah and Haggadah.

אפילו מעט מצוות (:4)—So grave a matter is the breaking of a vow that the "few" מצוות he did do not count. A grave עבירה may offset one's מצוות. The moral life is a unity, is a reflection of the unitary character of the self. This midrash, however, only implies that awareness since its explicit teaching embodies the concept of מדת הדין.

XVI.6 (361:1 f.)

[1] עובר על חמשה ספרי תורה (:5)—This is, of course, hyperbole, and the Munich MS. reads כאילו עובר. It is a means of emphasizing the evil character of לשון הרע (:4) (comp. WE, "Devices for Emphasis," pp. 31 ff.).

XVI.7 (361:7 ff.)

[1] אילון ציפריא קולנין וכו' (8:)—By involving the ritual of the birds with the concept of לשון הרע (8:), the ritual becomes not merely ritual alone, as it is in the Bible, but is drawn into the sphere of the ethical. But there are also other instances where the Rabbis draw matters of ritual into the sphere of the ethical (see, e.g., 72:4 f.). This means that there is an emphatic trend toward the ethical, an emphasis on the ethical. The emphasis on love is so dominant and so frequent, that we have usually treated it as an emphatic trend in its own right and as distinct from the general emphasis on the ethical.

[2] . . . ומה אם צפרים . . . (362:2)—The birds are not actually the property of a person, since they also dwell in the field. However, the food and drink they occasionally take from him constitute an obligation on the man's part. The concept is כפרה.

[3] כהן שנהנה מישראל וכו' (3:)—The concept of Israel is here stressed above that of קדושה. The twenty-four מתנות (3:) are the מתנות כהונה given by God and are קדושות, but here they are regarded as constituting an obligation of the priest towards Israel. Similarly, the concept of Israel is stressed as against that of כהונה. The stressing of one concept above, or as against another, is a characteristic of the organismic complex.

XVI.8 (362:5 ff.)

[1] אמ' ר' אחא . . . חלאים עליך (5 f.)

מאדם הוא . . . עליו (5:)—Based on the interpretation of מן הצרוע (Lev. 14:3) as *"because* of the צרוע." That is, he has been healed because his healing depended on himself, and his being healed is the result of his having done תשובה. The concepts of תשובה and God's justice, embodied in the interpretation of Lev. 14:3, illustrate a general matter, namely that the rabbinic value-complex interprets situations left uninterpreted by the Bible. והנה נרפא of that verse is not accounted for in the biblical text (see CA, pp. 92, 134, 142). Here, however, the general point is made that a man's good health is the result of his good conduct and is a reward by God. The concept of God's justice.

הרשון (363:3)—Lieberman (p. 874 here) suggests that רעיון in the parallel combines the two words, רע עין, that is עין רעה, begrudging the success of others, as in Abot II.11. In this sense עין רעה refers to a human trait belonging to the first phase of דרך ארץ (on this phase see WE, pp. 39 f. and 52), a trait immensely harmful to its possessor, the worst sickness of all (כל חלי, 3:). In the context of Deut. 7:12 ff., warding off this sickness by God is a combination of the concepts of God's justice (ibid., v. 12) and God's love (ואהבך, v. 13). Regarding this trait as a sickness is, of course, a true insight.

על דע' . . . שמים (5:)—All death is בידי שמים (6:), including death from diseases of the bile (מרה, 6:). The fact of death in the human race is interpreted by different authorities in accordance with different aspects of God's justice. The idea in the midrash here is that only one percent of human deaths is caused by diseases or events other than the disease of the bile, but it is assumed that every death is due ultimately to God's justice. (Comp. Tosafot B.M. 107b; s.v. תשעין.)

[2] בעין (364:1)—Here עין הרע refers to the superstition of the "evil eye." It has a kinship with folklore "science" because the measures taken against it belong to the category of techniques (see J.T. Shab. XIV.3, 14c). Such techniques do not involve concepts and hence עין הרע here is not related to עין הרע referring to a human trait. Although folklore "science" is given expression in some statements, as in the present midrash, it was not actually rabbinic thought but common to the peoples of the ancient world in general. The superstitious element in folklore "science" was usually reworked and purged by the Rabbis.

בצינה (1:)—The statement here expresses folklore science, not a superstition but the fruit of some observation. The same is true of the statement at 363:5.

[3] אנטונינוס . . . מחמתו (3: f.)—What obviously lies within your own power to correct or achieve does not justify resort to prayer. Implied, too, is rejection of the folklore science involved in צינתא (5:).

בפשיעה (365:2)—A view which rejects the several dicta of folklore science, since it insists that deaths are largely due to neglect of ordinary precautions.

XVI.9 (365:4 ff.)

If the נגע has been healed though no תשובה has been done, the teaching here is that the נגע will return. The healing of the נגע is thus no proof that the person is now righteous and so there has been a kind of "trial by ordeal." There is an emphasis here not on the judgment of others but on the subjective consciousness of the individual involved. If he has not done תשובה, he should not assume that he has been permanently healed, and he must therefore do תשובה.

[1] This is another instance of what is purely ritualistic in the Bible but is drawn into the sphere of the ethical by the Rabbis. And so again there is an emphasis on the ethical, here by means of the concept of תשובה. It is also another instance of rabbinic symbolism.

[2] אזנך . . . בתפילה . . . ר' יהושע (366:5 f.)—Refers to private petitions and not to the עמידה, for it speaks of spontaneous expression of prayer.

תכין לבם (367:1)—The proper expression of a petition to God is regarded as a sign, but also as itself a gift from God. The concepts here are תפילה and כוונה. On the other hand, the Rabbis are also aware that in כוונה in prayer there is the danger that it may become a kind of theurgy (see WE, p. 188, note).

. . . רפאני ה' (:4)—Apparently used here as a supporting verse to indicate restoration of health by God to a supplicant.

Chapter XVII

XVII.1 (368:2 ff.)

[1] אך טוב . . . נחלתו (:2 f.)—Interpretations of various verses have in common here the formula יכול לכל, תל' לו'—all of them thus teach that real differences mark off the צדיקים from the rest of Israel. These are differences of their more thoroughgoing commitment and dedication.

כוונת הלב (:3)—Who do מצוות with שלבן ברי במצוות. The word ברי is taken as בריא, healthy (as can be seen from MSS), i.e., a functioning heart or mind and hence, מצוות done with כוונת הלב.

אשרי . . . עוז . . . בלבהון (:3)—The word דאורייתא (:5) indicates that עוז (:4) is taken as referring to Torah (cf. Sifre Deut., 343, ed. Finkelstein, p. 398 and the references there), so that the verse is rendered, "Happy is the man who possesses Torah through Thee"—"through Thee," because any knowledge of Torah is given by God. (See OT, p. 45 f.)

ולישרים בלבותם (:6)—Not merely good people, but righteous, because of complete integrity.

ויודע חסי בו (:7)—Those who always trust in God and not only in time of trouble—the concept of בטחון.

לנפש תדרשנו (:7)—Whole-souled seeking.

לשארית נחלתו . . . (369:3)—This teaches, apparently, that only the צדיקים, "the remnant," are granted forgiveness for sin. On the other hand, elsewhere they are also spoken of as more subject to retribution than others (see Yeb. 121b).

[2] עם אבא בגיהינם . . . רשעים . . . (:5)—They regard גיהינם here and usually elsewhere as functioning in the present.

כי קנאתי . . . (:6)—His sin was that he was envious of the wicked, those who bring woe to the world.

בשלומן שלרשעים אראה (370:1)—This describes the proper attitude to the רשעים which he now has; he expects to see the punishment, the retribution, visited on the wicked. Instead of the
further description of their well-being as in the פשט, the concept
of God's justice is here injected. Another instance of the wider
applicability of the rabbinic concept of מדת הדין.

[3] כנען . . . ועם אדם (372:3)—The passage seems to teach:

נגעים do not mean that anyone so punished is a רשע. They come
as chastisements so as to bring about תשובה.

A person recognized to be a רשע is not subject to נגעים, but is
apparently punished on the יום הדין, an answer to the problem of
רשע וטוב לו.

מזהיר (5:)—According to this view, Lev. 14:34 does not simply
speak of something that may happen, but is a warning of a punishment. There is an injection here of מדת הדין, whereas that
concept is not involved in the biblical passage itself.

XVII.2 (373:1 f.)

[1] Another פתיחה leading to the interpretation of Lev. 14:34. Again, the
injection of מדת הדין where the Bible itself does not embody it.
The rabbinic concepts, among them מדת הדין, have a wider
application than their biblical antecedents, interpreting matters
left uninterpreted in the Bible. In this case, however, to make
their point the Rabbis are obliged to add to the biblical content.

[2] בגויה . . . יגל (1:)—The entire passage in Leviticus is given a new
turn: the refusal by a man to lend wheat or other products and the
refusal by a woman to lend household objects through disclaim-
ing possession of these things—all these matters are not biblical.
The biblical command, to clear the house of its effects, is made by
the Rabbis to have the purpose of exposing the lie and thus to
indicate the selfishness of the householder. If the passage is to be
interpreted by מדת הדין, there must be a reason for this punishment, and hence the matters added by the Rabbis.

XVII.3 (374:3 ff.)

[1] עין רעה . . . על עשרה‏ (3:)—The entire realm of ethics applies to the non-Jews as well as to Israel—that is what דרך ארץ, the rabbinic term for ethics, implies. Here a number of what are included in שבע מצוות בני נח are listed together with several other concepts, the "additional" concepts being: עין הרע and גס רוח, לשון הרע (5:). Since all of the things listed are grouped together because they are all punished by נגעים, they are obviously all of one kind, and if most of the things relate to the בני נח, so must all the rest. Furthermore, a non-Jew, גלית, is punished for violating one of these matters (376:1). In another list פרעה (347:9) is held guilty of a moral wrong.

[2] חילול השם (375:5)—An aspect of חילול השם consists of the effect on a Gentile of a bad act committed by a Jew (comp. Tos. Baba Kamma X.15). Here Gehazi erases the קדוש השם of Elisha's refusal to accept anything from Naaman (see מהרז"ו). It was קדוש השם because Naaman accepts in his own way the worship of God (II Kings 5:17, and see WE, p. 133 f.). In giving the instance of גלית, a non-Jew, the passage indicates that the list of "ten things" applies to non-Jews as well, but this also indicates that עבודה זרה and חלול השם are forbidden to non-Jews too, and that these matters are elements of דרך ארץ.

XVII.4 (378:1 ff.)

[1] ר' חוניה . . . תחילה (1:)—When God punishes, He does not begin with striking the person. This implies that He strikes first at a man's property. Why? Evidently to make him aware of the need to repent. This is made explicit in the details concerning נגעים (381:7), although it is only implicit in the other cases.

[2] בעל הרחמים (2:)—The concept of God's love is combined with that of His justice: the person has sinned but God gives him the opportunity to repent. The destruction of his property is a warning to repent. The term בעל הרחמים in a context of God's justice reflects an emphasis on God's love.

עוה"ב . . . וכי הבקר . . . חורש בקוצר (3 f.:)—Concepts of נס and עוה"ב.

ונגש חורש בקוצר (379:2)—The concepts of עוה"ב and ימות המשיח
are, of course, rabbinic, but here is an instance of how adumbration of these concepts is to be found in the Prophets. Such an
adumbration of a rabbinic concept consists in what can be
regarded as a "concretization" of the rabbinic concept. It is therefore characterized as: מעין דיגמא שלעולם הבא (1:).

אמ' ר' אבא . . . ומתו שם (3:)—Apparently this is an attempt to
indicate that the נערים were given time to repent but did not do
so. Still, repent for what?

[3] מיד מת . . . ואמלטה (4:)—See Mandelbaum's note on להגיד לך (5:) in
his edition of Pesikta de R. Kahana, p. 130.

[4] במצרים . . . אף במצרים (381:4)—Egypt likewise was first punished by
destruction of property, and only at the end by death of the first-
born. Loss of property ought to have warned them to let Israel go.
The narrative in the Bible itself already contains the idea of the
midrash although the notion of the בעל הרחמים is not explicit
there. But the Bible, of course, does not regard the plagues of
Egypt as only one example of a general proposition.

[5] מושבו . . . אף נגעים (7: f.)—The general proposition is illustrated in
detail here.

על ביתו וכו' . . . כתחילה (7:)—Opposite to the order in the Bible,
and all of the נגעים described there are taken as referring to the
same man.

XVII.5 (382:3 ff.)

[1] מתקללת . . . כי תבאו (3:) - רמזו (4:)—This is reminiscent of Gen. 3:17,
but here it is a particular land, and that particular land is bound
up with a particular people, Israel. The land and the people are
related in a kind of corporate entity, or, the land is an extension,
as it were, of the people. Again, not the land is punished but the
people, the householders.

[2] The biblical curse (ארור, 383:4) is removed from כנען and instead he is

given the status "blessed" (ברוך, 4:), an example of the rabbinic emphasis on love.

This is the reward of כנען, the עבד, for having served Abraham faithfully, אליעזר being none other than כנען. Thus the emphasis on love is found in a context of God's justice (see also XVII.4[1]).

XVII.6 (384:4 ff.)

[1] תני ר׳ שמעון . . . תחתיה סימא (5: f.)—In the Bible the concept embodied here (Lev. 14:34 ff.) is טומאה, but the midrash adds to this the concept of God's love. The procedure engaged in because of the טומאה brought prosperity to Israel. As described in the Bible, the plague on houses is a calamity. In this midrash, however, it turns out to be a blessing, a manifestation of God's love. Another instance of the emphatic trend toward God's love.

[2] אמ׳ ר׳ ישמעאל . . . מלחמה ונפלו (386:1 f.)—Medieval authorities attempt to reconcile the version in J.T. Sheb., VI.1, 36c with the Bible (see, e.g., Tosafot to Giṭ. 46a, s.v. כיון). However, on the sheer basis of the statement, especially as given in this midrash, there is certainly an attempt to avoid war and bloodshed. Notice הרוצה לפנות יפנה ולהשלים ישלים (2:). In other words, the concept of peace plays a much greater role than in the biblical narrative.

XVII.7 (387:3 ff.)

[1] כנגע . . . עבודה זרה . . . (6:)—What connection is there between the נגע and עבודה זרה (7:), an idol? The concept of טומאה, an idol being an original cause of an entire order of hierarchical טומאה (see WE, p. 231 f., and see also רד״ל and רש״ש to איכה רבתי, פתיחתא 21).

[2] אמ׳ ר׳ אחא בייא . . . דביתא (8:)—This refers, apparently, to the absence of גלוי שכינה in the Temple caused by the presence of the idol. טומאה, the opposite of קדושה, negates it and therefore prevents the sensory manifestation of הקדוש ברוך הוא. It is assumed that otherwise there was גלוי שכינה in the First Temple.

[3] הים . . . אמ' ר' ברכיה (9:)—The point made by the parable refers once more to גלוי שכינה in the Temple. Now, however, there is the additional implication that this is a manifestation of God's love, and this cannot occur when God is flouted by the presence of an idol in the Temple, an idol being, so to speak, a "rival" of God.

מקום טמא (1:) because it is not ארץ ישראל. ‫בבל—(389:1)‬ is ‫זו בבל‬

Chapter XVIII

XVIII.1 (389:6 ff.)

[1] . . . עד . . . ימי הזקנה (390:6 ff.)—From here to the application are inserted interpretations of the rest of the passage in Ecclesiastes. These interpretations usually regard the verses as describing the disabilities of old age but as a description given through metaphors, the interpretations being largely an attempt to relate the metaphors to sober physical phenomena. This is the opposite of Haggadah, for in Haggadah the plain literal meaning is the stimulus for imaginative interpretations. Again, the interpretations here are not Haggadah for the reason that they describe, largely, a physical condition only and hence do not embody, in the main, value concepts. On the other hand, the method employed is the same as in Haggadah, the midrashic method, and thus it may also be used to express a haggadic idea, that is, an idea embodying a value concept.

In the attempt to relate the metaphors to plain descriptions the method is midrashic not only because there is often a word-play involved, but also because, when this is not the case, the metaphors are seen as representing the physical phenomena by virtue of some analogical resemblance to them, and the use of analogy, especially in the form of parables, is a characteristic of the midrashic method.

[2] אילו ימי המשיח (391:1)—The correct reading, אלו היסורים (see Margulies: אילו היסורים), may simply be stating a fact, the lot of old age, and not involve מדת הדין as a value concept (see below,

400:4). The reading given here in the text does involve the concept of ימות המשיח. The idea of "the freedom of the will" is an auxiliary idea, for בחירה חפשית is not a rabbinic term and the idea here is tied to ימי המשיח, a rabbinic concept. (On auxiliary ideas, see RM, p. 52 and the Index there, s.v. auxiliary ideas.)

[3] ר' לוי . . . מקדמין אתו (4:)—This only looks like an example of the rabbinic method in which the same author gives different interpretations of the same verse. Rather, this is an attempt to give the prosaic meaning behind the biblical metaphor—one meaning for the scholars and another for the common people. Actually, then, there is an attempt here to give the פשט, and the metaphor makes two alternative meanings possible.

אדריינוס . . . ממנו כלום (394:2)—A haggadic idea embodying the concept of תחיית המתים.

[4] שלום . . . ותפר . . . לאשתו (395:1)—A haggadic statement embodying the value concept of שלום (2:). התאוה (1:) is a human trait, and thus belongs to the first phase of דרך ארץ (see WE, p. 39), but one which has ethical concomitants, as here.

כי הולך . . . למלך . . . עצמו (396:3)—A haggadic statement embodying the concepts of צדיק (4:) and עולם (הבא) (5:). עולם here can only refer to עולם הבא, since it cannot refer to עוה"ז. Apparently, therefore, occasionally עוה"ב does mean the life immediately after death, not the Age to Come. Notice that the phrase עולם בפני עצמו follows שהכל טועמין טעם מיתה (397:2). Emphasis on the individual.

[5] לאחר שלשה . . . חגיכם (398:1)—A haggadic interpretation embodying the concepts of גזל and חמס (1:). Hyperbole indicating how difficult it is for people in general not to give way in these matters to some degree.

וישב העפר . . . כף הקלע (399:2)—A haggadic interpretation embodying the concept of מדת הדין. The implication here is that only רשעים are not buried, as can be seen from נפש איביך (4:) in the prooftext (Sam. I 25:29).

והרוח (399:2) ונשמה (2:) refers to (400:2)—ונשמה . . . טהורה היא of the prooftext. The concept here is טהרה. The idea here is that if a person sins, the נשמה is no longer pure. Does that mean that only the נשמה of a perfectly sinless man returns to God? This is the implication here. The parable suggests that ritual purity and the moral purity of the נשמה are related in some fashion.

שורפה לפניך (3:)—An impure soul is destroyed, but what of the punishment after death? According to this view, apparently only the צדיקים survive after death.

[6] בזיבה וצרעת (4:) are thus punishments, but this means that the disabilities of old age do not come as a result of sin, are not punishments. That is the implication, too, of the story about ר' שמעון בן חלפתא on 395:2 f., wherein his infirmities are ascribed simply to his being old.

XVIII.2 (400:7 ff.)

[1] משפטו ושאתו יצא (7:)—איום ונורא . . . ושאתו יצא, the second half of this verse is interpreted in the same manner in all the examples of the section, namely that the punishment of the sinner named issues in some fashion from the sinner himself. However, איום ונורא הוא—the first half of the verse is applied in one way to Esau (Rome), to סנחריב, to חירם and to נבוכדנצר, and differently to Adam and to Israel.

[2] איום ונורא הוא (7:)—Adam's appearance was איום ונורא but there was nothing wrong in that—not even his doing, his fault, as it were.

[3] ד"א איום . . . ד' דבר (401:6 f.)

זה עשו (6:)—Refers to Rome and so also does אדום (8:). Rome inspired fear everywhere and hence איום ונורא (6:).

הגדול (7:)—Great and powerful and thus a characterization of Rome, and a text indicating Rome was איום ונורא (see רש"ש).

עובדיה . . . ממנו . . . עובדיה . . . דבר (7: f.)—עובדיה, who issued from Edom, prophesied the destruction of Edom, i.e., Rome, but of course did not cause its destruction; Rome still existed. Rome sinned because it spread terror (איום ונורא הוא, 6:). Rome was characterized as מלכות הרשעה (cf., e.g., Ber. 61b), and it ruled by terror.

[4] ד"א איום . . . סנחריב . . . אלהי וגו' (402:1)—In this example, the elements in the midrash are more fully utilized and so also in the next two instances.

איום ונורא זה סנחריב (1:)—But this is only part of the characterization.

מי בכל . . . הארצות . . . מידי (1:)—The verse continues with: כי יציל ה' את ירושלים מידי (Isa. 36:20). His sin, therefore, is חלול השם, one of the Noachian prohibitions. He regarded himself as more powerful than God, as all-powerful and indeed he did strike terror everywhere.

How was he punished? ממנו . . . אילו בניו . . . (2:). He was slain by those who issued from him (ממנו), his sons. Now those who issued from him are, so to say, an extension of him. He who thought he was all-powerful is, in the end, shown to be powerless.

[5] ד"א . . . נבוכדנצר . . . חרב (403:1 f.)—His boast of divinity and the fear he engendered are contrasted with his degradation, with the disrespectful dragging out of his dead body so as to convince his issue, namely his son, of Nebuchadnezzer's death. His חלול השם is given in Isa. 14:13–14.

[6] אני אמרתי אלהים אתם (404:5)—A statement embodying the concept of God's love and here indicating that the appearance of every Israelite was awe-inspiring (איום ונורא, 4:). A statement by God, not a boast by a man.

XVIII.3 (404:8 ff.)

[1] ביום שנטעתי וכו' (8:)—This and the following statements apparently attempt to answer the question: How could Israel have sinned after having experienced מתן תורה on Sinai? The answer: Even then it was only an outward acceptance of Torah and was not genuine. There was, therefore, no real change in character.

[2] אלה . . . חרש (405:1)—Attempted to deceive God.

שגשגתון . . . נכון עמו.וגו' (2:)—They did deceive God; concept of אונאה or גניבת דעת. This obviously is in conflict with the idea of

God's omniscience; however, there is no rabbinic term for God's omniscience and hence the latter is an auxiliary idea, not a value concept (see RM, p. 220). We should say that this midrash involves indeterminacy of belief, for it does contradict, after all, an idea held by the Rabbis, even though it is an auxiliary idea. An auxiliary idea does not have to be harmonized with a value concept, but it does have to be reckoned with. For an example of how this auxiliary idea is used, see CA, p. 97 (text and our comment).

Now the idea in this midrash is fully expressed in the supporting verse (Ps. 78:36–7) in the words יפתוהו בפיהם (2:). The conflict with God's omniscience is thus biblical; it is an example of the close relationship between the Bible and rabbinic thought. Even when the rabbinic concepts are new concepts, they always have antecedents in the Bible, and hence are always linked with the Bible. Rabbinic thought does represent a development, but an indigenous development. The attempt to make out rabbinic thought to be a derivative, in some manner, of Greek thought ought not to be taken seriously (see, e.g., Kaufmann, *Toledot* etc., IV, p. 347, on the concept of תורה שבעל פה and its so-called similarity to Greek thought).

[2] שלמלאך המות . . . נד קציר (406:1)—A later midrash pointing to the three interpretations of חרות at 407:3. They could combine those interpretations because they all interpret חָרוּת as "freedom" and none negates the others. An example of a later midrash based on an earlier one (see RM, p. 60).

[3] למה שהן בניי . . . אלהיכם (6:)—This is an interpolation. An entirely different reason is given here for the angel of death having no power over them than the reason just given. The concepts involved, accordingly, are also different: in the second reason the concept is solely God's love (בניי, 6:); in the first reason, the element of reward implies the concept of God's justice, perhaps in combination with that of God's love. These words are not found in the parallel in Canticles R. VIII.3.

[4] ביום נחלה . . . זב מבשרו (407:5)—Continues with the interpretation of the last clause in Isa. 17:11, the verse of the פתיחה. The giving of the Torah is here regarded not as a possibility for great benefits, as in the preceding midrash, but as involving the possibility of

punishment for infraction of its laws. The concepts here are Torah and God's punitive justice.

XVIII.4 (408:1 ff.)

[1] וכל זב . . . תני ר׳ שמעון—The association of ideas is dual. This midrash is associated with the previous one both because it too contains a teaching regarding זיבה וצרעת (407:8), a teaching here emphasized by the prooftext (Num. 5:2) in :7, and also because it begins with an idea related to the one in 406:3, a relationship extending to the wording as well.

[2] ובצרעת . . . ר׳ תנחומ׳ (409:3)

מליזין על הארון וכו׳ (3:)—The ארון is personified. This implies apparently that a deliberate malevolence was attributed by Israel to the ארון and hence a slander, since the deaths were caused by irreverence.

[3] פרוע . . . ורבנין (5:)—The concept here is not לשון הרע as in the two preceding midrashim but עבודה זרה. They were punished with זיבה וצרעת (5:) for the first time after worshipping the Golden Calf. This is an instance of the flexibility of the organic complex; there is no inevitable connection between a concept and any one concretization. While the idea that לשון הרע results in זב ומצורע is frequently met with, it is not the only one found, i.e., it is not a dogma—here זב ומצורע results from עבודה זרה.

[4] לאהל מועד . . . ר׳ יהודה (7: f.)—Israel was punished for the first time with זיבה וצרעת after the incident of the quail when they were guilty of gluttony, an aspect of דרך ארץ (first phase). The proof is given at the end of the midrash.

מהו לזרא . . . לאהל מועד (8:)—Various interpretations of Num. 11:20. The last apparently consists of an explanation of the word לזרא (8:) bearing on זיבה וצרעת.

XVIII.5 (410:4 ff.)

[1] נפשותיכם . . . אכסריה . . . ר׳ יהושע (4 f.:)—Acts of man which are
paralleled by acts of God. They serve as contrasts to the statement
at the end in which acts of God are not paralleled by acts of men.

הנני ממטיר . . . לחם מן השמים (411:6)—In order to make it a
parallel to an act of man, the aspect of נס is not taken into account
here. It is made a secondary matter at best. This ignoring of the
concept of נס, or practically ignoring it, is most unusual.

[2] מידי מציל . . . בשר ודם מכה (412:1)—The emendation of רד״ל is
necessitated by the prooftext, Deut. 32:39, which has מחצתי (1:)
and hence refers to God, not to man. This is especially applicable
in the case of an illness and to recovery therefrom. The illness is a
punishment and thus a manifestation of God's justice, whereas
the recovery from the illness is indicative of God's love. There is
thus, in this midrash, a combination of the concepts of God's love
and His justice. In the parallels of man's acts and God's acts, the
latter are mostly concretizations of God's justice and the rest,
those of God's love, but no combination of the two.

Chapter XIX

XIX.1 (412:7 ff.)

[1] האותיות . . . ראשו כתם פז (7 f.:)—The idea here is a good instance of
indeterminacy of belief. Torah here refers to the written Torah,
more specifically to the Pentateuch, but after all, much of the
Pentateuch is narrative and speaks of events that happened after
the creation of the world. The idea here, then, is obviously a
poetic notion and not felt to be a strictly literal matter (see RM,
pp. 132 ff., and see also our remarks below at 420:4).

אתמול . . . שתי אלפים קדמה תורה (413:1)—Another implication
of קדמה is: being of greater importance. Torah was created before
the world because it transcends the world.

במי שהוא משתיר וכ׳ (‎6.‎f)—The concept here is תלמוד תורה whereas in the preceding midrash it was תורה.

[2] אמ׳ ר׳ שמואל . . . של יהושפט (‎414:1 f.)—The concepts here are תלמוד תורה, בטחון and נס, as well as God's justice (reward).

מי יכין לעורב צידו (‎2:)—Apparently צידו refers to Elijah, Elijah's food; the נס here is biblical, and the implication is for their own day.

למוד . . . בתורה (‎2:)—The נביאים are also חכמים, scholars whose entire lives were devoted to תלמוד תורה. The נביא was, of course, inspired by God but what was he occupied with when he was not engaged in prophecy? With study of Torah; the נביא was thus regarded as a חכם to whom was *added* the gift of נבואה. נבואה was a gift, apparently, that was dependent upon devotion to study of Torah.

[3] אמ׳ ר׳ שמואל . . . תורה (‎415:1)—This midrash is based on the preceding one and the author may be the same for both. Asceticism in rabbinic Judaism was advocated by the Rabbis in order to enable one to study Torah, but not for its own sake. (See OT, p. 53 ff.)

ר׳ אסא . . . לערב צידו (‎4:)—This "experiment" is an example of folklore science. Despite the support this experiment attempts to give to the concept of נס concretized in Job 38:41 quoted in the conclusion, that concretization is explained away by the experiment which reduces it to a natural phenomenon, and thus the very quality characteristic of נס is lost, since the very characteristic of נס is its not being explainable. Although, as here, there are rabbinic statements containing folklore science, they are not compatible with the value complex.

XIX.2 (416:7 ff.)

[1] שכר יגיעה (‎419:2)—Reward is given for the effort expended, even if what was learned is forgotten. תלמוד תורה is a virtue in itself, besides being the means of acquiring knowledge of Torah.

[2] יוד שלירבה קיטרגו (‎420:4)—This is obviously a poetic idea, a play of fancy, and yet it does contain a teaching. Such ideas seem to

indicate that the indeterminacy of belief is characterized by a spectrum of ideas and that these poetic ideas are at the end of the spectrum. (See the example at 412:7 f. and our remarks there.)

[3] יהושע . . . ר' הונא (421:4 f.)—Altogether, beginning with 420:4, four different ideas personify the יוד here. These poetic ideas thus do not consist of an isolated phenomenon, an indication of how frequently the end of the spectrum of indeterminacy of belief was resorted to.

[4] לבלותך . . . כת' שמע (422:3 f.)—This passage belongs at 419:5, since it provides examples for the general idea there about how "the world may be destroyed" by what you see merely as small "strokes."

XIX.3 (423:4 ff.)

[1] כלפידים . . . ר' יהודה (4:)– . . . מראהו כלבנון (5:)—The relation of this verse and also of Nahum 2:5 to the concept of תלמידי חכמים (4:) is not clear as is evident in the commentaries.

[2] הרי הן עריבות עלי (424:3)—A criterion is not their appeal to man but their appeal to God.

זוב דמה . . . תדע לך (3:)—To indicate how we can tell that they do give pleasure to God.

XIX.4 (424:6 ff.)

[1] שנתעצלו ישראל (6:)—Meaning here that everybody refrained from quarreling (see רד"ל). Voicing the same spirit is the adage that it takes two to make a quarrel.

[2] גם עבים נטפו מים (425:2)—This verse, too, is taken to refer to the giving of Torah at Sinai. When Israel heard God's voice, their souls fled and God revived them by letting fall upon them the dew that will revive the dead (Ginzberg, Legends, III, p. 95). The concepts here are: תחיית and מתן תורה (reward), מדת הדין, שלום המתים.

[3] חטטים . . . ד"א בעצלתים (:6 f.)—This is not folklore science but an empiric knowledge of health rules. The negative concept of indolence is involved here, a concept belonging to the first phase of דרך ארץ.

ר' כהן . . . באשה . . . הערה (426:3)—The concepts embodied are זנות and צניעות; see also רד"ל.

בנידתה (:6)—Concepts are טומאה and מדת הדין.

[4] טביתא . . . לי נפשי (:7 f.)—Association of ideas. Tabitha was careful to be בודקת.

XIX.5 (427:4 ff.)

[1] ומי נתנבא . . . עזריהו בן עודד וכו' (:5)—Question and answer emphasize that this verse (II Chron. 15:3) was said by the prophet, an emphasis intended to indicate that 15:7 was *not* said by the prophet but by a בת קול (428:1). It is surprising that the commentaries did not speak of this, since it is the entire point of the midrash.

מדת הדין (:6)—Here the term refers to human justice.

ללא תורה (:4) is taken in the sense of הוראה, שסנהדרין גדולה (:7)—a function of the סנהדרין.

The midrash here (428:1) thus emphasizes God's love by an interpretation in which God comforts and encourages them, for the verse in Chronicles ends with כי יש שכר לפעלתכם.

[2] ר' יודן ור' פינחס . . . הרעים (:2)—Having adduced Isa. 35:3, interpretations of this verse are now given, interpretations that are unitary entities in their own right. The concepts embodied are צדיקים and רשעים.

[3] ר' הושעיה . . . חומתה (:5)—But where is the comfort to these "brokenhearted?" It is given in the continuation of Isa. 35:4 and in the verses following. A new redemption of Israel is foretold there, as well as the punishment by God of the oppressors.

רחוקין (429:1)—On the concept of קץ, a subconcept of גאולה, redemption, see CA, pp. 182–83.

This midrash makes more explicit the ideas in Isa. 35:4. By mentioning the concept of קץ (:1), the midrash makes evident that the verse refers to the redemption which is imminent, and by employing איה אלהיך of Ps. 42:11, the idea of גלוי שכינה is prepared for. The concepts are: מדת, אומות, ישראל, גלוי שכינה, בת קול, קץ, הדין. This midrash exemplifies the close relation between biblical and rabbinic ideas.

[4] ימים רבים . . . ימים רבים (:5)—Return to the verse of the פתיחה (II Chron. 15:3). These midrashim do not say that the ימים שלצער (:5, etc.) were punishment for sin. Apparently they are explanatory and not really valuational, teaching only that ימים רבים means צער. ימים של צער belongs to the first phase of דרך ארץ, a phase of the concept which refers to human traits and is thus merely descriptive (see WE, pp. 39 f.). Such midrashim are not פשט, of course, but neither are they valuational Haggadah.

ודכוותה . . . ומאת יום (430:4)—But why should this be the occasion for צער? יפ"ת refers to the midrash which says that the Jews saw the holy vessels of the Temple in the house of the king (Esther R. II.11).

הדין . . . ימים רבים (:5)—The צער is two-fold: physical pain and separation from her husband. There is also embodied the concept of טומאה.

[5] על אחת כמה וכמה (431:6)—How can there be any analogy between separation from a husband and separation from the Temple? The idea here, therefore, is that there was גלוי שכינה in the Temple, a visible manifestation of God at the occasions of the sacrificial worship and that when the sacrificial worship will be restored there will again be גלוי שכינה. See RM, pp. 239 ff.

XIX.6 (431:7 ff.)

[1] הגיע זמנו . . . לאו (432:3)—The time for the destruction of the First Temple was fixed by God, and hence the Sanhedrin ask about

that of Nebuchadnezzer who was to be the instrument of the destruction. The concept is God's justice.

[2] בידן . . . כיצד שילשלו (433:2)—The views here are instances of indeterminacy of belief. Two opposite views are supported by different verses and the third is a deliberate attempt to make the views more fixed through a reconciliation of the two. See our next comment.

[3] . . . מה עשה לו נבוכדנצר (6:)—The authorities here assume that יהויקים was killed by Nebuchadnezzer; apparently the first view given above is accepted. Did these authorities make independent statements which an editor wove into a connected story? This seems likely for they could not all have been together on one occasion. On the other hand the "pairs" named do give an impression of a kind of dialogue. Note this same style and the same terms used in the case of both proponents of a "pair."

הוא שנביא מקנתר וכו' (434:4)—The "three Amoraim" interpret the words: והנמצא עליו (4:), each one interpreting them, in different ways, to refer to transgressions relating to his body, whereas ר' יוחנן (435:1) apparently interprets ותועבותיו (434:4), a word used to refer to sexual sins (see Lev. 18:26). The concepts here are: עבירות and עריות, and, of course, מדת הדין.

ר' יהושע . . . שאגתו (435:2)—An interpretation drawn from another verse, and the concepts are: עריות, שפיכות דמים, מדת הדין, and גזל.

[4] הואיל . . . מפתחותיך וכו' (436:6)—An acknowledgment that they were unworthy to offer sacrifices. The concepts are: sin, קדושה, עבודה, and מדת הדין; the statement and act of the king imply repentance, and hence also תשובה.

חד . . . פיסת יד . . . מידו (7:)—To indicate that, indeed their worship was no longer desirable (נבחר מפנינים). The concepts are: עבודה, מדת הדין, and נס.

ומה . . . עולין . . . לגגות (437:1)—Without the Temple worship, there was no point in living. (See מהרז"ו for the connection of Isa. 22:2 with v. 1 in the interpretation.

[6] מה היה שמה וכו' (438:3 f.)—On this haggadah, see Brill's *Jahrbücher*, III, pp. 18 f. (Lieberman here, p. 876).

[7] ‏. . . וכן אתם . . . הדם שבסיני (439:5)—This indicates that תשובה may involve not just a specific experience but may be expressed in a steady adherence to מצוות disregarded heretofore. The king's observance is representative of the new attitude of the entire people.

‏שמחל לו . . . כל עוונותיו (7:)—God forgave all his sins, implying that his general attitude was involved in the fulfilling of this מצוה.

Chapter XX

XX.1 (441:2 ff.)

[1] This midrash teaches that the מדת דין visited on a man is not necessarily an indication of his character. The good name of afflicted persons was, in this way, protected even though the concept of מדת הדין was employed.

[2] מקרה אחד (2:)—ר' שמעון . . . מקרה אחד . . . ולרשע מקרה אחד in the verse itself refers to the common fate of all mankind and thus to that common event of death. In this midrash, however, the term is made to refer to the similarity of what happens in each case to the righteous and the wicked. By thus being particularized, the similarity of what happened is made more striking, and hence to suggest that a lesson be drawn.

[3] הכישו נחש ושברו ארי (5:)—This assumes the longer midrash in Ber. R. XXX.6, ed. Theodor, p. 272: He was a צדיק but here he was punished (and see also יפ"ת on Ber. R., l.c.). We thus have מדת הדין applied to Noah.

‏והקריב . . . תחתיו (5:)—The first כהונה is thus related to the ancestor of Israel, the ממלכת כהנים.

מנגנון (442:2)—The idea of a machine so constructed as to simulate a function of a living creature is an aspect of folklore science. Compare Daedalus of the Greeks.

מדת הדין (2:)—זה מת צולע . . . צולע similar in every respect, even as to both having been maimed by a lion; yet one is a צדיק and the other a רשע. The lesson is: Do not draw the conclusion from the same manifestation of מדת הדין that their character was the same. The goodness of afflicted persons was thus protected even though the concept of מדת הדין was employed.

שנולד . . . מהול (4:)—The foreskin was considered a blemish which was removed by circumcision, and being born without a foreskin meant that a person was perfect from the beginning (Ber. R. XLVI.1).

[4] טמאי שפתים (5:)—By uttering evil the spies became ולטמא אילו מרגלים (רד״ל).

איולו אמרו . . . אילו לא נכנסו וכו׳ (6 f.)—The מדת הדין is the same, but the specific sin here is only that of the spies, and hence the contrast. However, the Bible itself assigns this very punishment to Moses and Aaron for a different sin (Num. 20:12). Again the lesson is that a manifestation of מדת הדין is not always indicative of a man's character. The same punishment is suffered by men of diametrically opposite character.

זה מת . . . זובח (443:5)—Again a contrast between the act of Josiah and that of Ahab, and yet a similar punishment is visited also upon Josiah. (On Josiah's sin, see Ginzberg, *Legends*, IV, p. 283 and the notes.) The Bible describes Ahab as a wicked king and Josiah as a righteous king, and so here too the same מדת הדין visited on both is not to be taken as an indication that their characters are the same.

[5] נזכר לתלמודו (444:1)—David was an embodiment, so to speak, of Torah and seeing him made a person recall what he had been taught, an inspiration that amounted to a נס.

כחוטא . . . פרוק (1:)—But how could חוטא be contrasted with Torah? Knowledge of Torah has an immediate practical efficacy influencing a man's behavior, his conduct (see "The Efficacy of Torah," OT, pp. 68 f., especially pp. 70 f.).

[6] זה מת בניקור וכו' (5:)—Both are instances of מדת הדין. In regard to Samson, see Soṭah I.8, which is a case of מדה כנגד מדה. However, Samson is described as צדיק (Soṭah 9b—'Abaye); also, apparently the breaking of an oath was regarded as a greater sin and one of which Samson was not guilty.

XX.2 (445:4 ff.)

ר' לוי פתח . . . לעולם (4:)—Characteristics of רשעים.

[1] ולרשעים . . . לשמוח בעולמי (6:)—The רשעים make joy their objective in life, but they are not entitled to joy for there are צדיקים who did not rejoice. שמחה is a human trait and thus belongs to the first phase of דרך ארץ.

[2] אדם הראשון (446:1)—אדם הראשון: as indicating a conceptualization, Man, (see CA, pp. 12 f.). Notice that here Adam is among the צדיקים.

תפוח . . . כמה וכמה (2:)—"The diminishing of the sun" apparently is meant to indicate Adam's beauty.

ואל עפר תשוב (447:2)—Adam sorrowed when he was told he would die. His past glory only served as a contrast to his present unhappiness.

[3] אברהם . . . בשמחה לחמך (2: ff.)

ענן וכו' (6:)—A manifestation of גלוי שכינה.

עם הדומה לחמור (448:2)—This does not actually deny the humanity of non-Jews but indicates rather their incapacity to experience גלוי שכינה. Nevertheless, the expression itself is harsh. (On a concept reflecting a broader view, see RM, pp. 27 f.)

[4] כנגד שש תקיעות (449:2)—The תקיעות on the New Year, by being related to the sacrifice of Isaac, are thereby interpreted by the concept of זכות אבות. The plea for forgiveness on ר"ה is on the ground of the merit of Isaac, Isaac and his descendents being regarded as one corporate personality. This is an instance of the

integration of Halakah and Haggadah. A haggadic interpretation of a halakah.

[5] ישראל . . . לעתיד לבוא (:6f.)—This statement indicates that the רשעים spoken of at 445:6 are the wicked of the Gentiles since ישראל (:6) refers to Israel as a whole. Perhaps the רשעים there refer to Gentile advocates of hedonism.

לעתיד לבוא (450:1)—Apparently refers to the Days of the Messiah since גאולה is implied here.

[6] כביכול הקב״ה . . . לעתיד לבוא (:1)—God will rejoice only when there are צדיקים and no רשעים. לעתיד לבוא (:3) here probably refers to עוה״ב.

XX.3 (451:3f.)

[1] חתנים . . . ברכת אבלים (452:5)—On their close conceptual and literary relations, see "Berakot as Gemilut Ḥasadim," WE, pp. 151 ff.

הפטיר עליו . . . מהולל (:6)—The אהטרה, of which only the biblical text is given here, is found in some MSS and in parallels. The comfort offered consisted of the teaching of Haggadah, of Torah and only the verse interpreted (Koh. 2:2) was relevant to the occasion.

XX.4 (453:1 ff.)

[1] משרה שכינתי . . . מסלק שכינתי (454:1)—This refers to גלוי שכינה, a visible manifestation of God on the ארון in the holy of holies but filling the holy of holies too, apparently. על מימר פומך (:1, :2), "at your behest," is hyperbole. The Pesikta R. (ed. Friedmann, p. 190) tells that to pay honor (כבוד) to Aaron, God left His place on the ארון when Aaron entered and that He returned when Aaron went out. He did this, the passage implies, because when the Shekinah was present in the holy of holies it filled the place. When Aaron entered there was no גלוי שכינה on the ארון and this seems to represent the Pharisaic view as against that of the Sadducees, but see the discussion in RM, p. 245. We have here

another indication that the Rabbis did not have the conception of the "immanence of God," a philosophic idea. Immanence that is not permanent is not immanence.

[2] אילו לאילו . . . ואל יגביהו (455:5)—Apparently refers to arrogance in office and does not advocate egalitarianism. It belongs to that phase of דרך ארץ consisting of manners, and exemplifies the idea that "there is no real line of demarcation between manners and morals."

[3] העולם שבע . . . למרחוק (456:3)—Basically these are omens and belong to the sphere of "folk-science," even though they are attached to a verse. Astrology also employs the various directions as omens (Mekilta, ed. Lauterbach, I, p. 19). "Folk-science" is the result of observation but is usually characterized by inadequate data, as here. However, as in this case, its omen-like quality also relates to magic. The prayers of the High Priest just before this statement indicate how valuation concepts differ from science and magic. The prayer (תפילתו, 455:3) is not an expression of determinism, but of hope, of desire, is indeed prompted by uncertainty. Value concepts are essentially indeterminate.

XX.5 (457:6 ff.)

[1] ציץ . . . דומין . . . לא היו (:7 f.)—יפ"ת penetrates to the essential meaning here. The dead staff of Aaron, by being restored to bearing fruit and blossoms, indicates that the קדושה precinct was the source of life (מקור החיים). Then why did death come from there to the live sons of Aaron? Job 37:1 is interpreted to mean "shocked surprise," and this is said here of the contrast between what happened to Aaron's staff and what happened to Aaron's sons, implying that, notwithstanding the latters' sin, the role of the holy precinct in their death is surprising, and this further implies that the holy precinct is primarily a source of life.

In this midrash there is the idea that קדושה is primarily related to life, to revival of life and is thus associated with joy, not with dread and fear as described by R. Otto in "The Idea of the Holy." We have here the view of, and also the experience of the holy which is a positive aspect of קדושה, as well as the view of קדושה as love and קדושה as imitation of God (see WE, p. 267).

XX.6 (458:5 f.)

[1] בני אהרון . . . ר' ברכיה (5:)—Had the sons of Aaron died because I thus punished Aaron (for the Golden Calf), it would indeed not have been good, but I punished his sons for their own present sin. (See רש״ש and the comment by Mandelbaum in his edition of Pesikta de R. Kahana, p. 393.); emphasis here on the individual as against corporate personality.

[2] שהורו הלכה וכו׳ (459:1)—The biblical characters cited here are interpreted in terms of the rabbinic complex, i.e., as the חכם and his תלמיד. But the תלמיד of the חכם would know what the הלכה is, and hence, as far as the הלכה was concerned, the sons of Aaron were correct. Their sin was in deliberately ignoring Moses, their teacher.

ומעשה . . . מיתה (2:)—In an oral tradition the role of the teacher was predominant. When a student gave a legal decision (הורה, 2:) "in the presence of his teacher," not only did he show disrespect for the teacher, but also may have caused disrespect for the tradition.

XX.7 (459:6 f.)

[1] Association of ideas in relation to the preceding midrash.

[2] כמחנה ישראל (7:)—The חכם is not only the teacher of his students, but potentially of all Israel, of all who direct questions to him.

XX.8 (461:1 f.)

[1] על הקרבה . . . הכניסו (3:)—One of the concepts embodied in the first three sins mentioned is קדושה: entering the קדש הקדשים (see Mandelbaum, loc. cit.); the קרבן which was the קטרת (see ibid., loc. cit.); and the אש זרה (3:) which consisted of a "secular" fire instead of holy fire (Margulies).

[2] שלא נטלו . . . דכת . . . מזה . . . (4 f.:)—Consulting with another person is practical wisdom and thus belongs to the second phase of

דרך ארץ. However, the moral overtone implied in this phase would not in itself be sufficient to have incurred the death penalty for its violation, and it is only because, in this particular case, the result of this violation of דרך ארץ was the violation of קדושה that they were punished. Had they sought advice from one another, they would not have violated קדושה.

איש מחיתתיו . . . (462:1)—Refers to these violations of קדושה by each individual separately, not to the idea that in general they did not seek counsel from each other. The connotation of מחיתתו (1:) in its literal meaning is still retained, implying that the act of violating קדושה constituted מחיתתו (see also נבחר מפנינים). Implied is the idea that they were צדיקים, and that it would have been enough for them to have consulted each other for them to have kept to their true character.

[3] בלבד . . . אמ' ר' ירמיה (2:)—In these passages we have instances of indeterminacy of belief. The preceding passage tells of ארבעה דברים (461:1), whereas this passage emphasizes that there was only one sin. The second passage follows on the first with no attempt to reconcile them. Here it is even more strongly implied that they were צדיקים, since they had only one sin—a צדיק is not sinless, but he rarely sins.

[4] מתו . . . אמ' ר' לעזר (4:)—Again an instance of indeterminacy of belief. Emphasizes again the idea that they commited this single sin but adding also that they had no secret sins.

כמה קשה מיתתן וכ' (4:)—This assumes that sin is the cause of death and embodies the concept of God's justice, but death may be caused by many different sins, and hence this one sin is specified wherever their death is mentioned. God was "apprehensive" lest their death might make people suspect them of secret sins. This midrash, too, regards them as צדיקים.

XX.9 (462:8 ff.)

[1] . . . בשביל ארבעה דברים מתו (8:)—Of these ארבעה דברים only the first three refer to different matters associated with the same event, whereas at 461:1 all four were so associated. The fourth matter

here (463:6) refers to a sin independent of the others, an ongoing sin, and hence they could not have been regarded as צדיקים in the present midrash. Since the character of the sons of Aaron is thus different from the one in the preceding passages, the present passage is also an instance of indeterminacy of belief.

XX.10 (464:3 ff.)

[1] שחצים (3:)—A negative value concept like רשעים, to which it is related. (On negative value concepts, see WE, p. 24.)

[2] אימותיהן . . . ועוד מן הדא (7 f.:)

ועוד מן הדא (7:)—Proof from another verse that they were שחצים (3:), but this proof and the others following serve also to illustrate the function of value concepts. The various incidents represent different concretizations of the value concept. The term שחצים gives to the separate incidents a common, unfavorable character.

[3] ולא נהנו מן השכינה . . . ועוד מן (465:5 ff.)—This midrash obviously embodies another concept as well, namely גלוי שכינה. It seems to reflect a negative attitude toward those who deliberately attempt to cultivate such a phenomenal experience.

היו ראויין להשתלחת יד . . . (6:)—A combination of מדת הדין and מדת רחמים.

אכילה וודיי . . . חיים (466:2)—The experience was energizing and life-giving. Compare our remarks on the experience of the holy at 457. At the same time it did not make for ethical behavior, but on the contrary provided another occasion to express their arrogance.

ר' יהושע . . . ולא נהנו וכו' (4 f.:)—Moses had an opportunity to enjoy a visible experience of the Shekinah but did not take it and therefore he benefited, as a reward, from that occasion. The contrary was the case with the sons of Aaron.

משה לא זן עיניו . . . יביט (4 f.)—The visual experience of Shekinah which Moses later had was a reward מידה כנגד מידה, a reward for hiding his face, etc. The example of Moses' attempt to avoid experience of גלוי שכינה indicates again the Rabbis' own attitude.

ולא נהנו מן השכינה (467:2)—Since they suffered an untimely death. The concept of מדת הדין.

[4] אלא . . . מתים החייהם (4:)—Emphasizes God's sympathy with the parents. Concepts of מדת רחמים and צדיקים.

ר' פינחס . . . מאביהן (5:)—Emphasizes God's sorrow over the death of the sons of Aaron, twice as great as even that of Aaron. Emphasizes the concept of God's love.

[5] במדבר סיני . . . אהל מועד (7 f.:)—This refers not to an additional incident where they were שחצים but to the one at Sinai where they witnessed גלוי שכינה. The prooftext is different.

יום חתונתו (468:6)—The bridegroom is Israel and the bride is the Torah given to Israel by God on Mt. Sinai.

XX.11 (469:1 ff.)

[1] בכבוד (3:)—כבוד is a value concept. In this halakah it endows any specific office with significance.

נוהג כמנהג אבותיו (3:)—Here it seems to be an ethical rule of דרך ארץ.

[2] טומאה (470:2)—The other concept involved is, of course, כהונה, a form of קדושה. טומאה would temporarily disqualify Aaron. ר' חייא (471:4) implies that Aaron was never so disqualified, whereas ר' יצחק (470:1) says that both אהרן and אלעזר were at times temporarily disqualified by טומאה. (On טומאה as the obverse of קדושה, see WE, pp. 227 f.)

אמרה . . . מיימיי (471:1)—Concretization of the concept of צניעות.

וקריין עלה וכו' (3:)—Concepts of צניעות and God's justice as well as כהונה.

XX.12 (471:5 f.)

[1] שאפר פרה מכפר (472:1)—Atones for the Golden Calf; the concept of כפרה.

[2] כך מיתת מרים מכפרת (1:)—On the basis of all the parallels it should read: מיתת צדיקים. The concepts are: כפרה, צדיקים, and ישראל. (See the reading in J.T. Yoma I, 38b.)

מכפרת (על ישראל) (1:)—The death of the righteous is atonement for Israel; this is "vicarious atonement." The righteous men and women do not deserve to die and their death is atonement, not for their own sins which are few but for Israel as a whole. Involved here is the idea of corporate personality, the righteous of Israel and the people as a whole constituting a single personality.

Notice the plural (צדיקים, 472:5–6). As a value concept כפרה has more than one concretization. Notice that the death of בני אהרן (3:) was also atonement (see RM, pp. 319 n. and 358 n).

[3] כשיבור לוחות (3:)—Aaron is regarded as a living embodiment of Torah.

[4] שיום הכפורים מכפר (5:)—On the atoning power of the day itself, see RM, p. 182.

[5] ומנין . . . מאחרי כן (6:)—But the concept embodied here is גמילות חסדים, as is evident in Pirke R. Eliezer, Chapt. XVII, *not* כפרה. The original source of the passage is J.T. Yoma I.1, 38b, and what is given here at 472:5–7, is not found there.

PART THREE

Chapter XXI

XX.1 (473:2)

[1] אין הרשע . . . וכבודי להם (7 f.:)

עד שהוא . . . מתוך פיו (8:)—The concepts here are גזירות (אפופסים,
8:) and נבואה. Pharaoh is conceived as unwittingly uttering
decrees against himself, unwitting prophesies. (See other examples, again with Pharaoh as the subject, in CA, pp. 242 f..)

מוריש אני עשרי וכבודי להם (474:4)—The ביזת הים, the spoils at
the Red Sea is here referred to. This is never spoken of in the Bible
itself.

XXI.2 (475:1 ff.)

[1] ר' אבא . . . מלמד . . . אחזתו (4:)—The concept of נס. Of course, the
event is really declared to be such in the Bible itself, but that is
underlined here. The narrative in the Bible does relate Goliath's
death to an act of David's, but here there is direct intervention of
God.

[2] זממו אל תפק וכ' (476:2)—See Lieberman here, p. 876.

[3] ר' יודן . . . תחמודתיה (3:)—Goliath was a pederast, a fairly common
sin among Roman soldiers.

[4] בזאת . . . לזקני . . . ויאמר (477:2)—The idea in the manuscript commentary quoted by Margulies is that of corporate personality,

David and his ancestor Judah being regarded as links in the same personality. David trusts in God's help by reason of Moses' plea for Judah, and written by him in the Torah. The concept of בטחון is an abiding concept, but here we see that it may be strengthened. The concepts bearing on it here are Torah, צדיק (Moses), and prayer.

XXI.3 (477:4 f.)

XXI.4 (478:7 ff.)

[1] שרי אומות העולם וכ' (479:1)—Whatever their "origin" may have been, as they are found in rabbinic literature, they are angels. Now the function of "angels" in rabbinic literature is to bring into bolder relief, frequently, the concept of God's love and other rabbinic concepts. Here the complaints of these angels bring into relief God's love for Israel on Yom Kippur when He forgives Israel's sins.

אילו . . . דמים . . . (:2)—The three cardinal sins are given probably to imply that the accusations against Israel are exaggerations, since Israel, for one thing, are not idol-worshippers.

לגהינם (:4)—This is usually a hereafter concept as it is here, apparently. Nevertheless, it may not be a dogma.

[2] השטן (:5)—The word here refers not to a single individual being (as in the Bible), but to the שרי אומות העולם (:1). If the שטן is an "adversary," he is thus not an adversary of God but of Israel. The non-definiteness of the term here also suggests indeterminacy of belief. Notice, too, that a contradictory midrash is found in Pirke R. E. (cited by Margulies).

XXI.5 (480:3 f.)

[1] כי בתחבולות . . . את (:3 f.)—The "battle" is that of the מצוות (:5) against the עבירות (:4). The מצוה is done by the same organ of the body that had earlier done an עבירה, and the assumption seems to be that it will now be at least more difficult to do the עבירה. The

מצוה is thus given an additional function, namely, to make it more difficult to commit specific ethical transgressions. Since no indication is given as to just how this is achieved, we do not have here a form of טעמי המצוות.

ואתם עדי . . . ה' (481:1)—In *Kiddush Ha-Shem,* the martyr testifies to the פרהסיה present that God alone is holy.

[2] ר' יוחנן . . . מצוה (2:)—מצוה here refers to an ethical מצוה, for only such a מצוה requires one to be especially alert for it. Continous alertness is the idea involved in the image of קבירניט (3:).

[3] ר' יוסי . . . תחבל (3:)—It apparently refers simply to the need to be careful in the observance of the law in Exod. 22:25, for a busy man is apt to neglect it.

[4] ר' בנייה . . . משנה (4:)—The text is interpreted to mean "bundles" of משניות, and the study of these is referred to by the symbol of "battle" (see also מהרז"ו; on the symbols of Torah, see RM, p. 118).

XXI.6 (482:1)

[1] Here the כהן גדול (1:) is regarded not simply as High Priest, but as the representative of Israel. The מצוות, except for the קורבנות (7:) on יו"כ, are those observed by all Israel, and the block of other matters (שבטים, ירושלם [the sons of Jacob], etc.) are national in character.

[2] בזכות יהודה (5:)—Perhaps the term here relates to the משיח, a descendant of Judah.

XXI.7 (482:8 f.)

[1] This midrash is an interpretation of Lev. 16:2 and is thus associated with the preceding midrash which interprets Lev. 16:3.

[2] ממחיצתו (483:2)—Refers to the phenomenon of גלוי שכינה in the Holy of holies. גלוי שכינה is in a particular locale.

[3] לעולם (8:)—While the term here is concerned with time, in accordance with the other measures of time here, it is apparently limited to עולם הזה.

[4] בכל שעה שהוא רוצה ואל יבא (484:2)—This is an interpretation of ובלבד בכל עת (Lev. 16:2). Although imposing the condition שיהא . . . הזה (484:3), the rabbinic interpretation is an example of the rabbinic emphasis on God's love, for it is just the opposite of the simple meaning—it is an expression of God's love for Aaron. רד"ל cites Elijah Gaon who says that this applied only to Aaron, only he being permitted to enter the Holy of holies whenever he wished, whereas his descendants were limited to once a year on Yom Kippur.

XXI.8 (484:6 ff.)

[1] צפה . . . ברוח הקודש (485:3)—רוח הקודש here is a kind of clairvoyance which was attributed occasionally to the Rabbis (see Bacher, ערכו מדרש, on the term). (On לזווית (5:), see Lieberman here, p. 876.)

[2] אמ' . . . נפשה לגופה (486:2)—A נס in response to a תפלה. The other concept embodied in the statement is study of Torah.

[3] אמ' ר' שמעון . . . שלחבירו (4:)—Involved here are matters of ethical דרך ארץ (see יפ"ת).

דבר שבינו . . . בפרהסייא (5:)—That is crystallized in a concept, נבול פה (see מהרז"ו).

[4] והלא . . . ונשמע קולו (487:3)—The concept embodied is respect, כבוד. It is thus not merely a warning of one's presence.

XXI.9 (487:5 ff.)

[1] ר' ברכיה . . . באמנה . . . בן בנו (5: f.)—The conceptions of both corporate personality and individual personality are involved here. Corporate personality: the eighteen successive descendants of Aaron are regarded as though they were Aaron himself. Individual

personality: each of them exhibited a quality that can be projected only by a functioning individual, namely, the quality of אמנה (7:) or אמונה, "faithfulness, trustworthiness." In this statement both conceptions are combined and neither dominates.

[2] מתקצרות . . . מקדש שיני (488:1 f.)—Apparently, according to our text, the high-priesthood was bought only after שמעון הצדיק (2:) and also, apparently, only he served באמנה and hence was called הצדיק. This tradition about the indifferent character of the High Priests of the Second Temple seems to be the basis of calling them רשעים (489:5).

XXI.10 (489:6 f.)

[1] אתו . . . אלא כנגד מילה . . . (490:1)—The numbers of the garments is here given an interpretation whereas in the Bible, it is not. Underlying the interpretation is the idea that the High Priest is the representative of the people rather than just a high functionary, an emphasis on Israel and מצוות.

בריתי (1:)—The interpretation utilizes a different meaning of the word, the covenant of circumcision, and what in the text is limited to the priest is now related to the folk.

[2] בבגדי זהב . . . ר' סימון (2:)—ר' סימון does not object to gold as such, as do the two authorities who follow, but he regards gold as the symbol of the golden calf.

לסטן (3:)—Notice that in the parallels given by Margulies the שטן is not mentioned. Belief in the סטן (שטן) is thus seen to be indeterminate, since the same idea is taught without taking him into account.

[3] של ישראל . . . ר' יהושע (4:)—Integration of Halakah and Haggadah. The linen garments could not be used again, and the reason given is haggadah, embodying the concepts of God's love and Israel in combination.

[4] מלך . . . מפני גאוה (5:)—גאוה, pride, is a negative value concept, and מלך refers to God.

XXI.11 (490:7 ff.)

[1] בפר בן . . . יכפר עליכם (:7 f.)—The passage involves the *conception* of corporate personality, and the *concept* embodied is זכות אבות. The sacrifices brought by the High Priest recall the deeds of the Patriarchs, the idea being that atonement for Israel is merited because of the deeds of the אבות.

בזכותו שליעקב . . . יכפר עליכם (491:2)—The conception of corporate personality allows Jacob to "provide" atoning sacrifices for his descendants.

[2] ואין לי אלא . . . בד בבד (:6)—The merit of the אמהות (:6) is not specified as in the case of the Patriarchs here. Recalling the general merit of forebears is not an uncommon theme.

[3] כשירות שלמעלן . . . ילבש (492:1)—The concept here is קדושה. The holiness of the linen garments used by the High Priest is emphasized by associating them with those of the angel, the angel himself being holy.

XXI.12 (492:4 ff.)

[1] ולבשם . . . הדיוט (:4)—Concretization of קדושה in halakah. Halakah and Haggadah are related, both being concretizations of the same value concepts.

ר' דוסא . . . הדיוט (:5)—This implies that the holiness of the ordinary priest is no different in degree from that of the High Priest.

[2] וכל אדם . . . בבאו (:6 f.)—The angels show כבוד to the High Priest. There is also the implication that the angels are less holy than the High Priest. They are regarded in tannaitic sources as less holy than Israel (see WE, p. 224, 279n.).

[3] בשנה שמת . . . דעת (493:2)—ר' אבהו (:4) declares that the זקן (:3) was הקב"ה וכבודו (:5). A section in the Mekilta II (ed. Lauterbach, pp. 31–32) gives instances of גלוי שכינה, and one of them is God revealing Himself at Sinai as זקן מלא רחמים. Here, too, it is

evidently the same figure, for יום כפור is the occasion when the sins of Israel are forgiven by God. The concept of גלוי שכינה, though so different from the other value concepts, is part of the complex for it interweaves with the other concepts, as here where it interweaves with מדת רחמים.

וכבדו (5:)—Refers to גלוי שכינה.

Chapter XXII

XXII.1 (494:1 ff.)

[1] שלעולם הן . . . ר' יהודה א' (2:f.)—The concepts are God's love, man and עולם. God so made the world that there is nothing which man cannot find useful in some measure. This is not teleology, a philosophical idea, for in the examples given there is no element of design by God, the ends to which the things are put being left to man.

מלך . . . הנאה לו (495:1)—The overwhelming importance of agriculture. The concept here is דרך ארץ, first phase (see WE, pp. 39 ff.).

[2] מתן תורה . . . ר' נחמיה (496:3)—Both the concepts מתן תורה (4:) and תורה are involved here. The details of צצית, תפילין ומזוזה (4:) are תורה שבעל פה and are recognized as such, yet they are also regarded as having the force of מתן תורה, are included in that event.

ואפילו מה שתלמיד ותיק עתיד וכו' (497:1)—There is certainly an awareness that the student's statement is contemporary. The concept of Torah, like other concepts, has new concretizations. The concept of מתן תורה supplies authority for these new concretizations.

ותלמיד אין לו (498:1)—Refers to לא תבואה (Koh. 5:9). The concept of תלמוד תורה is embodied here. This concept connotes both studying and teaching. Notice that it is felt that if studying does not lead to teaching, nothing has been achieved.

XXII.2 (498:4 f.)

[1] ורבנין . . . והארץ (4:)

והארץ . . . אף הן (5:)—The insects appear to you superfluous.
The point in this passage is that you need *not* justify their existence; they are part of the created world. This is almost like saying
that you need not look for teleology.

[2] מלך . . . תחרש (6:)—Notice that this is an independent midrash, not
connected with the one preceding; concept of God's love here.

וצדקות (499:3)—Acts of צדקה.

XXII.3 (499:5 ff.)

[1] אמ' להן . . . שלוחים (5:)—The function of the prophet is that of a
נביא-שליח, as Y. Kaufmann says; association of ideas with what
follows.

[2] אמ' ר' אחא . . . יתוש (6:)—This refers to acts, not to a message and
hence it does not contradict the preceding statement. It interprets
ויתרון ארץ בכל (5:), and teaches that what seems to a person
superfluous in creation may be used by God as His agent.

[3] טיטוס הרשע וכו' (7:f.)—God punishes him not through the mighty
sea but through the little flea.

לא דמי . . . דידיה ונצח ליה (500:3)—Titus is regarded as having
fought primarily against God. The רשע (501:5) fights against
God and does not only oppress Israel.

XXII.4 (503:1 ff.)

[1] More examples of how God uses all kinds of things as His agents.
Most of the instances are apparently examples of God's punitive
justice even though this is explicitly indicated only in the cases of
the רומי (505:8) and the בולדר (506:5), stories about Romans. These
stories are all נסים. They indicate that נסים of this character and
folklore belong to the same category. The stories about the various

grasses and also their relations to snakes are obviously folklore and are found probably among other groups as well. Folklore is to be differentiated from folklore science. In folklore science, the grasses would be identified and perhaps even deliberately employed.

[2] מחיי מיתיא דארע דישראל . . . (509:3)—Reflects the idea that תחיית המתים will take place in Israel. His intention was presumption and therefore sin.

XXII.5 (511:5 f.)

[1] מועד . . . והיו אומות העולם (512:2)—Integration of Halakah and Haggadah. Often the haggadah involved consists, as here, of a "reason" for the halakah. (See CA, p. 26 and the examples there.)

XXII.6 (512:5 ff.)

[1] הרגן . . . ר' יוחנן אמ' (5 f.:)—He who robs from or steals from a person is accounted as though he has thereby murdered that person. This is not a matter which is rationalized by saying that the robberies, etc., may lead to the death of the victim. By means of concepts, the *valuation* of the act is changed, the act becomes not גזל but שפיכות דמים. Notice that even the robbery or the theft of שוה פרוטה (513:1) is stigmatized in this manner. The case of the Gibeonites, however, is in a different category for they were prevented from obtaining their livelihood.

[2] פן אשבע וכחשתי (514:4)—This refers to עבודה זרה (5:) as the sequel clearly indicates, and not to כפירה.

מצינו שויתר . . . לא תחללו עוד (5 f.:)—In עבודה זרה (5:), only the person who worships an idol is involved, but in חלול השם (6:), an act affects other persons by lowering, in some manner, their regard for God (see WE, pp. 132 f.). The Name of God is thus profaned in חלול השם but not in עבודה זרה.

והיו ישראל . . . אשר ישחט (515:2)—An aspect of חלול השם (514:6) which involves Gentiles. When the Gentiles' opinion of God is

lowered as the result of Israel's actions, Israel commits an act of
חלול השם. Integration of Halakah (איסור במה, 515:2) and
Haggadah (חלול השם).

XXII.7 (515:6 ff.)

According to the opinion of R. Ishmael, Lev. 17:3 ff. forbade בשר
תאוה and hence the halakic passage here. The halakic concepts
constitute a distinct group in themselves although they are part of
the complex as a whole. They are not connotative and are often
defined. התיר and איסור (:6) are denotative, "permitted" and "forbidden," and do not possess a penumbra of meanings. Some of
the halakic concepts are defined (such as פיגול). At the same time,
this halakic discussion is concerned with value concepts, for value
concepts are common to both Halakah and Haggadah. Some of
the value concepts here are: קדושה), 516:4; מצוות (concretized in laws of שחיטה here, 516:2); and בשר תאוה) עבירות—
ישמעאל ר'; נחירה, 2:); also מחשבה (:5), which is an aspect of כונה,
but has halakic implications.

R. Ishmael and R. Akiba can differ because, despite the deno-
tation of halakic concepts and the definitions, the setting, the
framework of value concepts, is organismic and thus allows for
differing views.

XXII.8 (517:3 f.)

There is a real difference between the reasons given by Maimonides for the sacrifices and the midrash here. In the midrash,
centralizing the sacrifices in the אוהל מועד has the *effect* of separating Israel from the עבודה זרה they had previously worshipped,
whereas that is not the point made by Maimonides. Nevertheless,
the similarity is strong enough to characterize the idea in the
midrash as a rationalization. There is, occasionally, a rationalistic
tendency to be recognized among the Rabbis, and Maimonides
utilizes it. This is certainly the case with the rabbinic rationalizations concerning a number of נסים (see RM, pp. 153 ff.).

XXII.9 (518:4 ff.)

This is another halakic passage, and it demonstrates how value concepts are concretized by Halakah.

[1] נביא . . . הבמה ניתרת (4:)—Concept of התר, a halakic concept; נביא, a value concept. מקריב (6:)—concept of עבודה, a value concept.

ובדבורך (519:1)—Concept of דבור, a value concept, also a sub-concept of גלוי שכינה.

[2] אמ׳ ר׳ אבא . . . מחוסר זמן (3:)—Indicating how a נביא is permitted to override the laws.

עצי אשירה . . . ונעבד (3:–4:)—Violations of halakot informed by the value concept of עבודה זרה.

וזר ולילה (4:)—Violations of the value concept of עבודה.

[3] אמ׳ ר׳ יוסי . . . שם ביתו (520:2)—There is a difference of opinion. This difference of opinion and the others here are characteristic of Halakah. The value concepts are organismic, permitting difference of opinion.

XXII.10 (521:1 ff.)

Another halakic passage in which halakot concretize value concepts.

[1] מה שאסרתי לכם התרתי לכם (3:)—This statement, here and in the following sections of the passage, contains the halakic concepts of אסור and התר, as in the preceding passages, but now the very halakic concepts are employed in a concretization of the concepts of God's love, a value concept. Because of God's love, the self-same things prohibited elsewhere are, in other situations, permitted.

[2] אסרתי לכם . . . אשת איש וכו׳ (522:1 f.)—Concretization of the value concept of עריות.

בהמות (2:), זיז (2:), לויתן (2)—Referring to תחת מה . . . אלף (523:1) (6:), the three being food for the צדיקים; embody also the concept of God's love and לעת"ל (probably the Days of the Messiah)—integration of Halakah and Haggadah.

[3] ישלח שרשיו . . . ר' יוחנן (523:6–526:1)—Each opinion differs from the others with respect to the food eaten by the animal בהמות and likewise, the opinions differ concerning the source from which it drinks. What is the reader or hearer to believe then? His belief can only be indeterminate. Indeed, through an instance such as this we can demonstrate the existence of indeterminacy of belief and its character. This indeterminacy of belief applies not to details alone but to בהמות itself, and if it applies to בהמות, it must also apply to what is the food of the צדיקים, i.e., to לויתן and זיז as well.

[4] זאת . . . אמ' ר' מאיר (526:2)—This certainly contains the idea of God's omnipotence but it serves the concept of God's love whereby these foods are provided. The idea of God's omnipotence is not crystallized in a rabbinic term and remains an auxiliary idea (see RM, p. 55).

Chapter XXIII

XXIII.1 (526:9 f.)

[1] רמיי (527:2, 3:), רמאין (3:), רמאות (6:)—A negative value concept.

[2] וצדקת (3:)—צדקת (and צדיק) has an ethical connotation, being the opposite here of רמאי. Notice that the concept is applied to women as well as to men: in spiritual character, both are equal.

[3] כולל את כולן ברמאות (6:)—Implied is the interpretation of Cant. 2:2. Jacob was not affected by the wickedness of his new environment—the mark of the צדיק.

XXIII.2 (527:7 ff.)

[1] ממצרים . . . גוי מקרב (528:1)—The concepts embodied here are: Israel, The Nations of the World (Egypt), עבירות, and גאולה. The people of Israel practiced the same customs as the Egyptians and thus committed what were, for Israel, עבירות, and hence did not deserve redemption. Margulies points out that this view differs from that of בר קפרא (XXXII.5, 747:4 f.) who says that Israel was redeemed because of the מצוות they practiced. But variety of opinion is characteristic of Haggadah since each haggadic statement is an independent entity. This is so because the organismic character of the value concepts allows the same situation to be interpreted by different value concepts. Thus, in our midrash, one of the concepts describing the conduct of the people of Israel in Egypt is עבירות, whereas the opposite concept, מצוות, interprets their conduct in the view of בר קפרא (see RM, p. 73.)

[2] לבית עלי . . . אילו . . . א״ר שמואל (4:)—There is emphasis here on God's love; it was preordained, so to speak, to overcome מדת הדין in this instance.

[3] שבעים ושתים אתיות . . . א״ר יודן (7:)—Theodor in his commentary on Bereshit R., p. 442, points out that the midrashic literature does not contain any explanation of this name of God. מהרז״ו at Ber. R. XLIV.19 says that this name has an esoteric meaning of which he has no knowledge. It is certainly not a matter that has to do with normal mysticism and apparently is an element in an esoteric tradition which was an eddy alongside the main current of rabbinic thought. Its mathematical character probably indicates that it is related to some aspect of theosophy.

XXIII.3 (529:3 f.)

[1] העולם (8:)—Here it means "the world," including mankind.

[2] כדאי הן ישראל שינצל כל העולם כולו בזכותן (530:4)—Because of the merit (בזכותן) of Israel, the whole world (כל העולם כולו) is to be saved. How can the merit of Israel extend to all of mankind if Israel and the rest of mankind constitute two distinct entities?

The answer is that they are not two entities. Mankind is conceived as possessing a corporate personality. The merit of Israel accrues, therefore, to mankind as a whole. We have here an instance of the emphasis on universalism, one of the great emphatic trends of rabbinic thought. (See WE, pp. 29 f.)

XXIII.4 (530:5 ff.)

[1] בגמילות חסדים (5:)—Here this value concept is used in relation to the leader's role in corporate liturgical acts. These acts are themselves characterized by value concepts.

[2] עשרה שנכנסו לבית הכנסת וכו' (5:)—The "ten" constitute a face-to-face צבור. When only one of them knows how to lead in these corporate acts of worship, he is the benefactor of the rest.

לפרוס על שמע (6:)—On the public recitation of the *Shema'* as a corporate act, see WE, p. 136. The value concepts embodied in the *Ḳeri'at Shema'* are תלמוד תורה and מלכות שמים. The two introductory ברכות were doubtless included.

ולעבור לפני התיבה (6:)—On the *Tefillah* as a corporate act, see WE, p. 143. *Tefillah* itself is a value concept.

[3] ברכת חתנים (8:)—The ... לעשרה (8 f.)—The ... להכניס ... לבית האבל and the ברכת אבלים (531:1) are acts of גמילות חסדים *incumbent on the* צבור *as a whole*. That is how these acts differ from the acts of worship in [2] above here, wherein the benefactor was an individual. Of course, here too, the knowledgeable leader is the benefactor of the "ten" who do not know these ברכות, even though these ברכות are incumbent on the צבור as a whole. Besides גמילות חסדים, these acts are concretizations of ברכה.

[4] ר' אלעזר ... קארו ... חסמא (531:2 f.)—This story indicates that the folk were obliged to rely primarily on the Rabbis to lead in corporate liturgical acts. The prayers and the ברכות were still fluid, i.e., the content was more or less fixed but not the language, and the leader was, therefore, to a degree, creative. See J. Heinemann התפילה וכו', p. 34. On the other hand, many Rabbis, as in the case of R. Elazar, did not feel that it was their function also to act

as שליח צבור. They felt that it was sufficient for them to be
scholars, teachers and judges. They may also have felt that they
did not have stylistic gifts or the quasi-poetic ability to inspire a
mood of prayer or thanksgiving. Notice how R. Elazar appears
simply to accept the forms given him by R. Akiba, for he certainly
must have known the *Keri'at Shema'* and the content of the
Tefillah.

[5] בכל מילה . . . ר' יונה (532:1)—The word אפי' (2:) (i.e., אפילו) indicates
that he taught them the forms, for, again, they must have known
the content of the *Tefillah*, etc., though evidently the ברכת חתנים
(2:) and the ברכת אבילים (2:) were not familiar.

XXIII.5 (532:3 f.)

[1] ר' חנינא . . . וגו' (3: f.)—The burden of the various taxes imposed was
so great that it made for hopelessness. Only a steadfast trust in
redemption by God could overcome such hopelessness, a feeling
that this redemption might come in their day. But the tax burden
was no doubt a cause for emigration from Palestine.

[2] לבם מכוון כנגד אביהם שבשמים (7:)—The concepts are: God's love,
גאולה, and אמונה. Awareness of God's love despite present conditions is expressed in the term אביהם שבשמים, and trust in
redemption in the latter part of Ps. 25:15.

[3] יצתו . . . ר' אביהו (533:1)—גאולה involves first, the punishment or
extermination of neighboring enemies. The concepts are: גאולה,
גוים, and מדת הדין.

בגאולה של מחר (1:)—The imminent redemption, and a term used
as against the redemption from Egypt.

XXIII.6 (533:8 f.)

[1] ולמעשים טובים . . . ד"א כשושנה (8: f.)—The joy of doing a מצוה does
not contradict the legal principle that מצוות were not given as a
means of acquiring enjoyment.

[2] מה שושנה . . . של ישראל (534:1)—The fragrance of the flower is associated with the entire flower, and so because of the צדיקים (2:) Israel as a whole will be redeemed. The metaphor completely expresses the idea that the צדיקים and Israel as a whole are a single corporate personality.

XXIII.7 (535:1)

[1] כשהייתם . . . החוחים—This interpretation of Cant. 2:2 patently contradicts the interpretation of the same verse at 527:7, an instance of the organismic character of rabbinic thought. The concept of מדת הדין is embodied at 527:7 but not here.

[2] למלך שהיה לו וכו' (9:f.)—The parable inserts the idea of the danger inherent in an evil environment.

XXIII.8 (536:7 f.)

[1] ועתה . . . ימים—A halakic interpretation of Job 37:21, but following this is a haggadic interpretation of the same verse. An instance of the interrelation of Halakah and Haggadah.

XXIII.9 (538:5 ff.)

[1] תני ר' חייא . . . כמעשיהם (6:f.)

שני פעמים וכו' . . . (539:1)—Interprets אלהיכם in Lev. 18:2 and in ibid., 4, to refer to מדת הדין. It operated in the past and will do so in the future.

שעושה כמעשיהם (2:)—Relates to Israel. The source in Sifra, ed. Weiss, 85c, reads here: ליפרע מכם אם תעשו כמעשיהם. There is here the emphasis on the universality of God's justice.

[2] אני ה', אני . . . ליפרע . . . כמעשיהם (540:7 f.)—The same formula as at 539:1, but now it is applied to individuals, and further, not only in punishment but also in reward—emphasis on the individual.

XXIII.10 (542:1 f.)

[1] There is a new idea here, and hence it probably is an independent midrash connected with the preceding one through association of ideas.

[2] ומהו סמיכה (6:)—The midrash here is an instance of indeterminacy of belief. There are other instances of this kind of belief also involving midrashim at variance with the Bible. See, for example, CA, pp. 212 f. On indeterminacy of belief, see RM, pp. 131 ff.

XXIII.11 (543:5 ff.)   וחטאתי לאלהים . . . אמ' ר' יוסי (5:)

[1] יצרן (5:)—Stands for יצר הרע, the personification of the evil impulses. Here the יצר הרע is personalized with respect to the different individuals named. For the full term, see 544:3 and subsequently in this passage; the biblical antecedent is: יצר לב האדם רע מנעוריו (Gen. 8:21). The good impulses are personified in the term יצר הטוב (see Jastrow, *Dictionary*, s.v. יצר), but see our next comment.

ונשבעו לו (5:)—This phrase implies that the personification of the יצר הרע goes so far as to be conceived as a being. The יצר טוב, however, is seldom so vividly personified.

[2] הרעה הזאת . . . שאיני חוטא (544:1)—So vivid is the personification that the words of the oath itself to the יצר הרע are discerned in Gen. 39:9.

[3] למי נשבע . . . תשחיתהו וגו' (2:)—An even stronger indication that the יצר הרע was conceived of as a being, for one authority regards the oath as primarily having been given to a human being. The personification is an imaginative means of making vivid a strong temptation. It is a dramatic, even poetic metaphor so often employed as to take on an almost casual character, and yet not an altogether prosaic literalness. Other personifications are *Middat Raḥamim, Middat Ha-Din* and *Keneset Yisra'el.*

XXIII.12 (545:5 ff.)

[1] . . . בעיניו . . . ועין נואף (5:)—This is perhaps an extreme example of the rabbinic emphasis on the inward life. There is an emphasis on the inward life in the sphere of morals, not only in religious experience (on the latter, see OT, p. 224; RM, p. 167.)

[2] לפרסמו . . . צר כל קטירין (546:1)—The child has facial features testifying to the sin of the adulterous couple; their sin is hence publicized and thus is a manifestation of God's justice. The concepts here are: sin, God's justice, and נס.

[3] לפרסמו . . . אמ' ר' לוי (547:2)—This is a striking instance of a parable which is not a real analogy. The referent says that the facial features of the child publicize the adulterer's sin. The parable, however, indicates that it is the sinner who is confronted with his sin. Since the referent or general statement is also given here: לפרסמו . . . הרי אני צר . . . כך (4:) as the conclusion, the parable adds to this idea that the sinner himself is made to face his sin. (On the character of parables, see CA, pp. 51, 252.)

[4] כוותיה . . . רפו ידיו . . . ר' יהודה (5: f.)—The teaching here is that the conception and development of the embryo are a נס, not only the changing of the features of the child to publicize the sin of the adulterer.

התשתם כחו שליוצר (548:2)—Notice that this idea is involved with the concept of נס here, characterizing the conceiving of the child a נס by God, which is then to be altered by another נס. It is an auxiliary idea having only a specific function, and it is absorbed, so to speak, by the concept of נס. Incidentally, the parable (נתחלף המלך, 547:7) is again not altogether at one with the נמשל.

[5] שניהן נהנין (4:)—The husband, since he is, after all, the father of the child, and the adulterer, since the child's facial features do resemble his features (Lieberman in a conversation).

XXIII.13 (548:6)

[1] תראינה ארץ with continues 33:17 .Isa—(6:) ר' מיישא . . . תחזינה עיניך
מרחקים and that is taken to refer to the World to Come; the
promised reward of גלוי שכינה is to be in the World to Come.
Refraining from illicit sight will be rewarded ultimately by
blissful sight.

Chapter XXIV

XXIV.1 (549:2 ff.)

[1] מדת הדין of concepts The—(.f 2:) ויגבה . . . עם הרשעים . . . במשפט
(3:) and קדוש השם are combined here in that aspect of קדוש השם
in which God Himself sanctifies His Name when He punishes
the רשעים (4:). That manifestation of God's justice magnifies His
Name in the world, i.e., He is acknowledged everywhere and everybody recognizes His holiness.

[2] התגדלתי והתקדשתי (3:)—The two words here are taken as equivalents.
On the close relation of these biblical verses to the crystallized
rabbinic concept, see CA, pp. 247 f.

XXIV.2 (550:3 ff.)

[1] ר' ברכיה . . . בנוהג . . . בעילויונה (.f 3:)—An instance of the interrelation of Halakah and Haggadah, the halakah being in Ber. IX.5.

[2] On מידת הטוב (6:) and מידת הפורענות (551:1), see RM, p. 219, n. 73.
This is followed by interpretations of other verses in Psalms in a
similar vein; all such interpretations are instances of the same
interrelation of Halakah and Haggadah. This haggadah attributes
the ideas contained in these *berakot* to David.

[3] אמר ר' תנחום . . . בין כך . . . דבר (551:4)—Assumed here is the rule
of interpretation in which אלהים is taken to refer to מדת הדין (5:)

and 'ה, to מדת רחמים (6:). However, this is not an iron-clad rule, as can be seen in the succeeding and in the preceding interpretations where 'ה refers to both מדת הדין and מדת רחמים.

[4] דינו . . . אמ' ר' יודן (9 f.:)—Here the rule of interpretation is applied. God's love is given added expression here in the idea that He took counsel with His court of justice and He did this so that someone might, perhaps, make a plea in defense (see our next comment).

[5] רעה . . . אמ' ר' לעזר (552:1)—In view of the teaching of Abot IV.8, 22 that God is the sole judge, the notion of a heavenly court is a matter of indeterminacy of belief (but see also Duran, מגן אבות on Abot IV. 8.)

[6] קדושה (553:2)—קדושה is not only distinctiveness, high status, but also the imitation of God in acts of love (see RM, pp. 169 f.)

XXIV.3 (553:4 ff.)

A folklore story despite the fact that it is told as the experience of an individual. It is unusual in two respects: The demon originally dwelling there is not a harmful one, whereas demons usually are. Furthermore, a value concept, מדת רחמים, is embodied in the idea of divine help, and this idea is the concluding thought of the entire story. Usually demons are not brought into the category of significance. The bit of dried blood (חררא דדמא, 554:7) reflects a belief in the physical constitution of demons; also that demons may engage in combat with one another.

XXIV.4 (555:6 f.)

[1] מקדש . . . עתיד . . . ד"א ישלח (6 f.:)—This midrash refers to the Days of the Messiah (עתיד, 6:) since one of the things that will take place will be the sounding of the שופר (556:2).

[2] מציון מעשים . . . מקידוש מעשים (556:4-5)—The commentaries differ on the meaning of these two phrases (comp. יפ"ת and מהרז"ו). Does not the passage itself, however, continue with an explanatory

statement? Both phrases refer to the imitation of God, and the two phrases thus relate to the two aspects of holiness implied in קדושים תהיו (7:):

מקידוש מעשים (4:) is explained by the word פרושין (6:), that is, by requiring that Israel "separate" themselves from what is impure and defiling (among them the cardinal sins); and מצוין מעשים (5:) relates, apparently, to the positive acts implied in קדושים תהיו, namely, to imitation of God in acts of loving kindness. Cf. Schechter, "Aspects of Rabbinic Theology," pp. 203 ff., and WE, p. 228.

XXIV.5 (557:1 f.)

[1] בה . . . בהקהל . . . תני (1:)—This פרשה (Lev. XIX) was taught by Moses to Israel, according to this interpretation, in such a way as to differentiate between it and other sections, בהקהל (1:) (see ראב״ד on the parallel in Sifra, ed. Weiss, 86c). The presentation in an "all-inclusive assembly" is obviously a device for emphasizing the laws thus taught. We have, then, a form of emphasis we have not hitherto discussed. (On emphasis as a feature of organismic thought, see WE, pp. 11 ff., 26 ff.) But emphasis, especially in Halakah, does not rule out what is not emphasized. The other laws were also regarded as having been taught by Moses to the people, although not in an all-inclusive assembly. The concepts are: תורה; תלמוד תורה; ישראל.

[2] שרוב גופי תורה (2:)—According to ראב״ד, l.c., this section is so characterized: מפני שיש בה מצוות הרבה ורוב עונשין של שלשים ושש כריתות—thus the reason for the all-inclusive assembly was not only the major character of the laws but also their large number (see also David Halivni, *Mekorot Umsorot*, II, 591 f.).

[3] כמוך . . . שעשרת הדברות . . . ר׳ לוי (2 f.:)—Another reason for the all-inclusive assembly. יפ״ת explains that just as the Ten Commandments were given by God at an all-inclusive assembly, so this section containing them was so taught by Moses; but the manner of giving them originally was obviously an emphasis. The concepts here are: תורה; מתן תורה; תלמוד תורה; ישראל.

[4] פרשת עריות . . . ר' יוחנן (558:2)—The same number of מצוות in the three sections apparently implies that no one of these sections is emphasized more than the others. Thus, this midrash seems to say, the section on קדושים תהיו (:4) was not given a special emphasis, contrary to the point made in the preceding midrashim.

XXIV.6 (559:1 f.)

[1] One of the aspects of the idea of קדושה (:2) is "separateness," to separate oneself (see 556:6-7, קדושים . . . פרושין . . .). In the present section, this aspect of the idea is established on the basis of biblical verses that concern refraining from unchastity or prohibited sex relations (ערוה, :2). The concepts involved are: ערוה (or עריות) and קדושה. This demonstration also allows us to recognize that this idea of קדושה is already inherent in the biblical meaning of the word.

[2] ולמה נסמכה . . . נקרא קדוש (:1)—The lesson is drawn from the contiguity of the biblical section on עריות (:1) to the section on קדושים (:1). If such contiguity occurs in various contexts, the demonstration of contiguity is really a demonstration that the contexts indicate that refraining from ערוה is characterized as קדושה, and this is the case with the juxtaposition of verses introduced by the phrase ואית ליה קריין סגיין (560:4).

[3] ר' יהושע . . . אמתיה . . . דמרי (:3 f.)—This characterization is not only rabbinic but was prevalent among the folk at large, as is to be seen from the instance אמתיה דר' ישמעאל (560:1) and its implication. (On אמתיה, see מ"כ.)

[4] ואית ליה קריין . . . קדושים תהיו (:4)—The various contexts here reveal that the Bible itself links the prohibitions of prohibited sexual relations with קדושה; in other words, that one aspect of קדושה is related to separateness, to abstention from some act. Already in the Bible, then, קדושה has an ethical connotation, whatever other connotations it may have, that is, the ethical is not something developed later.

XXIV.7 (561:1 ff.)

[1] ניבול פה . . . חלוני . . . אמ' ר' שמואל (:2 f.)—This midrash interprets
Deut. 23:15, as can be seen in the sequel, and it is given here
because of an association of ideas.

כהן אני ובדרך וכו' (562:2)—The printed editions have, correctly,
ובדרך טהור. The idea of טהור in the parable suggests or implies
that ערות דיבור (:7) is טומאה. The parable adds something to the
interpretation itself; it puts more explicitly the idea that God may
leave them.

ערות דיבור . . . ניבול פה (:7)—The word ערות indicates that this
was regarded as טומאה (on moral טומאה, see WE, p. 228). ניבול
פה is the regular value concept.

XXIV.8 (562:9 ff.)

[1] Two midrashim on Lev. 19:2 and ibid., 20:7 by the same authority.
Even the same authority can teach different interpretations of the
same verse, and even consecutively. Thus, no interpretation is
more authoritative than another. In Haggadah the text is a non-
determining stimulus (cf. RM, pp. 71 ff., especially p. 72 f.).
However, in the present case, as we shall see, in both midrashim
by ר' אבין, the interpretations of Lev. 19:2 and Lev. 20:7 are
practically the same.

[2] למלך וכו' (:9)—The parable indicates that the קדושה involved is that
of self-control, withdrawal. In contrast to the application, however, it emphasizes reward, thus suggesting, too, that the קדושה is
also of an added, mystical kind, a kind that is itself a reward.

הלווי בשתי קדושות יעמדו (563:7)—In hierarchical holiness, the
awareness that one thing possessed more of קדושה than another
almost gave to קדושה a character of substantiality. The idea that
Israel possessed two קדושות (:7) has a similar connotation, for
here too, the thought is that Israel has more of קדושה, is holier
than the angels, the latter having only קדושה אחת (:6). Unlike
the purely mystical hierarchical holiness, however, קדושה here
also has a moral connotation, namely abstaining, withdrawal.

Here then, two phases of קדושה reinforce each other. Though possessing several phases, קדושה is, after all, a single concept. (See רד"ל who suggests that the second קדושה relates to abstaining from what is legally permitted.)

מכתירים . . . שלש קדושות (564:3)—The angels praise God by proclaiming daily שלש קדושות and these prayers are called "crowns" (comp. אבודרהם השלם, p. 175, on "כתר"). They do not, of course, thereby create קדושה. However, when God confers two of these "crowns" on Israel, the crowns are no longer simply praises but mystical קדושות, as in the preceding midrash by the same authority, ר' אבין. That is why the prooftexts of Lev. 19:2 and 20:7 are appropriate here as well.

XXIV.9 (564:6 ff.)

[1] מגדולתך . . . והדין דבר . . . אמ' ר' שמעון (6 f.:)—This is a daring passage. It teaches that there is a status relationship between God and Israel, and that this status relationship consists of the hierarchical relationship of קדושה in which God's holiness is greater (קדושתי למעלה מקדושתכם, 565:5). But this teaching also indicates how wrong it is to speak of the remoteness of God to man in rabbinic thought. This midrash is, of course, characterized by indeterminacy of belief, for in the two preceding midrashim it is God Who confers holiness upon Israel and no status relationship is involved. The derivation of the idea of status relationship from the words employed in the description of the relation of Pharaoh to Joseph serves almost in the same manner as a parable about a king and his minister.

[2] לכשיבא אני שלהקב"ה . . . (566:1)—There will be גלוי שכינה when there will be the גאולה. The other concepts are: מדת, כבוד, ישראל, רחמים, ימות המשיח (the period of redemption and exaltation of Israel).

Chapter XXV

XXV.1 (566:6 ff.)

[1] אמרי . . . עץ חיים (:6 f.)—In this interpretation למחזיקים בה refers to those who themselves study Torah.

[2] זכות (567:2)—The keeping of the מצוות constitutes the זכות. The words of Torah are taught by God, but you must deserve such teaching by keeping the מצוות. Note זכות (:2) here is merit acquired by oneself, and thus there is an emphasis on the individual, whereas in זכות אבות the Merit of the Fathers, the זכות is that of the ancestors. However, because of being united with them in a corporate personality, we are rewarded for their deeds.

[3] ונתן בו קמיע (:4)—(:2)- ר' חוניא . . . ברייה—The parable speaks of an amulet but that does not mean that the words of Torah are likened to an amulet. The קמיע "gives" automatic protection and is magic or perhaps is folklore science. It is the idea of protection that prompts the parable, but no more than that.

כך אמ' . . . עיסקו בתורה וכו' (:5)—The Torah requires study, devotion, mental and spiritual activity. The protection given by it is the reward for study: this is מדת הדין; and the giving of Torah by God (teaching it) is מדת רחמים, so that its protecting quality is thus anything but automatic. Of course, a מזוזה is not a matter of engaging in Torah (עסקו בתורה, :6). (On the מזוזה and theurgy, see CA, pp. 111 f.) This protection, then, is by God, not really by the Torah.

[4] ר' הונא . . . למחזיקים בה (568:2 f.)

אם היה למוד לקרות . . . שני פרקים (:3)—Doubling the amount of Torah does not act as a talisman. By studying Torah more than was his wont, a man is indeed likely to repent sincerely, for study of Torah implicates conduct and molds character, and repentance, תשובה, always avails.

למחזיקים בה . . . לעמלים . . . ואם אינו (5 f.:)—By being a civic leader and a dispenser of public charity he can be the one who helps to support those who are engaged in study of Torah, and thus, in a sense have a share in such study. Apparently the consciousness of vicarious study also leads to true repentance and makes him committed to proper conduct. Note that the words יקים (569:2) and מחזיקים (3:) are taken to mean "to support" or "maintain" (see רד"ל). The concepts are: צדקה and תלמוד תורה.

[5] Outweighing study of Torah and teaching it and observing מצוות is the failure to protest against wrong deeds and to support scholars. Support of scholars concretizes a combination of the concepts of תלמוד תורה and צדקה. The concept concretized in admonition or protesting against wrong deeds is מחאה (or תוכחה); the denigration of the failure to concretize מחאה or תוכחה emphasizes them.

XXV.2 (570:1 ff.)

[1] This is connected with the previous midrashim because here, too, those who maintain or support scholars studying Torah are extolled. Again, the emphasis is on the combination of the concepts of צדקה and תלמוד תורה.

[2] לבעלי המצות (2:)—On מצוה in the sense of צדקה, see דברים רבה, ed. Lieberman, p. 36, n. 10.

בגן עדן (2:)—Regarded as existing in the present, apparently, and not a sub-concept of עולם הבא; also here, the concept of מדת הדין.

אמ' משמו (4:)—Difficult, for he did not say so in the name of his brother (see the suggestion of רד"ל).

[3] מדת הדין (5:)—Concept of נקראת הלכה על שמו.

נקרא הפסוק על שמו (571:3)—The verse is addressed to זבולון (see also מהרז"ו). The concept here is מדת הדין.

באהליך (4:)—The word is taken to refer to the tents of זבולון since the verse is addressed to him. באהליך here may well be a symbol for study of Torah, something made possible by זבולון and hence attributed to him.

[4] ונוצחין . . . אמ' ר' תנחומא (4:)—Based on the preceding midrash which tells of the support of זבולון for יששכר, thus enabling יששכר to study Torah. Here, however, the reward is military victory, even when they are only half-hearted.

[5] מאכל . . . דרש ר' יהודה (572:1)—This is an independent interpretation of Lev. 19:23, the verse with which the preceding section begins. There is really no connection between this midrash and the preceding midrashim. As we have shown at the beginning of this commentary, unless a compositional form of some kind unites interpretations, every interpretation is a unit in itself. The preceding interpretations here too are independent of each other *intrinsically*, although several emphasized the same combination of the concepts of צדקה and תלמוד תורה. The concepts here are: מצוות (those given Adam), and now ערלה (3:) and Israel.

אדם הראשון (2:)—The rabbinic usage reflects אדם as a concept. (See CA, pp. 12 f.)

XXV.3 (572:5 f.)

[1] אמ' ובו תדבקון . . . ר' יהודה (5:f.)—We have here the idea of the otherness of God, not strictures on anthropomorphism. Had the Rabbis here exhibited an aversion to anthropomorphism, they could not have gone on to say that God engaged in planting trees, surely an anthropomorphism. The idea of God's otherness is taught here to indicate that something is conveyed by Deut. 13:8 that is not the literal meaning of the verse (see RM, pp. 303 ff., especially pp. 320 f.)

[2] עץ מאכל . . . מתחילת (573:3)—Israel is to imitate God in planting trees immediately after entering the Land, before doing anything else, just as God planted trees in Eden before creating the world.

Often the idea of imitation of God is the imitation by man of God's acts of lovingkindness, but here, in fact, all this is gratuitous for God's act was to plant trees in Eden *first*, before the creation of the world, and it was this act of planting trees *first* which Israel was to imitate on entering the Land. If the planting took place before the creation of the world, it was not גמילות חסדים toward the world. The concept here is דרך ארץ, specifically its second phase concerned with practical wisdom (see WE, p. 40). Fruit trees do not bear fruit for a number of years after planting, and hence it is wise to plant them immediately upon entering the Land. The idea of the midrash is related to the familiar one, that Torah teaches: דרך ארץ.

XXV.4 (573:7f.)

[1] לאבות הראשונים (574:1)—Referring to Abraham, Isaac and Jacob, as indicated in Deut. 6:10. The phrase implies that others after these are also called אבות.

XXV.5 (575:3 ff.)

[1] מי שת . . . הארץ ונטעתם (:3 f.)—Again the same verse, Lev. 19:23, is interpreted as teaching that when Israel enters the Land, they are to do the planting themselves. In the Wilderness, all their needs were supplied by God, the midrash points out. The concepts here are: God's love, Israel, and דרך ארץ (in its first phase). The parable implies that God supplied Israel's needs in the Wilderness because their own efforts could not have availed them.

[2] אדריינוס . . . ולא פגין (576:5–579:7)—The story is given here because it enlarges not only on the need for planting trees, but because it exalts that activity. Here the concept of דרך ארץ is linked with גמילות חסדים, for the old man plants for his descendants.

כשם שיגעו . . . יגע לבני (577:5)—The first phase of דרך ארץ is thus here given an ethical turn. The concept of God's justice is embodied in the reward given the old man, he himself being enabled to eat of the fruit of the trees he planted in his old age, and in the gift given him by the king. The incident of the neighbor apparently is told to indicate that it was not the gift of fruit by the old man that counted but his fine conduct in general. The role played by the wicked Hadrian here is puzzling for his relations to the old man express the attitude of a pious man.

XXV.6 (579:8 ff.)

[1] This material is given here because Lev. 19:23 is a factor in the interpretation. The section illustrates the fact that midrashim are
intrinsically independent. Concerned with Abraham, the "proper"
place of this midrash would be with the interpretations of the
verses relating to Abraham. However, since it is an independent
entity, it can be placed anywhere, so long as there is some association of ideas. Here, the two kinds of ערלה constitute the
association.

[2] קלין . . . שוות (580:2)—On the other hand, there is also the idea that
Abraham observed "even the Rabbinical injunctions." (See Ginzberg, *Legends*, I, p. 292.)

[3] תני ר' ישמעאל . . . על דבריו . . . עליון (4:)—Always associated with
כהונה (4:) is the concept of קדושה, and had Shem been the person
from whom כהונה descended, it would mean that holiness would
not be limited in mankind to Israel alone. Abraham, as Patriarch,
is regarded as being within Israel. But קדושה has an ethical as
well as a mystical character. Shem is described here as lacking in
proper reverence for God.

XXV.7 (582:8 f.)

XXV.8 (583:3 ff.)

[1] מיוסדים . . . דברי תורה וכו' (4:)—Since no explanation is given, this
can only be a mystical idea in which the words of Torah are felt to
be the very foundation of the world. This idea is related to Abot
I.2.

[2] פרשותיה שלתורה נדרשות לפניהן ולאחריהן (584:3)—A connection is
to be found between a given passage and the one preceding it;
likewise, another connection between the given passage and the
one following it. This principle does not really limit the character
of the Bible text as a non-determining stimulus to haggadic
interpretations, for the passages by themselves can give rise to any
number of interpretations.

[3] לעתיד לבוא (585:3)—Apparently refers here to the ימות המשיח (notice the term at 587:1). Since they are not punished בעולם הזה (2:), this means that גיהינם, the place of such punishment, will be not after death but לעתיד לבוא (3:).

[4] שימצה דמה . . . אתה ממתין (7:)—The concepts here are: עבירה, מצוה, and טומאה (נדה). By implication, also קדושה, the holiness of the fruits of the fourth year. The observance of ערלה points up Israel's dereliction in analogous matters.

[5] המציאה לו . . . ורבנן . . . ר' חגי (586:4)—As against the opinion of ר' חגי, רבנן implies that Saul was not worthy enough to have God Himself provide him (Saul) with a sword; two different opinions of Saul.

[6] זרעם . . . לעתיד לבוא (587:1)—As we have pointed out, there is a close bond between the prophets and the Rabbis (RM, 291 f., 299, 300). The Rabbis crystallize here in a single term (לעתיד לבוא, 587:1) what the prophets speak of more concretely. These definite details indicate that the Rabbis had in mind ימות המשיח.

Chapter XXVI

XXVI.1 (587:5 ff.)

[1] ומלך עולם . . . מהו אמת (588:4)—Since His power is eternal, what He says will come to pass. The concept is אמת (4:). "Truth" here means that what He says will be actualized, will prove to be true.

[2] פרסה הוא . . . טהורות. ר' יודן (588:5 f.)—The concept here is an aspect of טהרה, purity, since the word in the verse being interpreted is טהורות (5:). Even in ordinary description or conversation, "unseemly" words ought to be avoided. Also, begin with the "pure" even if you must also speak of the impure or unclean— there is extreme sensitiveness in speech. The concept of טהרה, so often ritualistic, extends here to a kind of moral sensibility. We

take it that what they say of God here implies an ideal for man. We thus have here an indication of how necessary it is for the understanding of a midrash to be aware of the concept informing it. By identifying the concept embodied in these homilies as טהרה, we learn that an aspect or phase of this concept concerns moral sensitivity, though usually the concept has a ritualistic connotation. We show elsewhere that there is no real dichotomy between the ritualistic and the ethical (OT, pp. 102 ff.).

XXVI.2 (589:6 ff.)

[1] מביניהון . . . בימי דוד . . . ר׳ יוסי (:6 f.)—Purity in study of Torah and keenness in studying are outweighed by לשון הרע, an emphasis on ethical conduct, and see below at [3].

[2] טעם חטא (:7)—Pure from sexual sin, hence the study is characterized as אמרות טהורות (Ps. 12:7).

שהיו בהם דילטורין (590:1)—Not only informers fell in battle but also those who were free from לשון הרע, an instance of corporate justice in which the righteous of the generation were punished too, along with the wicked. Corporate justice implies a corporate personality. The concepts here are: מדת הדין and לשון הרע.

שכינה (:7)—באותה . . . שכינתך מביניהון is a term for God implying God's nearness (see RM, pp. 225 f.). There can be no greater punishment than the loss of it. David regards his generation as deserving of such loss. שכינה here probably refers to גלוי שכינה.

[3] אבל דורו . . . מפרסמי למלכא (:8 f.)—This further emphasizes ethical conduct and now extols refraining from לשון הרע and from acting as informers. The emphasis on the ethical is an emphatic trend in rabbinic thought (see OT, pp. 245 f.).

אבל דורו . . . עובדי ע״ז . . . ונוצחין (:8)—Idolatry is a heinous sin, yet here it is outweighed by the refraining from לשון הרע. This is certainly an emphasis on the sheerly ethical.

[4] א״ר שמואל . . . שנאמ׳ עליו (591:3 ff.)—Folklore-like parallel between לשון הרע and the poisonous snake preceded, through an association of ideas, by other folklore-like notions about the snake.

In folklore, analogies play an important role, even if the

analogy is the result of a metaphor, as here. The metaphor of גדרו של עולם (591:4) is an imaginative analogy to the literal גדירות (:3), a mixture of biblical narrative and folklore, for "they" hold converse with the snake.

אמרו לו . . . עילותא (:5)—The snake accounts for his peculiarity by asserting that he is the instrument of God's justice, a rabbinic idea.

מפני (:7 f.) . . . באבר . . . ברומי . . . העולם—Now there is a parallel between the bite of a snake and לשון הרע, a parallel drawn by the snake. He implies that the בעל הלשון (592:1) is more reprehensible.

ולמה נקרא . . . עליו (:2)—Here the parallel becomes a kind of characterization. לשון הרע is called the "third tongue," a reference to the snake who was regarded as having a three-forked tongue (see Lieberman here, p. 878, and his *Hellenism* etc., pp. 191 f.). This anatomical "observation" is folklore science as is evidenced from its use in Targum Jonathan, a Targum intended for the Aramaic-speaking masses. However, this term is interpreted here and given valuational content: לשון הרע slays three—the victim, him who utters it and him who accepts it, and God's justice punishes the latter two.

[5] ולא מיחה . . . ר' יהושע (593:1 f.)—Four concretizations of God's justice are given here, each one accounting for the slaying of אבנר. The first one embodies also the concept of שפיכות דמים; the second, the concept of כבוד, honor; the third, the concept of פיוס (להתפייס, :5). The last one is connected tangentially to לשון הרע, for his sin was that he should have protested to Saul against the killing of the inhabitants of נוב, but did not do so.

XXVI.3 (594:3 f.)

[1] פרה אדומה ופרשת המת (595:1)—The concept is טהרה, for the verse interpreted declares אמרות ה' אמרות טהרות (Ps. 12:7). Notice that here טהרה refers, as usual, to ritual matters, whereas the concretization of the concept at 588:4 f. is an ethical matter (see our comment at 588:5).

XXVI.4 (595:3 f.)

[1] יום ליום . . . יצא קום (3)—In contrast to the order "above" in which, at a certain season, the day borrows from the night and at another season, the night borrows from the day, and all this by a "word" alone, without discussion, the borrowing by men incurs making and validating promissory notes and much discussion. The ideal is represented by the order "above," and men are manifestly inferior. The concepts here are: דרך ארץ (first phase of it, WE, p. 39) and דין.

[2] רב שלום . . . יצא קום (:6 f.)—An unusual interpretation which contains a parable but which nevertheless teaches what is regarded as פשט, the simple meaning: in the early morning the light of the sun is soft, barely warming (Ps. 19:4), but at midday, when the sun comes into its own, as it were, its heat is intense (ibid., v. 5). However, the parable, by its personification, does contribute a poetic quality.

XXVI.5 (596:5 f.)

[1] שנכפו ומסר להם רופא קמיע מומחה (:5 f.)—Epilepsy was treated by the doctors with an amulet, and those affected were also warned to keep away from cemeteries. Because of the involvement of doctors and psychological factors, this treatment ought probably to be regarded as folklore science, rather than magic.

[2] כך לפי . . . ואמרת אליהם (597:4)—Though very much akin to the two midrashim at 562:9 ff., this passage has a different character. There the concept of קדושה plays a large role; here it is not even embodied. As a result, there is no implication here that Israel is holier than the angels. The omission here of the concept of קדושה in the thought of the midrash seems to be deliberate, for the text containing the concept, Dan. 4:14, is used here as well as above. The concepts emphasized in the present passage are: מצוות and man.

XXVI.6 (597:8 f.)

[1] Although related to III.6 (pp. 70 f.), this midrash has not been affected by it, since the concepts are different.

[2] יראת ה' (8:)—The concept is יראת שמים. The verse here is sufficient to teach that he possessed יראת שמים.

טהורה (8:)—The concept is טהרה, referring to the content of the פרשה; his reward for יראת שמים.

זכה . . . עד סוף כל הדורות (598:1)—An instance of corporate personality for it was the merit of Aaron alone that was thus rewarded. The concepts here are: מדת הדין combined with מדת רחמים.

פרשת המת (2:)—The מת is טומאה, and this concept has two obverses, טהרה and קדושה. The need for טהרה implicates here the concept of קדושה. The priests are obliged to observe טהרה since they are holy and not to be defiled by טומאה. Their holiness thus does not depend on their primary function as priests at the Temple worship and hence their distinction is basically related to פרשת המת (2:). This distinction remains even though the Temple worship no longer exists.

XXVI.7 (598:3 ff.)

[1] This section is devoted largely to Saul's recourse to אוב וידעוני (599:1, 600:9). The concept that interprets אוב וידעוני is עבודה זרה, or rather, a phase or an aspect of it, for there is no idol involved. Furthermore, this phase or aspect of עבודה זרה is regarded as having efficacy. Both the biblical and the rabbinic narratives tell of how Samuel is "brought up" and holds converse with Saul, whereas idols are usually characterized as powerless (see CA, p. 95). In the Bible, the prohibition against Moloch worship is followed by a similar prohibition against האובות והידענים, obviously because they are regarded as of the same character (Lev. 20:2–6). The injunction is not limited to these two things. In a list of prohibited practices and practitioners which includes Moloch-practice and אוב וידעוני, the מכשף, sorcerer, is also included (Deut.

18:10–11). However, the Rabbis employ not only this term but the abstract noun כישוף, as well (e.g., Sanh. 56b), and this means that they possessed a conceptual term for a form of עבודה זרה. כישוף, sorcery, is thus a sub-concept of עבודה זרה in our nomenclature. (On the distinction between a phase and a sub-concept, see RM, pp. 16–17.)

[2] בעלת אוב . . . מה כתי' (3:)—The conjunction of Lev. 20:27 and Lev. 21:1 is here accounted for. They are related for they are made to refer to two of Saul's sins, the former to his traffic with בעלת אוב, and the latter, to his killing of the priests of נוב. Involved also is God's omniscience, His foreknowledge, an auxiliary idea, since it does not possess a rabbinic term (see RM, pp. 53 f., p. 220) and is always in the service of a genuine value concept. In this case it serves the value concepts of sin and God's justice.

[3] ועמשא . . . דרך ארץ . . . א״ר יצחק (599:8 f.)—דרך ארץ (600:1) here is practical wisdom. The lesson is: do not set out on a journey accompanied by only one person (a servant).

[4] בדבר הזה . . . לאשה . . . ארשב״ל (600:7)—See comments at 598:3 ff.

[5] וראשו למעלה . . . מנא ידעא (601:4)—These details suggest that this form of necromancy was regarded as genuine even though illegitimate. Additional details are given at 9: (ולא . . . אלא שלשה רואהו). Evidently it gave rise to its own folklore.

[6] רבי הוה פשיט וכו' (602:6 f.)—All the verses quoted embody the concept of מדת הדין.

[7] במחיצתי . . . ולית לי א״ל (605:6 f.)—Saul could have escaped and, indeed, could have been victorious in battle, but he chose death and defeat, thereby demonstrating his repentance and acknowledging God's justice. He also earned the reward, therefore, of being, together with his sons, in Samuel's division in גן עדן. At the end of his life, Saul thus emerges as a צדיק.

אם צדקת עליך את הדין (8:)—Concept of צדוק הדין, acknowledging God's justice. Involved in this acknowledgment is תשובה, repentance.

א״ר יוחנן עמי במחיצתי (606:1)—Hence God forgave him (מחללו) for "that sin" (see 'Erub. 53b and Rashi there). God's forgiveness is an aspect of מדת רחמים. The passage utilizes here this earlier midrash, and this also implies that the entire idea of the passage is early. במחיצתי (:1) reflects a belief that the souls of the צדיקים ascend after death to גן עדן and that there are divisions there according to degrees of merit. The hereafter concepts are beliefs rather than value concepts (see RM, pp. 364 f.).

[8] שפוגעת בו . . . ארשב״ל באותה (:6)—The angels serve as background (למלאכי השרת, :6) against which God's love is stressed, as they often do elsewhere. Angelology has the function of supplying value concepts with vivid concretizations.

[9] מפני מראית העין (:8)—Here it means fear of the evil eye, but it also often means avoiding even the semblance of wrongdoing (see Jastrow s.v. מראית).

[10] ושמח על מדת הדין שפוגעת בו (:9)—"Joy" here means whole-hearted acceptance of God's punishment being visited upon him. Implied is whole-souled תשובה. Compare the way in which "joy" affects obligatory matters.

[11] על חמש חטאות . . . אסוף ידיך (:10 f.)—Five sins are enumerated by the midrash, whereas the verses (I Chron. 10:13–14) apparently mention only two (see רש״י and רד״ק). The midrash stresses the concept of God's justice, Saul's death and defeat being thus fully deserved. This is an example of the combination of value concepts. If Saul's sins and punishment are all foreseen by God, were then his sins not foreordained? In a religious philosophy, this would be a major problem. But rabbinic thought is not philosophy; it is concerned with experiential concepts, and God's omniscience is not a value concept, not a crystallization of experience. Not represented by a conceptual term, it is an auxiliary idea serving here the value concepts of מדת הדין and חטא. Furthermore, since rabbinic thought is not philosophy but is concerned with experience, it is experience which is decisive and not logic. Thus, though there are "contradictory" concepts such as רחמים and דין, both are crystallized representations of experience, and none of these

matters are built up by logical casuistry. The pattern of value concepts is indifferent to logical contradictions in Haggadah. In other versions of this midrash, it is Adam, not Moses, to whom God shows all the generations that are to come, their leaders, etc. There the idea of God's foreknowledge is in the service of the concept of Man, אדם (see Ber. R. XXIV.2, ed. Theodor, p. 231, and the notes there; see also Naḥmanides, Commentary on Gen. 5:2).

XXVI.8 (608:4 ff.)

[1] להדרש . . . כל מקום . . . ר' יוחנן (4:)—This is one of a number of similar statements implying that Midrash Haggadah is already inherent, as a method, in the Bible. Notice that it is not confined to any one Book. (Compare our remarks above on 8:1.)

[2] צדקה (609:1)—An act of charity. It was needed not on his own behalf, of course, but to carry out the command.

ר' יהושע דסכנין . . . תחת כנפיהם (3:)—Angelology, as we have pointed out, is always background for a value concept. Here, as often, it brings into relief God's love. Gabriel waited patiently while the coals were being dimmed in his handfuls, for six years, thinking that Israel might do תשובה, and decided finally, when they had not, to throw the still glowing coals on them and to destroy them utterly. But God made him desist, saying that there were among them men who do צדקה with one another.

יש בהם בני אדם שעושין צדקה אלו עם אלו (6:)—Only some men among them do צדקה with one another, but all are to be spared. Another instance of corporate personality as all of Israel is spared because of the virtuous acts of some.

צדקה, (610:1)—מה טעם צדקתך אלהים עד מרום charity, is regarded here as a quality or activity of God which not only man but also angels are expected to imitate, for it is as necessary for relations among עליונים (609:8) as for relations among men. Ps. 71:19 is given in answer to מה טעם (1:).

מי כמוך כובש על מדת הדין (2:)—The צדקה of God is expressed in His charity or mercy as it overcomes מדת הדין (2:). Notice that in our midrash here צדקה is regarded as *the* expression of God since it is God Himself who overcomes מדת הדין.

[3] באמירה ראשונה . . . אל תחוס עליו (4:)—The midrashic interpretation tells that Ahab disobeyed God, something not stated in the biblical narrative, and it thus indicates that the punishment contained in the prophecy of I Kings 20:42 was deserved. At the same time, the miraculous character of the defeat of בן הדד in the biblical narrative, and particularly the parable there in vv. 39–40, do suggest that בן הדד was not Ahab's captive with whom he could do what he pleased. In concretizing the concept of sin, therefore, the midrashic interpretation makes explicit what is implied in the biblical narrative.

[4] ודכוותה ויאמר המלך . . . המלכה (7:f.)—The value concepts here are: צניעות or חשיבות, and also יהודית (611:1), the latter referring here to the people and hence a subconcept of ישראל.

[5] אלא באמירה ראשונה . . . הזקק לו (611:4)—An ethical מצוה is thus an overriding מצוה. The ethical concept here is כבוד הבריות.

XXVI.9 (611:8 f.)

[1] מה כתיב . . . הגדול מאחיו (8:)—See the version in Tosefta Mo'ed Kippurim I.6, ed. Lieberman, p. 222; and see his *Tosefta Ki-Fshuṭah*, IV, pp. 727 ff.

[2] למה נקרא . . . ובשנים (8:)—Two value concepts at once are concretized in a כהונה: כהן and קדושה. All the priests are equally holy and the כהן גדול is no holier than the ordinary priests. In the ברכה before blessing the people, the priests say, "Who has made us holy with the קדושה of Aaron" (Soṭ. 39a [Num. R. XI.4]), but the term כהן גדול suggests that he is superior in some manner to the other priests, and if not by being more holy, then in other ways. The phenomenon in which several value concepts are concretized at one time is a feature of rabbinic thought. Situations and statements usually embody a number of value concepts (OT, pp. 192–6; RM, pp. 110 f.). An act as a whole may be interpreted by two concepts at once, as in the case of an ethical מצוה (WE, pp. 209 f.).

Another instance in which people have been "grasped," so to speak, by two value concepts at once is the rabbinic statement that the צדיקים of the former generations were חסידים (RM, p. 39).

בחכמה בכח . . . ובשנים (9:)—All of these concepts belong to the first phase of דרך ארץ consisting of phenomena or modes of behavior characteristic of mankind, a purely descriptive phase (WE, pp. 19 f., 51 f.). ובשנים (9:) is no exception, for it refers to the counting of years, a human characteristic. A better reading is in the Tosefta, l.c., which has ובמראה, since it certainly is not a matter of his being older than all the other priests.

הסתת (612:3)—Read איש חבתה, as in Tosefta Mo'ed, l.c., and see Lieberman, *Tosefta Ki-Fshuṭah*, IV, p. 728.

[3] ולא כהן גדול . . . ישכון לבטח (4:)—The concept emphasized here is מלכות, royalty.

מיד וילבש שאול . . . עין רעה (10:)—A נס took place and David grew taller so that the armor fit him. David is regarded by the Rabbis as the epitome of kingship in Israel, and were his stature to remain shorter than Saul's, he would thus be inferior. Notice that Saul's excellence was symbolized in *his* being taller than all his people (I Sam. 9:2).
see OT, p. 132 f., 135, 303.)

Chapter XXVII

XXVII.1 (613:2 ff.)

[1] צדקה (4:)—He acts toward them with "towering" love; that is, their recompense is far beyond justice. צדקתך (2:) (Ps. 36:7) is taken as "Thy love." (On צדקה as love, see OT, p. 132 f., 135, 303.)

מדקדק . . . עד תהום רבה (5:)—He acts toward them with precise, thorough-going justice.

ר' עקיבה . . . לעתיד לבוא (614:1)—He acts with precise justice toward both. Another concept is also emphasized, the concept of

לעתיד לבוא (3, 4:), for there the צדיקים (2:) will receive a "good reward" and the רשעים (3:) their full punishment. The teachings of R. Ishmael and R. Akiba represent only some of the ideas of the Rabbis concerning the workings of divine justice. There are a number of other ideas on that subject expressed, for example, in the concepts of ייסורין, Merit of the Fathers, and vicarious atonement, the latter two involving the idea of corporate personality.

[2] משל . . . . במרעה . . . . שאולה וגו' (614:5)—The righteous and the wicked are designated metaphorically by their respective future dwelling places. The idea of reward, or more likely, love, is conveyed by צדקתך of the verse (Ps. 36:7) and, of punishment by משפטיך of the verse, whereas the metaphorical designations are respectively כהררי אל, the reward itself, and תהום רבה, the punishment itself. The concepts here are: the righteous and the wicked, לעתיד לבוא, God's love, God's justice.

[3] גיהינם (615:3)—Interprets שאולה of Ezek. 31:15. This midrash reflects the kinship between valuation and art, both being aspects of the category of significance (see RM, pp. 111 f.). The cover of a גיגית (615:1) is made of earthenware just as the vessel itself is made of that material, and the reason given is מפני שהוא ממינו (2:). The cover and the vessel are thus of the same kind, an aesthetic, not a utilitarian criterion. Similarly, it is fitting that תהום (3:) which is "darkness," should cover the רשעים (3:) who are "darkness," in גהינום (3:), which is "darkness." The word חשך (3:), darkness, characterizes all three with a negative valuational connotation, taking on the connotation of (מדת הדין) גיהינום and רשעים, although by itself it is a cognitive concept. The idea of fittingness is taken from the realm of art in this midrash, and employed in the realm of valuation.

[4] מעשיהם שלצדיקים (6:)—Since this interprets צדקתך of Ps. 36:7, it must refer at once to the deeds of צדיקים and to God's love which is the steady concomitant of those deeds.

כובשין על הפורענות . . . לעולם (616:1)—The deeds of the righteous prevent what would otherwise be the effect of the deeds of the wicked. There is thus implied the idea of corporate personality, for the whole world benefits from the deeds of the righteous. In this midrash the benefit is here and now. Compare our remarks on the workings of God's justice at 614:1.

לעולם (1:)—"The world" refers to all, not only Israel apparently, as is suggested by the analogy. There are also צדיקים among the Gentiles.

[5] למתן שכרן (2:)—The limitless reward of the righteous; interprets צדקתך of Ps. 36:7, and hence the statement embodies a combination of God's justice and His love.

משפטיך . . . יעשה לו (5:)—Punishment, not reward.

[6] מעשיהם . . . גלויים . . . צדקתך ד"א (7:)—But how is מעשיהן שלצדיקים (8:) related to צדקתך (7:), and how is מעשיהן של רשעים (9:) related to משפטיך of the verse being interpreted? In the two midrashim preceding there is a relationship, since both tell of reward and punishment for deeds. This midrash, apparently on the basis of those interpretations, makes of "deeds" alone the teaching of the verse, but this means that all three midrashim were taught as they are given here. In other words, these are not fragments of sermons at all, but demonstrate that Midrash Haggadah was taught as such, probably to scholars.

[7] כל החיה . . . ולא עוד אלא (617:4)—By calling attention to the others, including the animals, also "remembered" by God, the midrash emphasizes God's love.

[8] ומשפע . . . על העמודים (618:2)—The pillars are given personality and thus treated "poetically"—a form of indeterminacy of belief. Poverty was regarded often, but not always, as punishment for sin (see OT, pp. 140, 196, 314 n. 56.) Again, divine justice is felt to be present also in this world. (Compare our remarks at 614:1 and at 616:1.)

[9] מן נשיא . . . מעשה (5: f.)—Embodies the concept of wisdom, a trait of man, belonging to the first phase of דרך ארץ (see WE, pp. 39 f., 52).

דינכון אתית . . . מן גזילה (620:4 ff.)—The concepts are דין and גזילה. The latter is given its full force as a negative concept. (On negative value concepts, see WE, p. 25.)

זבנית ליה . . . חד מינהון (621:1)—Embodies the concept of צדיק.

אמ' ליה מטרא . . . דבזכותא . . . מפני בהמה תושיע ה' (622:3 f.)— [10]
Rain falls and the sun shines when these are deserved (God's
justice), but their laws reveal that the people of the land are
wicked. These things do take place in that land, however, only
because of the merit of the small cattle (apparently because they
harm no one) and thus, you too are saved (דבזכותא דבעירא . . .
משתזבין, 5:). A very unusual use of זכות, since it always implies a
corporate personality, and perhaps the word here, therefore, means
that "you" are saved incidentally, i.e., because the cattle on the
land deserve the rain and the sun. A MS reading: אדם מפני (623:1).
בהמה תושיע ה' suggests the latter idea for it is evidently meant as
a further explanation.

כך אמרו ישראל . . . תשקם (623:1)—The text is difficult. See also
the parallel in Pesik. de R. Kah., ed. Mandelbaum, pp. 149 f.

לפי שאנו נמשכין אחריך (2:)—Although conscious of our sinful-
ness, we long for Thee. Involved here is the concept of גלוי שכינה,
a longing for direct experience of God.

ולהיכן . . . תשקם (3:)—If, indeed, our wilful sins are taken by
Thee as unwitting sins (כבהמה תושיענו, 2:), then we shall behold
Thee in גן עדן (3:).

XXVII.2 (624:1 f.)

מי הקדימני . . . ישלם לו (1:)—Interprets Job 41:3 *not* as a question but [1]
as a declaration (see Pesik. de R. Kah., ed., Mandelbaum, p. 150,
note). He who has performed a good deed before he was obligated
to do so, I shall reward measure for measure. The statement
assumes that God's justice is to be expected in the here and now.

עתידה בת קול . . . שכרו (3:)—This relates to the future (עתידה, 3:), [2]
and רד"ל makes the likely suggestion that Num. 23:23 points here
to Isa. 40:9 and, hence, we should say, to ימות המשיח. It is then
that he who has done good deeds will be rewarded. The concepts
here are: מצוות, God's justice, and ימות המשיח. The statement
implies that God's justice is not in the here and now.

או עז . . . ורוח הקודש (:6 f.)—Now Job 41:3 is interpreted as a rhetorical question: Who has performed מצוות before I had recompensed him for doing them? No one. This is in contrast to the בת קול (:4), and in consonance with the statement (:1) above. This statement assumes that God's justice is manifest in the here and now, in this world. Furthermore, its very purpose is to contradict the statement on the בת קול and to stress the latter's inadequacy, so to say. This can be recognized also in the distinction between רוח הקודש (624:6), standing here for God's word (see the beginning of the speech in Job 40:6), and בת קול (:4), a distinction which is made even more strongly elsewhere. (See RM, p. 261.)

מי הקדימני ואשלם (:6)—The verse (Job 41:3) continues with לי הוא תחת כל השמים, a clause taken to embody the concept of מלכות שמים and thus to emphasize that the gifts to be mentioned come from God. Also embodied in the verse as a whole, as here interpreted, is a combination of God's justice recompensing the individual beforehand, and God's love, His giving these things to the individual in the first place.

מי מל לשמי . . . או עז (625:1)—Although most of the מצוות in this list are ritualistic, מעקה (:2) and פיאה (:4) are ethical. This intermingling of the two types of מצוות bespeaks a common bond. Indeed, the ritualistic מצוות of תרומה ומעשר (625:5) and חלה (:6) had the ethical functon of providing the priests and the Levites with food (see the discusson in OT, p. 102 ff.). It is in the very character of the מצוה, something done at God's behest, that an ethical מצוה is not something done for man alone but, so to speak, for God as well. Notice: מי הפריש לי פיאה (:4), although פיאה concretizes the concept of charity.

XXVII.3 (625:8 ff.)

[1] ולא יהיה . . . מזכיר עון (626:4, 6)—God does not want symbols of Israel's sin of the golden calf to be seen or used. The same emphasis is employed in regard to the reminders of their other sins also—the heinous sins of adultery and buggery—and hence the reason behind all the occasions for the use of this expression must be the same. The reason is God's regard for the honor of the

persons involved, as is stated elsewhere, specifically in the case of buggery (see Pesik. de R. Kah., ed. Mandelbaum, p. 36 and the references there). The concepts involved are: God's love, honor (of Israel or man), and sin.

שכינה (1, 2:)—The concept here is גלוי שכינה, a visible manifestation of God.

השופרות . . . שלעגל (4:)—Israel in the present must not employ a reminder of the sin of Israel in the wilderness, for the sounds of the שופר are a plea for forgiveness of sins now, implying Israel's corporate personality in time.

[2] ומתה . . . תני מפני מה (6 f.:)—On the Halakah involved, see Lieberman, p. 878 here.

XXVII.4 (627:8 ff.)

Introduction: An important aspect of rabbinic thought is indeterminacy of belief. A haggadic interpretation can even be taught and then be brushed aside for a later idea. The attitude toward a whole series of interpretations is indeterminacy of belief when such interpretations are preceded by the term דבר אחר, "another interpretation." Sometimes a rabbinic interpretation obviously contradicts a biblical narrative, and that is possible only because of indeterminacy of belief (see CA, pp. 212 ff.). Again, indeterminacy of belief makes possible divergent representations of the *shirah* of the angels. But there are some beliefs which have a dogmatic character, notably the hereafter concepts that point to events in the future which will occur in a consecutive order. These future events are successively the Days of the Messiah, the Resurrection of the Dead, and the World to Come. These hereafter concepts, though combining organismically with the value concepts, are not of an experiential character, but are beliefs to which all must subscribe. They differ from the value concepts, therefore, in demanding an assent of the mind. On the one hand, the hereafter concepts, like the other concepts with which they interweave, leave room for difference of opinion despite their dogmatic quality, and, on the other hand, because they require assent of the mind, their concretizations may be supported by what are regarded as relevant arguments. The future events of which the concepts are generalizations will be נסים, and support for belief in them consists of pointing to similar נסים described in biblical narratives.

[1] ר׳ יהודה . . . בתוך הים מה שהיה (8-629:7:)—In the statements of both ר׳ יהודה (8:) and ר׳ נחמיה (629:4), there is first a reply to a question raised regarding a matter related to a נס in the future. The statement goes on to tell of a נס which will take place in the future and to point to a similar נס described in a biblical narrative. The purpose of the question and the reply is to supply a background of נס in the past and in the present for the specific נס that will occur in the future. After all, the questions, including those about the future נסים, do not reflect genuine doubt but really invite an affirmative reply.

[2] סגיד . . . ר׳ אחא בש״ר שמעון (629:7 ff.–631:4)—This passage is connected with the preceding one by an association of ideas. Most of the נסים of the future mentioned here are quotations from the Book of Isaiah and these quotations are taken as so many concretizations of the concept of the Days of the Messiah or perhaps of another hereafter concept. The kinship here exhibited between rabbinic thought and the Prophets is another indication of the bond uniting the Rabbis with the Prophets. (For other examples, see RM, pp. 291 f., 299, 300; WE, pp. 176 f.)

בעולם הבא (630:1)—The Munich MS reads לעתיד לבא, a more likely reading since the midrash goes on to speak of תחיית המתים, usually conceived as a stage before the עולם הבא. Moreover, what follow are matters foretold in Isa. 43:2, things that are certainly more appropriate to ימות המשיח than to עולם הבא, a perfect state presumably in no need of such נסים.

XXVII.5 (631:5 f.)

[1] והאלהים יבקש וכ׳ (5:)—The Paris MS explains the term יבקש by the words מבקש את הנרדפים ואוהבם, that is to say, those who are persecuted elicit, by that very fact, a manifestation of God's love. (See below here on the use of the word בחר, on 632:5.)

[2] אפי׳ צדיק רודף רשע (8:)—Even though the רשע is altogether unworthy and the צדיק may be justified. Emphasizes here God's love, since it disregards the merits of the case otherwise.

[3] ר׳ יוסי . . . מיד רודפים (9: f.)—This is an independent interpretation of Koh. 3:15, and is an interpolation here. Unlike the other interpretations, it is a concretization of God's justice, not of God's love.

בחרת (632:5)—The rabbinic connotation of the word here and also of בחר (7:), of בחירו (9:), of יבחר (10:) and of בחר (11:) is primarily "love," for only God's relation to the persecuted matters here. This connotation may be, indeed, the basic rabbinic connotation of the root בחר. (See RM, pp. 56 f.; WE, pp. 90 f., 140; see also E. Garfiel, *The Service of the Heart* (New York, 1958), p. 154.)

קרבנות (11:)—קרבנות are קדושה, and one of the connotations of קדושה is love (cf. RM, pp. 169 f., 219). Animals and birds of prey are not eligible as sacrifices, for their dominant characteristic makes קדושה impossible in their case. This statement is one of a number of rabbinic interpretations according to which sacrificial worship is interrelated with ethics.

XXVII.6 (633:1 ff.)

[1] אמ׳ ר׳ שמואל . . . בבטן . . . עם בנוי (636:5-2:)—The three midrashim here are united by a single theme, and hence it is sufficient for only one of them to be an application of Micah 6:3, the application being the second midrash (634:1).

ושמחו אומות העולם . . . מן העולם (633:3; 634:1; 635:1)—The Nations, all of them, are the enemy of Israel and rejoice in the expected annihilation of Israel by God. The world is divided into Israel, on the one hand, and the rest of the Nations regarded as a unit, on the other.

כיון שראה הקב״ה . . . בנוי (633:5 f.; 634:3; 635:2)—An emphasis on God's love. That love changes a stricture or a chiding into what is only playfulness. The hatred of the surrounding nations, the Rabbis felt, calls forth God's compassion toward Israel.

[2] בזכות אהרן . . . ומה הלאיתיך (636:5 f.)—The concept of זכות, merit, implies the idea of corporate personality. Were it not for these three, Israel would not have had these things. The merit of these leaders made possible the survival of the entire people.

[3] או עז . . . יהודה ר' אמ' (637:5 f.)—In limiting the animals that may be sacrificed to the three kinds near at hand, and hence not imposing on Israel the hardships involved in procuring the other kinds, God manifested His love for Israel. Animal sacrifices are thus not only offerings to God but are themselves also manifestations of His love for Israel.

XXVII.7 (638:5 ff.)

[1] או עז . . . אתם הן ד"א (639:5 f.)

כאין נגדו . . . ברכיה ר' אמ' (:5 f.)—There is a dichotomy here between Israel and the Nations of the World. Israel alone is God's nation but this may be the result of Israel's character as against the character of the other nations.

הגוים (640:1)—Taken here in the literal meaning of the word as "nations," for the word relates to אומות העולם (639:6).

[2] נעשה ונשמע . . . ופעלכם (:1)—The good things happening to Israel are reward for their unequivocal acceptance of the Torah; the concept of God's justice.

או עז . . . תועבה (:4)—By decreeing an ox to be one of the sacrificial animals, God demonstrated that He forgave them the sin of the golden calf; the concept of God's love.

XXVII.8 (640:6 ff.)

[1] אלהיך ישראל . . . הונא רב (641:4)—The mixed multitude, the converts (גרים) made the golden calf and even taunted Israel with it. A remarkable emphasis on Israel, in view of the biblical account, and a denigration of גרים.

[2] בעקב . . . ידעה לא והיא . . . יהודה ר' אמ' (642:1)—Connected with

the preceding passage by an association of ideas. When the prophets say that Israel did not know God, it was really the case that Israel rebelled against Him. The concept here is פשע, rebellion. (On the entire idea, see RM, p. 342.)

XXVII.9 (642:5 f.)

The sacrifices are a privilege given Israel because of the deeds of the Patriarchs. The concept here is זכות אבות; implies the idea of corporate personality.

XXVII.10 (643:3 f.)

[1] קרבן . . . והיה שבעת (3:)—This is a Halakah interrelated with a haggadah which latter is introduced by ד״א (6:). The concept here is קרבן (4:). It is also one of the concepts in the haggadah which follows (9:).

[1] ר׳ יהושע . . . קרבן . . . בלא שבת . . . ירצה (7 f.:)—This haggadah, however, is not only interrelated with the halakah preceding it but is also integrated with halakot taught in the very same midrash, the haggadah supplying the reason for those halakot. The parable has the effect of characterizing שבת (9:) as a מטרונה (8:), a haggadic characterization. Now the שבת is objectified and differentiated from other holy days by the Halakah, and especially by those halakot which prohibit anything classed as "labor." These halakot certainly engendered the feeling of קדושה, but the haggadic characterization adds an emotional quality that is projected only by a person, and here by a personification. The parable, as usual, is not a complete parallel. We do not think that it extends to a mystical relationship between God and the Sabbath.

XXVII.11 (644:4 f.)

[1] ושור או . . . ולאבד (4 f.:)—An emphasis on God's love; in contrast to the wicked who have no compassion for anyone, God shows compassion even towards birds and animals. The concepts are אכזריות אכזרי) , 644:6; 645:3) and מדת רחמים. אכזריות is a negative

value concept, i.e., a type of value concept stigmatizing immoral acts (see WE, p. 25).

[2] ‏ולאבד‎ . . . ‏אמ׳ ר׳ לוי‎ (645:3 f.)—The aim of all the wicked men is to destroy Israel, and each of them prides himself on his being more realistic in such destructiveness than his predecessor. Their treatment of Israel is thus not a test of their wickedness, for they are all equally wicked, but of their vicious efficiency. It has remained for the Nazis of our day, utilizing scientific methods, to prove to be the most diabolically efficient of all. R. Levi's insightful appraisal has, alas, been confirmed by the unspeakable events of our times.

[3] ‏כל הארץ‎ . . . ‏אמ׳ ר׳ לוי אף‎ (646:3 f.)—R. Levi concludes with a fantasy projected into the future in which Gog, feeling himself to be more realistic than all his predecessors, declares that he will first do battle with Israel's Patron in heaven and after that, with Israel. The point here is that to destroy Israel, the wicked must first overcome God—that is to say, Israel will never be destroyed.

[4] ‏בגוים ההם‎ . . . ‏אמ׳ לו הקב״ה‎ (6 f.:)—The concepts embodied are: ‏גלוי‎ ‏שכינה‎ and ‏ימות המשיח‎ in combination. Isa. 42:13 and Zech. 14:3 state the ideas of the prophets used here to concretize the concepts of ‏גלוי שכינה‎ and ‏ימות המשיח‎ in combination, and this indicates again the bond between the Rabbis and the prophets.

‏כל הארץ‎ . . . ‏ומה כתיב‎ (647:1)—This embodies the concept of ‏מלכות שמים‎. After the time of Gog, God was recognized as King by everybody. Despite the dogmatic quality of the hereafter concepts, there could be wide differences of opinion in regard to projected concretizations (see RM, p. 362 f.). R. Levi's fantasy about Gog's challenge to God may have appealed to rather few.

XXVII.12 (647:3 f.)

Chapter XXVIII

XXVIII.1 (648:2 ff.)

[1] מה יתרון . . . א"ר בנימן . . . של תורה (2:)

מינות (648:3; 649:1)—This is not heresy in the sense of denying prescribed doctrine; it is denying a relation to God which had at one time been actualy experienced (see RM, pp. 341 f.). This denial often takes the form of a מין declaring that there is no divine justice, "no judgment and no Judge," (649:4).

בעמלו . . . בעמילה של תורה (6:)—Labor in the study of Torah does bring reward. The concepts are: תלמוד תורה and מדת הדין.

א"ר שמואל . . . אמ' שלמה (7 f.:)—An affirmation, ultimately, of God's punitive justice.

[2] ר' לוי אמ' . . . אורה (649:8 f.)—The light of the sun is the reward for engaging in מצות ומעשים טובים (8:). The first part of Koh. 1:3 is taken as a question, and תחת השמש (648:5) as an answer.

רבנן אמרי . . . בגבורתו (650:1)—Koh. 1:3 is again taken as a question and an answer. The reward of the צדיקים (1:) for their מצות (2:) ומעשים טובים is the light of their faces לעתיד לבא (2:), a light as great as the sun. לעתיד לבא refers here to עולם הבא. The concepts are: מצות ומעשים טובים, צדיקים, the world to come, and the combination of the concepts of God's love and His justice. Evidently the reward in [2] above is for those who do only a modicum of מצות and Good Deeds, and is strictly God's justice alone.

[3] א"ר יונה . . . את העומר (3:)—God's love as evident in what He does to provide plant food for man.

XXVIII.2 (650:7 ff.)

[1] **בעסק גדול** . . . **א״ר בניה** (651:2)—Because the midrash is introduced by a haggadic statement, we have here an instance of the interrelation of Haggadah and Halakah.

[2] **מהו צריך** . . . **א״ר ברכיה** (:10 f.)—The metaphor here regards the act of offering the עומר as a *prayer* for the success of the barley crop, for the proper conditions that assure its growth. The figure is of a cook or baker who tastes of the dish he is preparing so as to know what is still needed. The omer-offering is thus a prayer to God to do what is still required for the crop. Another instance of an act having the function of prayer is the blowing of the shofar (see 674:1 and our comment there). The concept involved is תפלה.

[3] **סנטירותי** . . . **ר׳ יהושע** (652:2)—The metaphor here regards the act of offering the omer as a thanksgiving for the safeguarding of the crop from harm. The concept here is הודאה. The act of offering the omer can be given different, though related, meanings.

באות בהן . . . **א״ר אלעזר** (:3 f.)—After the rains there is need for God to protect the grain from heat and harmful dew—in accord with the preceding midrash.

באות בהן . . . **ואימתי** (653:2)—See Lieberman's note here, p. 879.

[4] **וכמה** . . . **ומה העולם הזה** (655:1)—This world a person shares with all the rest of men, whereas in העולם הבא (:2) each צדיק is given a world for himself (see 397:2.)

[5] **שיעמול לרוח** . . . **א״ר סימן** (:2)—Even after plowing, reaping, etc., there is still need for the wind to winnow the harvest, and the omer-offering is the "price" for the wind. Dropping the metaphor, the offering is thanksgiving to God (הודאה) for the winnowing wind. Even in the very last process of the harvest, you are the recipient of God's love.

XXVIII.3 (655:6 f.)

[1] The interpretation here of Lev. 23:10 is not directly led up to by the long פתיחה which precedes it. However, like the various state-

ments in the פתיחה concerning the omer-offering and embodying the concept of God's love, the interpretation here also concerns the omer and tells of God's love. In contrast to the gift of manna by God which involved an omer to every individual Israelite, this single omer offered up by the entire people is very meager and of poor quality, but it must be offered at the appointed time. The emphasis is on the omer-offering as a קרבן and as such it must be offered at the appointed time.

XXVIII.4 (656:4 ff.)

[1] אלא בתפלה ותחנונים (6:)—(and in other interpretations in this section)— But through prayer and supplications that God answered by performing a נס. The concept is not only תפלה but also נס.

[2] אלא במעשים טובים (657:13)—The reward for the good deeds was the נס of the defeat of סיסרא.

XXVIII.5 (658:11 f.)

[1] טללים קשים . . . והניף את (11 f.:)—Waving the omer is a prayer to God to dispel bad winds and harmful dew. The same act is interpreted in the following statement in valuational terms and as an act of thanksgiving, and hence we have good reason to assume that the present statement interprets it as an act of prayer, thus maintaining the pairing of prayer and thanksgiving characteristic of the interpretation of the omer-offering in general. The alternative is to regard the present statement not as embodying a value concept but as a technique for dispelling undesirable dew and winds, a meaning the act perhaps may have had in very early days but certainly did not have in the biblical-rabbinic context (see OT, p. 218; RM, p. 158 n.).

[2] שלו . . . ר' סימון בשם (659:2)—It is interpreted as a thanksgiving for the harvest, expressed by acknowledging that the world belongs to God. This is, of course, similar to the acceptance of עול מלכות שמים in קריאת שמע, except that the latter is the daily practice of the individual. The concept of מלכות שמים, thus implied in the act, parallels its inclusion in the words מלך העולם of the ברכה

formula. The waving of the omer is hence an act constituting a kind of ברכה in itself. The passage exemplifies the integration of Halakah and Haggadah.

XXVIII.6 (659:6 ff.)

[1] . . . שבזכות (659:6 and on 660:2)—זכות here characterizes the omer-offering as having an inherent merit which constitutes the ground for God's rewarding justice.

[2] תשמור . . . שבזכות מצות (6:6 f.)—The omer-offering was the first new מצוה performed by Israel after coming to the Land and it was in reward for this future act that Abraham inherited the Land (מהרז״ו). The concepts here are: קדושה (the Land of Israel), מצוה, קרבן, זכות, אבות (Abraham), God's justice. What is involved here is the idea of corporate personality; the Israelites who came to the Land and Abraham constitute links in a single personality, and Abraham is rewarded for the act of his descendents.

[3] ר' שמעון בן לקיש . . . לאשתו (660:1)—מצות העומר is here extolled by associating it with מנחת סוטה (Num. 5:15 ff.), both consisting of an עומר of barley meal and both requiring תנופה, waving. The harmony established between man and wife is, by association, attributed to מצות עומר. The concepts are: זכות, שלום, קרבן, מצוה.

    The omer-offering is a קרבן צבור; yet it is associated here with a sacrifice by an individual, another illustration of the emphasis on the individual.

[4] מן הצדיקים (661:1)—The presence of צדיקים would have saved them from the enemies; the צדיקים and the folk constitute a corporate personality. The concepts here: God's justice, צדיק, the Nations, נס, קרבן, זכות.

[5] רבנן . . . ר' יהושע . . . עמהם (5:5 f.)—The role of the זכות deriving from the omer-offering seems to be secondary here. יפ״ת explains that the merit of Ezekiel saved them from famine, and מהרז״ו says that Ezekiel's suffering atoned for Israel's sins, and that puts the emphasis on the concept of כפרה, vicarious atonement. What

saves Israel, then, is Ezekiel's suffering rather than the merit of the omer-offering.

מצטערים עמהם . . . שכל זמן (662:3)—Here the צדיקים are individuals who have not sinned, whereas the rest of the people, designated collectively as ישראל, have sinned and suffer as a result. The mark of the צדיק is that he cannot be at ease when the others suffer.

לעולם אודך . . . מן דרכיב (666:6 f.)—Even המן (667:4) recites a verse from Ps. 30 so that all who are mentioned in the story participate in the recital of the Psalm. The story seems to be on the borderline between indeterminacy of belief and pious entertainment.

Chapter XXIX

XXIX.1 (668:2 f.)

[1] לעולם ה' דברך נצב בשמים (:2)—This verse is taken to refer to God's promise to Adam that his descendants would, like Adam himself, be placed in judgment on Rosh ha-Shanah and then forgiven (669:4).

[2] את מוצא . . . באחד לחדש (:7 f.)—The twelve hours of Adam's first day ended with forgiveness for his sin of disobedience: נתן לו דימיס (669:4), an emphasis on מדת רחמים at almost the beginning of the world.

אדם הרי . . . אף בניך . . . לחדש (669:4)—Adam is symbolic of his descendants in that regard. On Rosh ha-Shanah, the day of the year when he was forgiven after being placed in judgment, his descendants too will be forgiven after being placed in judgment. A recurrent manifestation of מדת רחמים (see יפ"ת).

XXIX.2 (669:7 ff.)

[] מדבר ביעקב (670:2)—This accords with the Rabbis' emphasis on the individual, for the verse speaks of the people of Israel.

והלא לא היו אלא שרי אומות העולם (4:)—The angels in Gen. 28:12 were not מלאכי שרת (4:) but "princes," guardian angels of the Nations who ruled over Israel from Babylon onwards. However they were conceived, here they merely stand for those nations. In the dream the number of rungs the ladder they climb foretells the number of years of the rule of each of them over Israel. Only the "prince" of Edom (Rome) seems to continue to climb, but God reassures Jacob that Rome will fall and then the reign of the Nations will end. The concepts are: אבות, מלכיות, אומות העולם, ישראל (Jacob).

ואעפ״כ . . . ר' ברכיה . . . ולא עלה (671:4)—Jacob was afraid and did not ascend despite God's assurance. Having thus sinned, Jacob forfeited the opportunity Israel had of being the ruling nation of the world. The Rabbis try to account for the fact that Israel was not a ruling nation, and they relate this failure to a sin of Jacob, and thus to a moral failure. The concepts are: sin and אבות. But note: now a concept, sin, has been injected into the story and an entirely different turn has thus been given to what had before been a familiar biblical story. What kind of belief could be accorded to the story as "corrected" by the midrash, a story diverging from the Bible story? An indeterminate belief.

אמ' לו הקב״ה . . . לאדום (6:)—Jacob sinned but his descendants are punished—the idea of corporate personality.

ושקט ממדי . . . מאדום (672:2)—The lands or powers named here oppressed Israel on its own land.

[2] בייסורין (6:)—A subconcept of מדת הדין. The punishments decreed for the individual are, in the long run, for his benefit, enabling him to inherit עוה״ב.

XXIX.4 (672:8 ff.)

(See Margulies, p. 672, footnote 28, regarding the numeration.)

[1] ר' יאשיה . . . פניך יהלכון (8:)—When the חכמים gather to intercalate a month, God causes His Shekinah to dwell among them and enlightens them concerning the הלכה (674:1). Reflected here is the Rabbis' experience of normal mysticism when studying and teaching Torah. As background, however, the midrash employs the concept of גלוי שכינה when it speaks of God leaving His heavenly councilors and thus emphasizes His love. The concepts involved are: גלוי שכינה, God's love, תלמוד תורה, זקנים (673:1).

[2] אשרי . . . באחד לחדש (674:1)—The act of blowing the shofar is an act of prayer to which God responds by changing מדת הדין (5:) to מדת רחמים (6:). We saw that the act of waving the omer is also interpreted as a prayer. (See our comment at 650:10 f.)

XXIX.3 (674:7 f.)

(See Margulies, p. 672, footnote 28, regarding the numeration.)

XXIX.7 (675:6 ff.)

[1] ליצרו (676:2)—Refers to יצר הרע (on that term see above at 544:1). Two ideas are apparently combined here: God prods the individual to walk in the right way, but the individual himself must make every effort to control his יצר הרע; if he gave way to it, he would lose both this world and the world to come. However, the idea about the control of the יצר הרע has no supporting verse, and hence may be a later addition.

[2] מדריכך . . . בחדש השביעי (3: f.)—In a manifestation of His love, God Himself tells Israel to invoke זכות אבות (6:) and thereby to be acquitted in judgment on ראש השנה (7:). The three Patriarchs are named here and hence it is זכות אבות literally. The concept of זכות אבות involves, of course, the idea of corporate personality, and by invoking זכות אבות the individual senses a direct bond between himself and the Patriarchs.

XXIX.6 (677:5 f.)

This section is an instance of the interrelation of Halakah and Haggadah. Ps. 81:4 is given a halakic interpretation which is followed by a haggadic interpretation of the same verse.

[1] בחדש (:5)—Both in the biblical verse and in the subsequent rabbinic interpretations in this section חֹדֶשׁ means "new moon." In Exod. 12:2 the biblical meaning of the word is "month," whereas a rabbinic interpretation renders it "new moon" there and in another rabbinic interpretation in another connection, renders it "month." The word thus has the same dual meaning both in the Bible and in rabbinic usage, an indication that there was no real break between the Bible and the later rabbinic development. Similar examples are the meanings assigned to: צדקה, גוי, ישראל, אדם, and מצוות, as well as עולם.

[2] ד"א בחדש . . . באחד לחדש (:8 f.)—The blowing of the shofar is here regarded, apparently, as a call to Israel to improve their deeds. The concept embodied is תשובה, repentance, the blowing of the shofar a call to תשובה. In turn, if this improvement takes place, the shofar itself is a symbol of God's forgiveness (see רד"ל). A combination of God's love and His justice is involved here.

XXIX.8 (678:3 f.)

[1] ר' חייא . . . זה לזה (:3 f.)—The marriage of a man and a woman is ordained by God at their conception. It is not something agreed upon by men but a נס going back to their existence as embryos. "Marriages are made in heaven," so to speak.

[2] כדי אברהם אבינו לכפר . . . (679:2)—Often the concept of כפרה means vicarious atonement and involves suffering or even death on the part of the person who thus atones for others. Here, however, it involves the idea of זכות. Abraham's merit is so great that it atones for all the sins of Israel in this world. This midrash thus brings to the fore the kinship between כפרה and זכות. Both these concepts imply the same idea of corporate personality. Elsewhere we describe the two concepts as overlapping concepts (see RM, p. 318 n. and the references there).

XXIX.5 (679:6 f.)

[1] כלה . . . אבל ישראל (680:4)—Only Israel had laws of charity. The difference between Israel and the Nations is thus of an ethical character. There is an emphasis on the ethical in rabbinic thought (see OT, pp. 243 ff.).

XXIX.11 (680:7 f.)

[1] לעולם שביעי חביב (7:)—Although עולם usually means "world" in rabbinic literature, it also retains, as here, the biblical meaning of "time."

[2] שביעי חביב (7:)—In folklore, the number seven has a kind of magical function, but the Rabbis use it to stress significance.

[3] למעלה שביעית חביבה (7:)—Assigning a heaven as a dwelling place of God serves as a negation of pantheism; it is, however, compatible with normal mysticism. (On the pantheism of Epictetus, see WE, p. 226 n.)

[4] באבות שביעי . . . האלהים (681:3)—There were not only three, but seven אבות, and Moses, the seventh, was the most beloved. Others are also designated as אבות. The concept of אבות, hence, like the other value concepts was an indeterminate concept.

XXIX.8b (681:10 f.)

Here the number seven stresses significance by the teaching that the seventh month is the occasion for performing seven מצוות. However, the association of "seven" with significance is by no means a necessary one. In the midrash here introduced by ד"א (682:2) and exhibiting the same stylistic form as the midrash it follows, the number seven is dropped in the interpretation and the word is made to convey the idea of "plentiful."

XXIX.9 (682:4 f.)

[1] שאני גואל את בניך (5:)—These words, it seems to us, have been interpolated because of the section which follows. In the present
midrash, Abraham asks God to forgive Israel's sins on the ground
of the binding of Issac—that is to say, זכות אבות—and hence the
oath implied refers to what takes place on ראש השנה, one of the
familiar themes of the liturgy of that day. Again, the idea seems to
be that God recalls the oath on the seventh month each year, and
this patently refers to forgiveness from sins.

[2] ולא השבתיך (683:2)—Abraham trusted in God; the concept of אמונה.
It seems to teach that neither Abraham nor Isaac expected that the
sacrifice would not take place.

XXIX.10 (683:5 f.)

[1] נאחזין בעונות ומסתבכין בצרות (684:5)—The צרות are punishment for
the sinning.

[2] וסופן ליגאל וכו׳ (5:)—The גאולה is redemption from servitude, from
the צרות (5:). In rabbinic Judaism there is no "redemption" from
sin; the individual himself does תשובה.

XXIX.12 (684:8 ff.)

[1] Interrelation of Halakah and Hagggadah, for Num. 29:2 is interpreted
first in a halakic discussion and then in a haggadah.

[2] אמר להם . . . לא חטאתם לפני (686:3)—The Rabbis felt that the study
of Torah implies repentance, and thus a withdrawal from sin.
Here the knowledge imparted in מתן תורה has a similar effect.
That is why, when they accepted the Torah, it was imputed to
them as though they had never sinned.

[3] מכיון שנכנסתם . . . חדשה (5:)—Because you have done תשובה and
therefore were judged favorably, you are not the same persons you
were when you were sinners (מהרז״ו). A person is not "twice-born"
but made anew at every ראש השנה.

PART FOUR

Chapter XXX

XXX.1 (687:2 ff.)

[1] בייז מסכתי . . . למה תשקלו (:4)—Because you neglect the study of Torah, you are punished by having to pay enormous taxes to Rome and to labor while the Nations have plenty. The concepts are: Study of Torah, God's justice, Nations of the World.

[2] מתן שכרה . . . ר' ברכיה (:7 f.)—Even collectors of charity will be punished for collecting from the poor by force. Only teachers of Bible and Mishnah (to children) are allowed to be paid and even then only as compensation for "interrupted labor" (Jastrow). The concepts are: God's justice, charity, and Study of Torah.

וראשי חדשים (688:4)—ראש חדש was evidently classed with festivals, for the additional expenditures are given by God as they are given for Sabbaths and Festivals. The concepts are: God's love and שמחת יום טוב.

[3] על דלא שבקת לסיבותך כלום (689:4)—Evidently neither ר' חייא nor ר' יוחנן himself expected, on the basis of God's justice, that He (God) would provide for him, and that his devotion to study of Torah would thus be rewarded. This contradicts the preceding midrash—something which occurs so often in Haggadah—for there it is implied that a person can expect to be recompensed by God for what he expends on his childrens' tuition. At the same time both midrashim stress the study of Torah.

עולם כולו . . . אבל התורה . . . לילה (:6 f.)—By regarding עולם as inferior to תורה, its significance is diminished.

[4] דמים . . . לולב שעומד (691:3)—It is assumed that a לולב is expensive, and hence, embodied here is the concept of הידור מצוה. (On the connotation of this concept, see WE, p. 235.)

XXX.2 (691:5 ff.)

[1] חיים את בעי (691:7, 9; 692:1)—Refers to לחיי העולם הבא of 691:6. These opinions, and the fourth that follows, represent what each of the authorities regards as the *summum bonum* of life. The variety of views indicates that there was no consensus on the part of the Rabbis concerning the *summum bonum*. Indeed, in the case of ייסורין (691:9) it is not true that what leads to עוה"ב is a *summum bonum* at all. All this is in line with the absence in rabbinic thought of an ultimate criterion in ethics (see WE, p. 31 ff.). An organismic complex of thought cannot be reduced to a single value or a single rule or a single criterion.

[2] שובע . . . ואגדות (692:4)—Studying each branch of Torah brings with it its own particular joy.

[3] מכחה שלתורה . . . שלמצות (693:9)—In this view the most beloved group consists of those who studied Torah and performed מצוות. It is a view commonly held, of course, but the question אי זו כת החביבה והנעימה שבהם (8:) indicates that there were other groups that might be considered "the most beloved," that תורה and מצוות are not the only criteria (see also our comment in [1] above).

אלו סופרין (10:) . . . בימינך נצח—Standing "at the right hand of the Holy One blessed be He" are the teachers of children. They are superior to those who are themselves devoted to the study of Torah and who teach Torah to adults.

[4] אורח חיים (2:)—תודיעני . . . ליום הכיפורים (694:2) refers to the life here. The annual ten days of תשובה at the beginning of the year constitute the way to life for that year.

שמחות (3:)—שובע שמחות . . . ושמחה (3:) is equated with מצות (4:), the joy of the מצוה.

מהו נעימות (5: f.) . . . ביום הראשון—The period from ר"ה (695:1) to סוכות when the לולב is taken is regarded here as a unit, for

Israel's victory on ר"ה is symbolized by the לולב held in the right hand. However, what the victory consists in is not stated, and it may refer to Israel's sheer survival.

XXX.3 (695:4 ff.)

[1] כי יעטף . . . פנה אל (:4 f.)—David is regarded here as a prophet who forsees the future (צופה, 696:2, 4). The idea of corporate personality is not involved here, for his descendants, some of whom are righteous and some of whom are wicked, are distinct from David. David is gratified or disappointed, as the case may be, by their characters, and this means that he judges them and is not identified with them.

[2] כי ה' הוא האלהים—אלהים (697:8) is taken as מדת הדין.

[3] מהרז"ו—(698:4) אלא תפלה זו בלבד relates this to ערער of Ps. 102:18 which is thus a characterization of prayer as the single means left for the present generations by which to approach God. Evidently לא מלך . . . ותומים (:3) is a cliché describing Israel's helplessness, but what are relevant here are the last three matters mentioned.

תכתב זאת לדור אחרון (:5)—God always accepts the repentant sinner even to the last generation.

שהקב"ה . . . ברייה חדשה (:6)—For after God has accepted them and forgiven them, they are as newly born.

[4] שהם נטויים למיתה (699:1)—The present generation is always in imminent danger from Rome. This attitude may have been affected by memories of the Hadrianic persecutions.

שהקב"ה עתיד לבראת וכו' (:1)—The word עתיד indicates daily expectation of ימות המשיח, a dogma.

ומה עלינו . . . ביום הראשון (:2)—Praising and thanking God now, for His redeeming of Israel is certain and imminent.

XXX.4 (699:4 f.)

[1] ישפוט תבל בצדק (700:2)—בצדק is taken to mean "with charity" and accordingly, the clause means: He judges the world with charity—that is to say, His justice is tempered with charity, mercy. That is why the world rejoices. (For a parallel idea, including a similar use of the term צדק, see WE, pp. 99 and 263, n. 27.) An emphasis on love.

XXX.5 (700:5 f.)

[1] ארחץ בניקיון (:5)—is probably given a valuational meaning, symbolically in the Bible itself.

[2] במקח ולא בגזל (:5)—This is an instance of the emphasis on the ethical sphere in rabbbinic thought, more specifically here, on the dominance of the ethical as against the ritual sphere. (For the emphasis on ethics in general, see OT, pp. 243 f.) In an organismic complex, however, the ritual and the ethical are intermingled or interrelated.

XXX.6 (701:7 ff.)

[1] לכם, לכל אחד ואחד מכם—An emphasis on the individual in Halakah. (See WE, pp. 28–29; CA, pp. 8, 10, 187 f.)

[2] משלכם ולא מן הגזול . . . קטיגורו (702:1 to 704:4)—This is an instance of the interrelation of Halakah and Haggadah. משלכם . . . גזול (:1) is a halakah, and it is followed by a parable leading to the idea that the stolen לולב cries out to God that it has been stolen. Not only the same concept (גזל), but precisely the same situation is embodied here in the halakah and in the haggadah.

לזכות בו (704:2)—The term here apparently implies that the waving of the לולב is an act of prayer, especially since a stolen לולב "speaks," as it were, though against him. (See also מהרז"ו.)

ומלאכי השרת וכו' (:3)—The angels usually function as dramatic background and, in that role, sometimes call attention to man's failings.

XXX.7 (704:5 ff.)

There is an emphasis here on God's love, on His forgiveness during the period from ראש השנה through יום הכפורים. However, the midrash also goes on to teach that the reckoning will begin anew. The emphasis on God's love does not mean that there are not other occasions when God's justice is concretized. Emphasis is a valuational mode, not a logical principle.

XXX.8 (706:7 f.)

This section exhibits an interrelation between Halakah and Haggadah. Most of the material here consists of halakic opinions, but the interpretations of the word הדר (707:1) are imaginative word-plays, a haggadic approach. This is also true of the preceding statement.

XXX.9 (707:8)

This midrash begins a series of different interpretations of the words standing for the four species (ארבעה מינים). They are intended, apparently, as ideas one is to bear in mind when taking up the לולב, but being different interpretations—ideas to choose from—they are only suggestions. As is indicated by the ברכה on the לולב, the מצוה itself consists solely of the act of taking up the לולב. The series of midrashim here show how to enrich that experience with other concepts beside מצוה. All are instances of the interrelation of Halakah and Haggadah.

An aspect of the concept of כונה relates to the attempt to achieve sheer awareness of God, and it is to that experience, an evanescent experience, that the present midrash points. The words describing each of the four species are made to refer to "The Holy One blessed be He." On taking up the לולב (the four species) a person ought to try to have an awareness of God, sheer awareness of Him, an experience not embodying a concept. In normal mysticism, however, this awareness is never an experience in itself, but is immediately associated with an experience that does embody a concept. Here this sheer awareness of God is associated with the act which embodies the מצוה of taking up the ארבעה מינים. (For other examples of this aspect of כונה, see WE, pp. 192 f.; CA, pp. 68 f.)

XXX.10 (708:1)

[1] Another interpretation of Lev. 23:40 teaches a different idea on taking up the לולב, namely, that one should have in mind the אבות and אמהות. The four מינים represent the four אבות and the four אמהות. Since on this Festival judgment is passed on the matter of rain for the coming year (Rosh ha-Shanah I.2), it was זכות אבות that was thus invoked and the act of taking up the לולב is hence a kind of prayer for rain, a plea that God be mindful of the Merit of the Fathers and give rain to their children. The idea involved in זכות אבות is that the Patriarchs and their descendants are links in a single corporate personality, so that the descendants may be rewarded for the good deeds of their ancestors (see, e.g., CA, pp. 47, 101, 225).

XXX.11 (709:1)

This interpretation of Lev. 23:40 says that the four species symbolize the members of the Great Sanhedrin, the scholars who ask them for halakic decisions (see אמרי יושר), the three rows of students sitting before them and the two scribes standing before them. These details, as symbolized in the four species, made the Sanhedrin not just an institution of the past but almost a present reality. The Sanhedrin acquired a function in the present, so to speak, the function of concretizing Torah as an ongoing process. It is this unique institution a person is to bear in mind when taking up the לולב—an act which is now a plea for rain for Israel on the ground of the merit of this institution of Israel, its Great Sanhedrin. (I discussed this midrash with Dr. Simon Greenberg.)

XXX.12 (709:6 f.)

This interpretation, too, teaches that the individual is to bear an idea in mind on taking up the לולב, and it also provides a background for that idea, namely, the unity of the people of Israel.

Subjectively, it is a consciousness that he, the individual, is an inseparable member of that people. The background for this idea is a symbolical interpretation in which each of the four species represents an element in Israel, and all these four elements are united when the four species are "bound" (יוקשרו, 710:3) together in the act of taking the לולב. Three of the elements are classified by means of the concepts of תורה and מעשים טובים (709:7, 9; 710:1), and the fourth is characterized by their absence. The idea that those with merit atone for those without it is, of course, also background, and it indicates that the Festival is associated with יום כפור. The midrash concludes with a statement that when the people of Israel thus demonstrate that they are a united people, God is exalted; support for this statement is adduced by an interpretation of Amos. 9:6. The concept here is מלכות שמים. (Compare the versions in Midrash Tannaim, ed. Hoffmann, p. 213, and Midrash Samuel, ed. S. Buber, p. 32a.) God's sovereignty is a reality when the Jewish people, unified through תורה and מעשים טובים thereby acknowledge His sovereignty.

XXXX.13 (710:8 f.)

[1] אמרתי . . . פרה . . . על הטמא (711:1)—The concepts here are: God's love, טהרה, and טומאה. טומאה has also another obverse, the concept of קדושה, and the latter has also far-reaching ethical implications.

[2] אמרתי . . . שאדור . . . לוקחין (3:)—The idea of "taking God" is surely not even a metaphor, for God is not a thing and therefore cannot be "taken." The idea is used only together with the idea of God's dwelling among Israel, that is, in the Tabernacle or Temple.

קחו אתי ואדור ביניכם (4:)—"Dwelling" in the Tabernacle, to which this passage refers, meant to the Rabbis that there was גלוי שכינה in the Tabernacle, sensory manifestation of God, in contradistinction to the normal mysticism of nonsensory manifestations of God (see RM, pp. 235 f.). This sensory experience of God in a definite locale allows the Rabbis to say He told Israel to take Him into the Tabernacle that He might dwell among them, an idea only expressing God's love and not really alluding to a physical act.

[3] אדם . . . אור . . . אמרתי (5:)—Passages of this kind have often been regarded as softening or mitigating biblical anthropomorphism. However, this passage, quoting Dan. 2:22, simply declares that God does not need light made by man. What underlies this and similar passages is the rabbinic idea of God's otherness, that He is not like man, indeed, that He is like none other (see RM, pp. 303 ff. and especially pp. 315 f.).

ולכפר על נפשותיכם (7:)—The lamp in the Tabernacle was felt to have the same efficacy as the sacrifice brought in the Temple—that of atoning for Israel.

נר אלהים נשמת אדם (8:)—This verse is interpreted as saying that there is something analogous between the soul of a man and the lamp of God, and the midrash adds the idea that the lamp atones for the sins of the soul. The word נפש (7:) is an alternative here for נשמה (8:).

[4] מטר . . . לזכות . . . ועכשיו (8:)—God rewards Israel for the מצוה of taking the לולב by sending down rain. No "magic or technique" is involved.

XXX.14 (711:11 f.)

The similarity in appearance between the four species and the major members of the human body is interpreted symbolically to mean that God is to be worshipped with a man's entire being (see יפ״ת). This, too, is among the suggested ideas to bear in mind when taking up the לולב. Another instance of the interrelation of Halakah and Haggadah. The concepts here are: מצוה, אדם, and עבודה (worship).

XXX.15 (712:4 f.)

[1] The role of the חכמים (713:7) in the interpretation of the תורה שבכתב is regarded as given them by God. It is an aspect of the תורה שבעל פה, for it is not made possible just by wisdom, as witness Solomon's difficulties. This midrash, too, exhibits an interrelation between Halakah and Haggadah.

[2] ישב לו תמיה . . . עליהן (5:)—Prov. 30:18 has a literal meaning which is entirely ignored here except for the numbers. The interpretation is an extreme example of how the biblical text may act only as a stimulus to a rabbinic idea and how, at times, the biblical context may be disregarded. (On the text as stimulus when the context is not disregarded, see RM, pp. 114f.)

[3] פרי עץ . . . שהוא אתרוג וכ' (7:)—Solomon was aware, then, of how the חכמים identified the four species described in Lev. 23:40. This implies that, according to the Rabbis, the academic and legislative body of which the חכמים were members already functioned in biblical days. The concepts here are: תורה שבעל, תורה שבכתב חכמה, תהלה, ישראל; חכמים, מצוות, פה (the first phase of דרך ארץ; see WE, pp. 39f., 51f.).

XXX.16 (713:9f.)

This midrash is, apparently, an enumeration of the *successive* events of the Days of the Messiah, ימות המשיח. First, there will be גלוי שכינה, then He will punish Rome (Esau), then He will build the Temple, and finally He will bring them the Messiah, and the משיח will thus come at the end of the Days of the Messiah, the beginning of which is signalized by גלוי שכינה. This period is here spoken of as reward for the מצוה of taking the לולב.

Chapter XXXI

XXXI.1 (714:7f.)

[1] אשר עשית . . . לאורן של ישראל (715:1)—God gives light to the whole world, and yet He desires the light brought by Israel, although He obviously does not need it. This involves the idea of the otherness of God discussed above at 711:5f. But here this idea serves more patently, perhaps, as background against which God's love is made to stand out.

כובש על מדת הדין (4:)—For the first part of Ps. 71:19 reads: וצדקתך אלהים (714:7) and emphasizes צדקה as love (see also רד"ל). Despite man's sins, God gives light to the world daily.

XXXI.2 (716:1)

The purpose of repeating a passage in the Torah several times is to make it clearly understandable (יפ"ת). Repetitions in the Torah are thus accounted for. The concept is תלמוד תורה.

XXXI.3 (716:5 f.)

Here, too, the idea of the otherness of God serves as background to emphasize God's love.

XXXI.4 (717:4 ff.)

[1] בר קפרא . . . בני ישראל (4:)—In view of the prevalence of the idea of God's otherness in this connection, both above and in the following sections, that idea is most likely assumed also in this midrash. However, here the concept embodied is God's justice rather than His love, and the emphasis is on performing a מצוה.

[2] ראשך . . . ארגוונא (8:f.)—An emphasis on God's love. The "poor" in Israel, a designation for those who have done only a few מצוות or good deeds, are as beloved of God as Elijah, David, and Daniel, each of whom, the contrast indicates, was a צדיק and performed מצוות.

אם אין לנו זכות הבט הברית (718:3)—Elijah's plea accords with the spirit of the midrash. He pleads that God regard Israel with favor even though they may have only the merit of the מצוה of circumcision.

[3] אמ' ר' ברכיה . . . במדבר צין (719:3 f.)—This is a striking instance of the emphasis on God's love. In Num. 20:12–13, where the event is described, and elsewhere also, the Bible indicates that the sin of Moses is a grievous one, so serious indeed as to be the single reason why he could not enter the Promised Land. In this

midrash, however, though the sin of מי מריבה (5:)‎ remains the reason why Moses could not enter the Land, the entire account is given a different turn. Here, it was an act of love for God to describe the event in the Bible and He did so at the request of Moses. Moses felt that otherwise Israel might account for his exclusion from the Land by saying he had falsified the Torah or had included in it something he had not been commanded to say. The sin of מי מריבה is thus made to seem a comparatively minor one, and its very inclusion in the Torah is made out to be an expression of God's love. The parable of the woman who sinned by eating the unripe figs is a complete analogy to this midrashic interpretation but, by the same token, is no analogy at all to the gravity of Moses' sin as described in the *biblical text*.

ר' שמעון . . . כי נעמו (720:6 f.)—This midrash is an even more striking instance of the emphasis on God's love. Here the three verses in the Bible referring to the sin of מי מריבה (721:2) are interpreted to be expressions of God's sorrow. Moreover, what the parable here describes is not a sin, but an accident, almost as though to imply that מי מריבה was an accident.

[4] ר' נחמן אמ' . . . בני ישראל (721:5)—God is the King of Israel as well as the King of the whole world, and this is the view in the Bible itself, and especially in the Prophets (see Kaufmann, תולדות האמונה, I, pp. 39 ff.), as well as being that of the Rabbis. Moses is described here as having been appointed by God to be king of Israel, but only in the sense of having the authority to issue commands, not in the sense of one to whom Israel owes allegiance.

XXXI.5 (722:1 f.)

[1] גברים כת' . . . נקבה (1:)—The angels are here characterized as males. (See our remarks in RM, p. 184, where we have mentioned other physical characteristics attributed to angels and where we concluded, on these grounds, that the word "angel" is a cognitive concept.)

[2] ויורד עוז . . . בני ישראל (3: f.)—All three opinions interpret the word עוז (722:4, 6, and 723:1) to mean Torah, and apparently all of them do so by employing the same prooftext, Ps. 29:11. This is

one of the cases (see also Sifre Deut. ed. Finkelstein, p. 398, note) where rabbinic inerpretation takes a biblical term to be almost a symbol for a rabbinic concept.

ה׳ עוז לעמו יתן (4:)—The verse is taken here to embody the concept of מתן תורה.

שכל מי שהוא . . . בני ישראל (723:1)—In contrast to the end of the preceding section, here, everyone who labors in the Torah, i.e., all the scholars (and not Moses alone) issue commands and others obey. Moses is thus not placed in a category by himself.

XXXI.6 (723:4f.)

[1] אבל לגדודיו אין מספר . . . (724:1)—The concept embodied is מלכות שמים, the countless numbers of servitors (angels), implying the unbounded majesty of God. The Rabbis employ angelology only in exposition of a concept or to give it dramatic background (TE, pp. 88 ff.).

[2] ורבנין אמרי . . . שהיה עולה (2:)—Only when the number of angels was countless, was the praise of God (קילוסו, 3:) His proper praise. The praise was קדוש השם by the angels, again an instance of angelology in exposition of a concept. However, when the Temple was destroyed, God decreased the number of angels and now one of the concepts embodied is גלוי שכינה, since the Temple is associated with a sensory revelation of God. Another concept is God's love, for the decrease in the number of His פמלייא (4:) is considered an indication of His sorrow at Israel's loss (of the Temple).

XXXI.7 (724:9 ff.)

[1] Obviously, everybody recognized that the light of the day was given by the sun. This passage, then, is an instance of indeterminacy of belief. The Temple was associated with גלוי שכינה and in the idea that the light of the world came from the apertures or windows of the Temple, the thought was expressed that God gave light to the world directly, that it was thus a direct manifestation of His love.

[2] אמרה לו בלחישה . . . ר' שמעון (725:7 f.)—The light spoken of here is the primordial light created on the first day before the creation of the sun and the moon on the fourth day, and hence the word יצא (8:) is in the past tense (see the parallel in Ber. R. III, ed. Theodor, p. 20 and the notes there).

XXXI.8 (726:8 ff.)

[1] This passage clearly shows the work of an editor: the formula at the beginning, the one before each grouping, the same rhetorical question at the end of each statement, the conclusion of each statement embodying R. 'Aḥ'a's interpretation of Isa. 42:21. The passage apparently consists of a discussion in an academy that was reworked by an editor.

[2] ר' אבינא . . . אני צריך (727:1)—What need could God have of the light kindled in the Temple? When the wheel of the sun which is only one of the thousand thousands of God's sun-like servitors (see מהרז"ו) goes out to the world no creature can bear to look at it directly. Besides saying that God has no need of a light made by man, this statement implies that God is not like any creature (בריה, 2:) at all, that He is other. It is a statement teaching the idea of the otherness of God. (On the wheel of the sun, see Ginzberg "Legends," I, p. 26.)

אמ' ר' אחא . . . לזכותך (3:)—צדקו here means "His love." He commanded you to kindle the Temple light only to make you more worthy (לזכותך, 4:) by fulfilling a מצוה. (See Lieberman here, p. 880.) The concept of God's love is emphasized once more through the idea of His otherness.

הגלגל הזה שלעין וכ' (7:)—Folklore science.

XXXI.9 (729:2 f.)

[1] This midrash and the others in the passage attributing qualities of personality and consciousness to the sun and the moon are instances of indeterminacy of belief. The daily liturgy speaks of God as renewing daily the creation of the world and gives as proof Ps. 136:7, interpreting the verse to mean that God makes "the

great lights" now, in the present. In this statement no personality
is attributed to the lights (Prayer Book, ed. Singer, p. 39; and on
מעשה בראשית, see RM, p. 36, n. 4). On the other hand, the
Sabbath liturgy contains a hymn, apparently of later origin,
which says that the lights "rejoice in their going forth and are
glad in their returning" (op. cit., ed. Singer, p. 129). The hymn
thus does attribute human qualities to the lights. However, it is
not a matter of an earlier or later idea, for a tannaitic midrash
speaks of the heavenly bodies (and, later, of the earth, etc.) as
conforming to their rule or mode (מידה), and then goes on to
attribute speech and joy to the sun (Sifre to Deut. 32:1, ed.
Finklestein, p. 332). Such contradictory ideas certainly reflect a
belief that is indeterminate.

[2] ולא בהתין . . . ולא יודע (730:5)—The sun and the moon suffer eclipses,
are "smitten" by God. Yet their worshippers are not ashamed of
worshipping them despite the admonishment of ordinary reason.
Inferential reasoning is employed here to negate the concept of
idolatry.

XXXI.10 (730:7 ff.)

[1] למלך שמרדו . . . לא מרד בו (731:1)—The first part of the parable here
relates to an earlier midrash (see יפה תואר and his reference to
Ber. R. XXVIII.8). Even the earth, through its plant and vegetable
life, rebelled against God by bringing forth unnatural fruit. The
only tree that was not corrupted was the olive tree, as will soon be
indicated, and hence, as reward olive oil was the only oil used in
the Temple light. By teaching that animal and plant life also
sinned, the Rabbis account for the destruction of the entire world
in the Flood and not only man. The rabbinic concept of God's
justice has, thus, a wider application than its biblical antecedent.
(See CA, p. 92 and the references there.)

[2] אמ' ר' ברכיה . . . מיתעבדא (731:5)—Had the dove not killed the tree
by tearing off the branch, it would have grown to be a large tree.
That is, Noah recognized it to be a true and healthy specimen of
plant life. This is to say, the olive retained its full original character, did not rebel, despite the rebellion and corruption of other

plant life. The concept is מלכות שמים, as the analogy in the parable indicates.

[3] ר' לוי אמ' . . . ביום זעם (732:1)—See Lieberman here, p. 890 on the text. In the parallel in Ber. R. XXXIII.6, ed. Theodor, p. 311, the idea that the Land of Israel was not inundated by the Deluge is associated with the preceding statement here, and so also in a number of other sources (see Theodor, a.l.). The concept embodied is קדושה, holiness, and that concept is concretized in both statements. Because it was to be holy, the Land of Israel was already differentiated from other lands. Since holiness has a moral connotation (see RM, pp. 169 f.), there is probably also the implication that the Land of Israel, in contrast to the rest of the earth, did not rebel, an implication that seems to be reflected in לא לקת (:2), "was not smitten."

[4] אמ' ר' יוחנן . . . נימחו במים (:4)—Since the Land of Israel is differentiated by being holy, the objection of ר' יוחנן—if the text is correct—could easily be answered by saying that the Land of Israel was different. But the statement of ר' יוחנן does not belong here. It is not found in the parallel in Ber. R. nor in the Munich MS (see Margulies), but it is found in Ber. R. XXVIII.3 and XXX.8 where the Land of Israel is not involved at all. This is one of the many instances where the awareness of the concept embodied helps to solve a textual problem.

XXXI.11 (733:1)

[1] The people of Israel will be rewarded for setting up the light in the Tabernacle and the Temple, a reward which will take place at the end of days.

[2] אמ' ר' לעזר . . . תפתה (:1)—According to this midrash, the reward will consist in the people being saved from the fire of גיהנום, from which apparently the other nations will not be saved. The reward relates to Israel as a people since setting up of the lights is not an act of a personal or private character. However, there is also a belief that גיהנום is the punishment after death in the here and now, and as such it relates to the individual. Notice, for example,

the fear expressed by ר׳ יוחנן (Ber. 28b). A belief which has thus several forms is not a fixed belief.

[3] ערוך מאתמול תפתה (3:)—That is, גיהינם was created before the world was created (מ"כ) and is therefore a haggadic concretization of מדת הדין, since it was not conceived to have been at first a matter of experience.

אמ׳ ר׳ חנן . . . נלך (3:)—According to this midrash, the reward is to see the Messiah. The Days of the Messiah, one of the "hereafter concepts," functions as a belief as well and even has a dogmatic quality. Nevertheless, it is characterized by decided differences of opinion and hence it, too, is not a belief that is rigid.

Chapter XXXII

XXXII.1 (734:1)

[1] גן עדן (4:)—בשעה שהצדיקים . . . בעולם הזה (3:)—here is an eschatological belief, for it is contrasted with עולם הזה (6:), this world, and the situation described is represented as something that is connected with the time when God will exalt Israel (and that will be in the Days of the Messiah). Elsewhere there is also the belief that גן עדן is the reward of the righteous after death (see, e.g., Ber. 28b—the anxiety expressed by R. Johanan). Like גיהינם, it is not a fixed belief and it is obviously a parallel to גיהינום. Although the צדיקים (3:) rejoice at seeing the punishment of the רשעים (3:) in גיהינום, their rejoicing is not gloating but joy at having undergone ייסורין (6:) in this world for their sins and for which they now offer thanksgiving. The concepts are: גיהינום, צדיקים, רשעים, עולם, מדת רחמים combined with ייסורין, מדת הדין, הודאה, גן עדן הזה.

[2] מהם . . . ואמרת (6:)—The רשעים (3:, 4:) are here described as אומות העולם (7:), and this implies that the צדיקים (3:) are Israel.

[3] יתהלכון . . . עד מתי (735:1)—Ordinarily there is no attempt to refute a haggadic derivation of an idea. Here, however, the refutation is needed in order to adduce the opposite idea.

וכעס וגו' . . . היא כיצד (2:)—Here the eschatological גן עדן (3:) seems to be conceived as permanent, but not so the eschatological גיהינם (3:). There is obviously nothing dogmatic about these eschatological beliefs.

לכשירומם הק' מצות בזויות בעולמו (4:)—Refers to the Days of the Messiah. In this world the מצות named here are בזויות, despised by the Nations. They despise the laws observed by the Jews alone (see WE, p. 44 f. and p. 212 where we show it is not a matter of ethical as against ritualistic laws).

אבי שבשמים . . . מה לך יוצא (5:)—In the Hadrianic persecutions the observance of these laws resulted in martyrdom, קדוש השם. The questions here are not a rhetorical device. They indicate that the act of קדוש השם took place in the presence of other Jews, for such an act involves the effect upon other Jews.

שבשמים . . . הה"ד (8: f.)—Refers to the beating by the פרגל (7:), the question here being similar to the other questions before it. It indicates that this is another example of קדוש השם, although the martyrdom does not result in death.

[4] מחוץ למחנה . . . אימתי (736:1)—On the basis of the interpretation of Lev. 24:14, the ממזר referred to here is also a מקלל (cf. the compassionate passage on ממזרים as such at 754:5 f.).

XXXII.2 (736:4 ff.)

[1] ולא יבין . . . גם במדעך (4: f.)—The verse itself (Koh. 10:20) declares that it is imprudent to curse a king or wealthy man. The midrash here, however, omits the matter of prudence entirely and instead forbids the reviling of any man on ethical grounds. The rabbinic interpretation, as against the biblical verse, thus contains an emphasis on the ethical. This is a good illustration of how the first phase of דרך ארץ, the phase of the concept which refers to general human characteristics, is not just descriptive, but contains traits that are not morally neutral. מדע (736:5), thought as

expressed in speech, is taken here to be *the* human characteristic in contrast to sight and hearing which man shares with cattle, animals and fowl. But this special characteristic of man, though one of his several traits, is not morally neutral; it must not be used by a man to revile other men. מדע as a trait of דרך ארץ is not morally neutral here because it is associated with the negative ethical concepts of חירוף and גידוף (7:).

[2] כבודך (7:)—The concept is כבוד הבריות, the honor of mankind. Here it is applied to mankind as a whole, but elsewhere it is also applied to an individual.

טובות (737:1)—ולא יבין . . . כמה טובות here refers to numerous other ways in which God has acted out of regard for the principle of כבוד הבריות, ways of which man is not aware. This is how the words אדם ביקר ולא יבין (1:) in the verse are interpreted, for יקר = כבוד.

כי עוף . . . טיארין (3:)—Augury and divination were, of course, prohibited (Deut. 18:14). Notice that they are included in the prohibitions of forms of עבודה זרה (ibid., v. 10). However, this midrash indicates that there was a belief in the efficacy of augury and divination. The poetic metaphor of "the fowl of heaven" is reduced here to an accepted method, and the danger warned against is thus made to appear more imminent.

ואזנים לדרך ארץ (5:)—The trait referred to belongs to the first phase of the concept of דרך ארץ (WE, p. 52). צניעות is required when attending to natural functions, lest that be heard—even this trait is not morally neutral here since it is associated with a value concept, צניעות. This interpretation of the last part of the verse is obviously not connected with that of the first part.

[3] ד"א . . . לדוד . . . שגיון לדוד וגו' (5: f.)—This midrash retains in part the biblical meaning of the verse but, instead of the prudential, it has an ethical admonition.

שגגות (738:3)—לא תעלה . . . זדונות אלא שגגות are inadvertent sins and this plea implies that David repented of his sin and asked forgiveness for it (cf. Yoma 36b).

[4] מלכו שלעולם . . . עשירו שלעולם אל תקלל (:4 f.)—The prohibition of
ברכת השם is one of the Noachian laws and is repeated here to
indicate that the verse as a whole relates to God.

אמ' ר' לוי . . . לטובה . . . לרעה . . . דברו (739:2)—In accordance
with what was said, the voice was, in the one case pleasing to
God, and in the other, it displeased Him. The same expression,
"And the Lord heard the voice of your words" (:3, :5) is used in
the Bible with regard to both instances, the midrash seems to
indicate, so as to teach that what made the difference was the
content of "your words."

[5] ר' חמא . . . למנוחה אחרת (:6 f.)—Another interpretation of Deut. 1:34,
the last verse adduced in the preceding midrash, and constituting
thus an independent interpretation. There is an emphasis here on
God's love, for the verses here are interpreted as a retraction of
God's oath and a promise of a future "rest," although the verse
actually consists of God's oath, that the people would not enter
"into My rest."

[6] הגוף אמ' (740:7)—Here it is the גוף that sins, and not the נשמה or נפש
(but see our discussions at 87:4 ff. and 90:1 f.).

לנשמה . . . לנפש (:7)—Here each term refers to a separate entity.
At 89:5–6, the terms נפש and נשמה are alternates for the same
entity (see our remarks there).

XXXII.3 (741:6 f.)

[1] ויצא . . . איש הבינים (:6)—יצא מעולמו (:6) may mean "he left,
excluded himself from, Israel," for עולם is frequently a term for
Israel (see, for example, above, 9:5).

[2] ר' ברכיה . . . מאחד עשר (:7 f.)—An element in this midrash is the
Halakah in Men. XI.9, and hence the midrash is an instance of
the integration of Halakah and Haggadah. The mocker assumes
that God eats, a notion the Rabbis elsewhere emphatically insist
is totally wrong. (See RM, pp. 315 f.)

XXXII.4 (742:6 ff.)

[1] מבקש להורגו . . . כיצד (743:1 f.)—Justification for the killing of the Egyptian by Moses: the Egyptian was a cruel taskmaster; he cohabited with the wife of the Israelite; he was bent on killng the Israelite.

היציצה רוח הקודש . . . מבקש להורגו (744:3)—In thus informing Moses God indicated that the would-be murderer was to be killed lest he succeed, by his persecution, in committing the murder. It was thus tantamount to a decree by God, although Moses was not himself named to execute it. The Mishnah states as a general law (Sanh. VIII.7) what we have inferred here to be a decree in this specific case (see Exod. R. I.29 at the beginning).

[2] השם והרגו . . . ר' נחמיה א' (745:1)—השם (:1, :2) was a substitute for the Tetragrammaton. Out of piety and reverence, the pronunciation of the Tetragrammaton was avoided in the synagogue and tended to take on a more or less esoteric character in the Temple, in the sense that pronunciation was deliberately blurred (see Allon, מחקרים, I, pp. 199 f.). This esoteric character of The Name meant at first that it was known to comparatively few and, second, that in contrast to the names of God publicly known, it could be used for magical purposes—and it is so used here. Moses used it to slay the Egyptian after he recognized that there was nobody about who knew and could use the esoteric Name. Basically, then, the Tetragrammaton did not have a magical functon.

רוח הקודש . . . ורבנין אמ' (:2)—The concepts are: (prophecy) and גר (convert).

XXXII.5 (745:6 ff.)

[1] גן נעול . . . פרעה וגו' (:6 f.)—The concepts are: ערוה (746:3) or גלוי עריות, Israel, גאולה, and God's justice.

[2] ר' חונא . . . בזכותו (747:2)—Implied here is the idea that the Gentiles, too, were forbidden גלוי עריות, the latter being a negative מצוה among the seven laws given to the Sons of Noah. The women of Egypt were given the moral strength to observe this law because

of the merit (בזכותה, 3:) of Sarah who observed it, and the men of Egypt were given this moral strength because of the merit (בזכותו, 4:) of Joseph who observed it. Notice that in the next midrash the word בזכותו (5:) can only mean "merit" for which a reward is given. In the present midrash, Sarah's merit is given a corporate reward in the moral strength of the women of what is now her country, to observe the law of chastity incumbent upon them, and similarly in the case of Joseph's merit. This is a very unusual instance both of a corporate reward and a corporate personality, but it is not correct to give the word זכות the meaning of "example," as do some. At the same time, there is an emphasis here on the individual also, in the roles given to Sarah and Joseph.

[3] בזכותו . . . ר' חייה אמ' (4:)—As in [2] above, the practice of chastity is said to be a cause for the redemption from Egypt, and so also in the next midrash. Now the redemption from Egypt is taught by the Rabbis as a paradigm for the redemption from Rome, and thus the people are assured that by practicing chastity now, they would be rewarded by redemption from Rome. (See Lieberman, Sinai IV, pp. 227 f. and also see רד"ל here; for our comments on details in the passage, see the remarks in CA, pp. 75 ff., on the version in the Mekilta.)

XXXII.6 (749:6 ff.)

[1] למטה דן . . . ר' שמעון אמ' (6: ff.)—Neither a person's tribe nor any external factors make for praise or denigrate a person but only his deeds which, if they are good, cause him to be praised and if they are bad, cause him to be despised (יפ"ת). The concept here is God's justice. The last example is an interpretation of the verse in the lection (Lev. 24:11).

[2] און . . . ר' חוניא א' (751:5 f.)—On the one hand, the ממזרין (6:) constitute an element that is periodically eliminated, but, on the other hand, God has such compassion for them that their identity is not disclosed since כשירין (7:) are likewise slain at the same time. Are the ממזרין inherently wicked? It would seem so, for they are called בית מרעים וגו' (9:), but if so, then their death as ממזרין ought to

have been made manifest. Further, are non-ממזרין to be slain with them merely so as not to disclose the identity of the ממזרין? This ambiguity of thought reflects the unsuccessful attempt to unite two opposite attitudes toward the ממזר, a harsh attitude and a compassionate one.

ואתייה . . . החטאים (752:1)—By itself this statement constitutes an emphasis on God's love. When the sinner brings a sin-offering in public, the sinner, according to the law, is not revealed as such. Integration here of Halakah and Haggadah. This statement however, is said to agree with the previous one and thus also to imply that the ממזר is inherently a sinner.

XXXII.7 (752:3 ff.)

[1] חיי הוא . . . זעורה ר' (3 f.:)—Public awareness of his status saves, as it were, the life of a ממזר. At the same time, of course, it helps prevent illegal marriage. The concepts are: Israel and ממזר.

[2] חיי הוא . . . כההיא (6 f.:)—The attitude of both ר' ברכיה and of the ציבור (753:1) toward the ממזר (753:3) is one of compassion. The ground on which ר' ברכיה made his appeal to the public (ציבור) in behalf of the man was דהוא ממזר (3:), an appeal to which the public responded with contributions. Furthermore, in thus publicly announcing the ground for the appeal, ר' ברכיה did not mean to shame the man but to save his life.

[3] הטינוף . . . ר' מאיר אומ' (7:)—The harsh attitude—even in the Days of the Messiah (לעתיד לבא, 7:), ממזרים (7:) will not be made pure and hence will never escape their status.

ר' יוסי . . . הממזרות (9 f.:)—The compassionate attitude and the argument from interpretations of Ezek. 36:25 in which ר' יוסי seems to disprove the arguments of ר' מאיר and hence to establish that ממזרים will be purified לעתיד לבוא.

א"ר חונא . . . הדורות (754:4)—"Hapless indeed are the generations if the law is not according to ר' יוסי!'' This is not only a statement expressing deep compassion for the ממזר, but a daring one. It expresses sorrow at the possibility that the status of the ממזר will not ultimately be changed and thus implies strong disapproval of the present status, the status obtaining during "the generations." Notice also that in contrast to this statement, none is given indicating agreement with the view of ר׳ מאיר.

XXXII.8 (754:5 f.)

[1] איכפת לו . . . חנינא (5:)—A statement going beyond compassion and calling the status of ממזרות unjust; integration of Halakah and Haggadah.

[2] איכפת לו . . . חנינא (5:)—They are punished though they themselves have not sinned (on עשוקים (6:), see Lieberman here, p. 881).

[3] בקהל ה׳ . . . ואין להם (8 f.:)—The Sanhedrin are called "oppressors" even though they are forced to exclude the ממזרים because of the plain injunction in Deut. 23:3. They are apparently assumed to be unwilling oppressors (see also the different explanation by רש״ש).

Chapter XXXIII

XXXIII.1 (756:2 ff.)

[1] חיים ביד לשון . . . רבי יניי . . . ר׳ חייה . . . א׳ (4:)—Another application of Prov. 18:21 by extension, for the statements refer to eating, not to speech. (On the punishment by death, see מהרז״ו.) The concepts are מצוות, holiness (תרומה), and God's justice.

[2] לית דביש מיניה . . . רבן גמליאל (6 ff.:)—This incident is of a literary nature rather than a factual one. (Notice the similar instances described by Lieberman here, pp. 881 f.)

[3] את אחיו . . . לפיכך (758:4)—The concept of אונאה which the Rabbis see embodied in Lev. 25:14 is both a negative ethical concept and a negative מצוה. In an organic complex an act may often be grasped by two concepts at once, and this is always the case in

regard to an ethical act (cf. WE, p. 12). However, according to the Rabbis, this verse prohibits אונאת ממון, acts of fraud or over-reaching, whereas Lev. 25:17 prohibits אונאת דברים, injury or wrong through words. In the present context Lev. 25:14 does seem to be applied to אונאת דברים.

XXXIII.2 (758:6 ff.)

[1] ושטרו בידו . . . ובידו אנך (7:)—Here ושטרו בידו relates to impending punishment because of אנך, i.e., for אונאה. In the statements that follow, the same phrase is a cliché also telling (but with regard to other matters) of impending punishment—the concept of God's justice.

[2] עוד עבור לו . . . ויאמר ה' (759:4)—The Rabbis often regard the evils that befall a person in this world, בעולם הזה (6:), as chastisement (יסורין, 6:), so that having been "corrected" here, he will not be punished after this world (לעתיד תבוא, 6:).

XXXIII.3 (760:3 f.)

Up to the application to Lev. 25:14 at the end of the paragraph, this section deals with גזל, regarded here as the most salient sin of all, or even as great a sin in itself as idolatry, murder and incest combined. By adducing at the end of all this the injunction against אונאה, the passage obviously indicates that אונאה is a form of גזל, robbery, or—to put it in our terminology—that אונאה is a sub-concept of גזל. Of course, Lev. 25:14 is now interpreted to refer to אונאת ממון. Now, אונאת ממון thus has a dual character, being at once a sub-concept of אונאה and a sub-concept of גזל. It is thus apparent that אונאת ממון, fraud or overreaching, is con-nected with גזל, since it shares in the same ground, i.e., taking something illegitimately. But what kind of kinship can אונאת ממון have with אונאת דברים, injury or wrong done through words, the other sub-concept of אונאה? Since אונאה is, like all value concepts, a folk concept at bottom, though built up by the Rabbis, it testifies to the ethical sensitiveness of the folk, for a wrong done by means of words was felt to be as real a wrong, as palpable, as downright fraud. If this kinship between the two sub-concepts is not readily grasped, it is because we have no modern ethical equivalent for this concept as a whole.

[1] סנקליטין שלו . . . ויאמר הך (3:)—This is one of the cases in which a biblical text is used by the Rabbis as a metaphor.

XXXIII.4 (761:4 f.)

[1] אהרון ומשה . . . לפיכך (762:5)—Moses was pre-eminent, but this did not mean that the Rabbis conceived him to be in a category by himself. Here the honor due Aaron takes precedence over that due Moses.

XXXIII.5 (763:1)

[1] שלשה ימים . . . ויכו בהם (1:)—The interpretation at :6, asserting that it was אביה (7:) who was stricken by God, relates also to the midrash here. He was punished for his calculated cruelty in making it impossible to legally establish the identity of the men of Israel killed in battle—an instance of the integration of Halakah and Haggadah.

[2] ולא ביערה . . . בבית אל (3:) is the (764:2)—ורבנין . . . עבודה זרה . . . בבית אל reading also in several of the versions. In some MSS, and in Ber. R. LXVIII.20, ed. Theodor-Albeck, p. 735, and in Midrash Samuel XVIII.5 (ed. Buber, p. 50b), the reading is ולא ביטלה, a reading which cannot be correct because the concept involved cannot be used here. בטול is a value concept connoting, in this case, cancellation of the idol, but only a Gentile who had worshipped a particular idol can cancel it by demonstrating that it no longer has, for him, the significance of a deity. This is an instance of the integration of Halakah and Haggadah.

[3] והרי דברים . . . כמ' וכמ' (764:5)—A king may act in this manner for reasons of state and not in order to vent his personal feeling (see מהרז"ו).

XXXIII.6 (764:7 ff.)

[1] **ר' חייא . . . מלכא וגו'** (7 f.:)—The derivation of the interpretation from
Lev. 25:14 is not clear and the commentaries are not very helpful.
Still, a rabbinic idea is to be discovered, one that involves normal
mysticism. In time to come, you will be sold to the Nations of the
world, that is to say, you will be exiled, but you must exhibit the
kind of attachment to your Creator that was exhibited by חנניה
מישאל ועזריה (765:1) and not vex Him. We take this "attachment"
to imply normal mysticism because in exile, the individual will
not have the experience of גלוי שכינה associated with the Temple.
The words apparently referring to God in Lev. 25:14 are forms of
"friend" and "brother," words expressing different aspects of
human relationship and hence reflecting a relationship to God
which can only be mystical (see RM, pp. 207 f.). "Friend" and
"brother" imply also relationship of love and are thus indicative
of God's love, a concept often embodied in normal everyday situations. Again, since לברייכון (765:1) relates to these terms of relationship of love contained in the biblical text, ברייכון is likewise
here connotative of God's love.

[2] **א' ר' יוסה . . . ר' יהודה . . . צדו** (765:5 ff.)—Common to all of these
interpretations is the idea of corporate personality, since it was
certainly not חנניה, מישאל ועזריה who had engaged in idolatry,
and yet the king, by quoting verses, could accuse them of having
done so. Again, those verses as interpreted do indicate that the
people were involved in idolatry, and it is thus implied that their
exile is to be regarded as justified and as an example of God's
justice.

[3] **ר' יהודה . . . עקילס . . . צדו** (767:1 f.)—This interpretation mentions
other sins of the people as well as idolatry, namely, drunken
debauches and homosexuality, and thus implies how richly
deserved was the exile.

[4] **ר' שמואל . . . לא למיסגוד . . . צדו** (768:6 f.)—The contemporary relevance of this series of interpretations becomes apparent here with
the reference to emperor worship and to the taxes imposed. The
king now quotes Deut. 4:28 to the effect, apparently, that Israel is
commanded to worship idols in the land of its exile, and the reply

is that this servitude is limited to the taxes imposed and does not refer to worship. The reply, of course, relates to Roman insistence on emperor worship.

[5] כצרצרא . . . ורבנין (769:2 f.)—Here the king quotes Jer. 27:8, a verse which applies specifically to Nebuchadnezzer, and the midrash also uses Dan. 2:16. Furthermore, there is no play here on הצדא but, instead, the midrash closes with riducule of Nebuchadnezzer. It may well be, therefore, that this version of the midrash represents the way in which the idea of limiting the servitude to Rome to its many taxes was the one actually taught the folk.

Chapter XXXIV

XXXIV.1 (771:6 ff.)

[1] אשרי . . . ערש דוי (:6 ff.)—Except for the first, the deeds named here are concretizations of the concept of גמילות חסדים, Deeds of Lovingkindness. The rewards for doing them are instances of מדה כנגד מדה, measure for measure (see יפ״ת).

[2] יצר הרע . . . מיצר הרע על דעת׳ דאבא (772:4)—The יצר טוב and the יצר הרע (:5) are not two distinct entities despite the fact that a man can make the יצר טוב rule over the יצר הרע. There are negative value concepts such as murder, lying, stealing, fornication, etc., concepts that connote a negative valuation and which thus stigmatize immoral acts. Such concepts have a drive *away* from concretization. But this drive *away* from concretization of the negative concepts is, at times, overcome by the evil impulse, the יצר הרע, thus allowing free rein to evil acts. On the other hand, when the drive away from concretizing the negative (evil) concept is not overcome by the יצר הרע, the Rabbis say that the יצר טוב has been made to rule over the יצר הרע. In time, the individual needs less effort to deny the prompting of the יצר הרע, and in this fact the Rabbis see God's reward for the effort exerted earlier.

ייסא אמ׳ . . . לעני (Return to 771:7)—This is the only act in the list in which דל (:6) is taken literally; the rest take the word in a borrowed sense. The act is a concretization of צדקה, but the concepts of צדקה and גמילות חסדים are used interchangeably (see OT, p. 138, and WE, p. 21).

ר' הונא (772:1) . . . מתיבין . . . מרווחין לו—An unusual instance in which a haggadic statement is questioned.

[3] אמ' ר' יונה . . . נתתיו לך (773:2)—Does this not involve lying to a man? But this is a case where one concept, צדקה, is emphasized above another, the negative concept of שקר. Such emphasis is a major feature of the rabbinic complex (see our remarks at 70:6, on a similar instance). Far from condoning a wrong act, the present midrash, on the contrary, brings out the full, rich connotation of צדקה, charity, as an act of love and deep compassion (see our remarks at 781:1, below).

XXXIV.2 (774:4f.)

[1] מלוה ה' . . . ישלם לו (4:)—Another turn is given the idea of צדקה in this passage, namely, that an act of charity constitutes a loan to God and that He will repay the giver for the good deed. This point is already made in Prov. 19:17. The midrash, however, adds to that idea by saying that the giver of charity, in hastening to do that מצוה, does what is usually done by God "who giveth bread to all flesh" (Ps. 136:25). Although the concepts of God's love and His justice are common to both Prov. 19:17 and this midrash, the latter adds the concept of מצוה and indicates thereby that to give charity is obligatory and not just a gracious act. The midrash is thus more than an enlargement of the idea in the biblical verse.

[2] ר' פינחס . . . ימוך אחיך (775:1)—An interpretation, primarily, of the second half of Prov. 19:17. God's recompense for an act of charity is for what was achieved by the money, not the repayment of the few coins, i.e., the saving of a man's life. God's recompense is that, on occasion He saves the giver's life. The concept of God's justice is combined here with that of His love.

XXXIV.3 (775:7 ff.)

[1] גומל נפשו . . . הלל הזקן . . . וכמ' (7:.ff)—Certain acts done for oneself have in them an element of piety. Bathing the body is among the modes of behavior common to all mankind and this belongs to the first phase of דרך ארץ, the purely descriptive phase, but Hillel teaches that bathing is a מצוה, a new view to his students, and this demonstrates that the first phase of דרך ארץ is not morally neutral. The midrash also indicates that something usually regarded as morally neutral may be shown to be not so. Since the reason given for this מצוה is that man is made in the image of God, the concepts here are not only דרך ארץ and מצוה but also Man and God's love.

[2] גומל נפשו . . . חסיד (777:5)—Rashi on Prov. 11:17 explains this to mean that the pious man acts with kindness to his relatives. The word נפשו here is thus taken as speaking of a corporate personality.

[3] אמ' ר' נחמן . . . אחיך (778:2)—Continues to interpret Deut. 15:10. The verse itself contains the theme here. The midrash only adds to the theme by pointing to the ever-present possibility of changes in circumstances, a phenomenon now explained as due to God's justice. The concepts are: charity and God's justice. This seems to be a valuational interpretation of the commonly observed phenomenon of "the wheel of fortune." See the way in which this midrash has been reworked in both Tanḥumas cited by Margulies.

XXXIV.4 (778:4 ff.)

[1] רש ואיש . . . לעשותו חכם (4:.f)—The concepts of צדקה and תלמוד תורה are related in that both giving charity and teaching adults Torah are obligatory for those to whom these things are possible, and this relationship is reflected in the utilization of these verses in Proverbs for ideas on the teaching of Torah. Poverty and wealth here represent degrees of knowledge of Torah. Indeed, the kindness of the איש תכבים shows that teaching Torah to adults is an act of גמילות חסדים as well as an act of תלמוד תורה and גמילות חסדים is a concept that may be interchanged with צדקה (OT, pp. 138 f.).

[2] העולם הבא . . . שניהם (779:1)—Reward for knowledge of Torah is given to the pupil as well as the teacher.

[3] עם דכוותך . . . עשיר ורש (1:)—The scholar refuses the ignorant man's request to be taught "one chapter of Mishnah." He regards it as beneath him to teach such easy chapters as could be understood by the ignorant man. The rudeness of the scholar and his overweening pride present a contrast to the kindness of the איש תכבים in the preceding statement. The midrash thus points to an unpleasant, almost immoral, characteristic more often found among the scholars than among others and it constitutes a stinging indictment of the scholars as a class. However, we ought not to forget that the whole haggadic literature indicates that many scholars did go out to the people and taught Halakah as well as Haggadah.

לעשותו חכם . . . עושה כולם (4:)—This statement is certainly a warning to the scholars, but it is also intended as encouragement to the ignorant.

[4] ימוך אחיך . . . עשיר . . . ד״א רש (5 f.:)—An interpretation embodying the concept of צדקה itself, and referring literally to the states of poverty and wealth the text speaks of. There is a correspondence between the two parts of the midrash. Here it is again the תכבים, now an ordinary working man, who responds to the plea, and it is again "the rich man," now in the literal sense, who rejects the poor man's plea. This midrash no doubt reflects the general impressions gathered from observation.

הבא . . . ה' שניהם . . . מצוה . . . ד״א רש א (5:)—The poor man gains חיי שעה (8:), life in this passing world, since his physical need has been met, whereas his benefactor acquires the life of the World to Come, life in the permanent world, as reward for his deed. Yet the text מאיר עיני שניהם ה' (7:) makes no distinction between what each man has gained. This implies that the Rabbis' belief in the World to Come did not mitigate their concern with this world (see also OT, p. 82 f.).

אמ' עשיר . . . דהוה ליה (780:3)—When the rich man not only refuses to give the poor man charity but goes further and tells the poor man to go to work, seeing he is physically so strong, the rich man's wealth will surely be lost. He has given gratuitous offense.

עין רעה (5:)—Folklore science.

XXXIV.5 (780:7 f.)

[1] עין רעה . . . ר' תנחום (7 f.:)—Apparently if a person does not truly rejoice at a friend's good fortune, he only causes him to be subject to the "evil eye."

[2] מתן שכרו . . . א״ר אחא ביום (781:1)—To find ways to help a friend in his misfortune in order (כדי, 3:) to earn a reward from God is certainly doing צדקה from an ulterior motive. And the end of the midrash telling that the rich and the poor benefit each other in no way mitigates this idea, for here, too, the poor man only gives the rich man the opportunity to earn a reward. In this midrash, the stress is on the concept of God's justice since reliance on that concept is the motive for the act, and hence the stress is on the צדקה itself, the act being prompted by compassion and love, the connotations of צדקה. The point here is strikingly illustrated by the version of our midrash at 773:3 which is the original statement since there alone is the midrash a play on a biblical text. That version does not contain the ulterior motive at all, and it goes on to give an example of how compassion directs the author of the statement to avoid offending the sensibility of the recipient of charity. The far greater frequency of צדקה itself as a motive goes back to the basic difference between the two kinds of motive. In contrast to צדקה, which is a genuine emotional drive, the concept of God's justice does not possess a drive in its own right, being only an interpretive concept (see WE, p. 64). A motive which depends on a mental factor alone obviously cannot compare with a motive which is an emotional drive.

XXXIV.6 (782:1 f.)

[1] דל הוא . . . פעמים רבות (1:)—Connected by association of ideas. The frequent servitude to the empires was punishment for idolatry, but as soon as they did תשובה (2:), they were again redeemed. The

obvious lesson was that if Israel truly repented now, they would also be redeemed immediately.

[2] אחיך . . . שבעה שמות (5: f.)—The definitions or explanations of these names are largely פשט but they also reflect keen observation by the Rabbis. The explanations include psychological insights both by the Bible and the Rabbis, and testify to the deep concern for the poor, a concern which is equally characteristic of the Bible and the Rabbis. These names are concepts belonging to the first phase of the concept of דרך ארץ and thus are concepts in which the role of the folk predominated.

XXXIV.7 (783:5 f.)

[1] גרמך בי . . . תורה . . . זעירא ר' אמ' (5:)—According to ר' יפ״ת, what זעירא (5:) says is that even everyday talk of the people in the Land of Israel involves an interpretation of a biblical verse (תורה היא, :5), his examples being an implied interpretation of the first part of Lev. 25:35, to the effect that in helping a poor man the giver acquires merit for himself (the same interpretation and terminology as at 781:7). Schechter (*Some Aspects of Rabbinic Theology*, p. 126) takes תורה היא (5:) to mean, "It conveys an object lesson," although he goes on to speak of the idea in the midrash at 781:7.

XXXIV.8 (784:6 ff.)

[1] וראה מה פרע הקב״ה לבניו (785:2)—Corporate personality and corporate justice, for Abraham did the good deed and his children (בניו, :2) were rewarded.

[2] דרך ארץ—אמ' ר' לוי דרך ארץ . . . ובמשתה (786:2)—דרך ארץ referred to here is that phase of the concept, the fifth phase, which consists of ethical rules which are also good manners. The rule here points to an act which is both courtesy and an act of גמילות חסדים and hence is used as an instance of the latter.

[3] ווידיי . . . גשי הלום (788:3 f.)—Teaches the פשט.

[4] ומאכילה . . . אמ' ר' יצחק (790:1)—A man ought to do an act of גמילות חסדים or צדקה (both are included in מצוה, 2:) with joy for then he will do it handsomely, completely.

[5] לפניו . . . ר' כהן (7:f.)—In view of the preceding midrash which speaks of מצוה as an act of charity or of גמילות חסדים, the word מצוה (8:) here, undoubtedly means an act of charity or of גמילות חסדים. This statement is an instance of indeterminate belief, for the prooftext (Mal. 3:16) is often given other interpretations (see, for example, Abot III.2 where the concept embodied is תלמוד תורה).

[6] שנתן לי . . . תני (791:2)—Here the idea that an act of charity benefits both him who gives and him who receives (see 781:6) is given another dimension. The recipient feels that he benefits his benefactor much more than the giver benefits him. Obviously, this idea saves the recipient's self-respect.

XXXIV.9 (791:7 ff.)

[1] משפטי נפשו . . . אמ' ר' אבין (8:f.)—This midrash embodies the concept of God's justice. At the same time the midrash also reflects normal mysticism, for only a person who has had experience of God which is not of a sensory kind can understand that God may stand at the right hand of the poor man who is at his door even though no one can actually see God there. The interpretation of Ps. 109:31 literalizes what is no doubt only a figure of speech.

XXXIV.10 (793:4 f.)

[1] מיד היה נענש למיתה (5:)—The word מיד (5:) is also found in all the parallel sources. What is stressed here is the need for responding immediately to a poor man's plea, despite the possibility of an impostor.

XXXIV.11 (794:8 f.)

[1] על ה' . . . ר' יהודה (8:f.)—Two concepts at once interpret an ethical act, the concept of מצוה and the ethical term designating the act.

In the case of מצוה, the word is used not only in the general sense of "commandment" but often also in the sense of צדקה. Here, in the phrase מצות העני קלה (8:), the word is obviously used in the sense of "commandment," whereas at 807:2, for example, it is used in the sense of צדקה. This interpretation of an act by several concepts at once is made possible by the organismic character of the value-concepts, a conceptual organization enabling the maximum number of concepts to be concretized in any given situation (OT, pp. 194 f.). The failure to recognize the nature of value concepts has led modern writers to say that the Rabbis knew only מצוות as a motive and had no ethical motives. These writers, furthermore, fail to realize that the very designation—charity, etc.—of an act is itself an ethical designation.

Punishment or reward is always associated with a מצוה and is indicative as to whether the מצוה is light or grave.

XXXIV.12 (796:1 ff.)

[1] Connected with the preceding statement on p. 795 by association of ideas. The belief in dreams as foretelling the future was not incompatible with the value complex. Here such a dream is made the framework of a story concretizing the concept of צדקה. The entire field of folklore was utilized by the Rabbis to convey teachings concerning value-concepts. Even what were originally magical acts and superstitions were reinterpreted by the Rabbis so as to become a potent means of embodying value concepts. See Lieberman's valuable study in *Greek in Jewish Palestine* (New York, 1942) pp. 97–114. It seems to us, however, that in a few instances there, the materials proved to be intractable.

XXXIV.13 (799:4 ff.)

[1] בית . . . שירדו . . . מנערותן . . . אילו (800:1)—These classifications of poor men describe human phenomena and hence belong to the first phase of דרך ארץ (see WE, pp. 39 f.).

[2] בית . . . מורין . . . ומרווין . . . אילו תלמידי חכמים (801:2)—The derivations here from the word מרודים (3:, 5:) take the word, as the commentaries point out, to be a notarikon and hence these deriva-

tions are the result of mere hints. Such derivations are not only
entirely compatible with the midrashic method but actually
emphasize its character. A haggadic statement is the result of the
impact of a biblical text on a creative mind; that is to say, a
biblical verse is a stimulus. Often there is a distinct visual
resemblance between the biblical word and the rabbinic idea
derived from it as, for example, the relation between מרודים and
the rabbinic idea of ירוד or ירידה in the earlier interpretations in
this passage. However, since the resemblance does not constitute a
logical inference but is the result of a stimulus, sometimes what is
produced bears hardly any resemblance at all to the original
stimulus, so that the biblical word can only be described as a hint
(see CA, pp. 20 f., where the midrashic method is more fully
described).

A verse can act as a stimulus for a rabbinic idea because in
the first place, the Bible as a whole is both related to and yet
different from rabbinic thought. A rabbinic idea embodies rabbinic
concepts—that is, concepts possessing conceptual terms largely
found in rabbinic literature rather than in the Bible, and where
found also in the Bible, have a different meaning there. For
example, מלכות שמים and תלמוד תורה are purely rabbinic terms,
whereas גר in the sense of proselyte and גוי in the sense of non-Jew
are biblical terms given a different meaning in rabbinic usage. On
the other hand, *every* rabbinic concept has its *roots* in the Bible.
For example: תלמוד תורה, the concept embodied in the midrash
here, has as one of its antecedents the idea in Deut. 6:7. Hence,
despite the new rabbinic concepts, rabbinic thought and the Bible
are in the same universe of discourse. At the same time, any particular rabbinic idea, an idea embodying a rabbinic concept, is a
new idea produced by a creative mind. But a new idea to be thus
struck off needs a stimulus and this stimulus is a biblical verse, a
verse related to the new idea because it is in the same universe of
discourse. The commentators are not aware that a biblical verse is
only a stimulus to a haggadic interpretation, so they regard the
latter as an answer to a "problem" or a "difficulty" the verse is
said to present. (See for example, מהרז"ו on הלא פרס at 795:5.)
This type of connection between a verse and its interpretation is
indeed to be found in many instances but there are also many
instances of mere word-play. In general, therefore, the connection
between a verse and its haggadic interpretation reveals simply

that the verse has played the role of a stimulus and the interpeta-
tion is not the result of a fixed logical method.

Because the rabbinic concepts and the Bible were in the same
universe of discourse, the Rabbis did not "outgrow" the Bible
when they possessed the new rabbinic complex of concepts. If the
biblical texts acted as a stimulus for the Rabbis, it was because
they knew, had absorbed the Bible's literal meanings. Thus they
sometimes employed the conceptual terms in their biblical meaning, despite their usual rabbinic meanings. However, they did
differentiate between the literal biblical meaning and their own
rabbinic interpretation, using the term ודאי to designate the
former. Again, because of the common universe of discourse, they
sometimes assume that a rabbinic interpretation represents a text's
literal meaning. In OT we have attempted to account for some of
the ideas presented here by the theory of "organic levels."

XXXIV.14 (802:1 ff.)

[1] Continues with the interpretation of Isaiah 58:7. The concept of צדקה
obviously dominates this passage and it interweaves with the concepts of: חכמים, תלמוד תורה, עניות, עריות, תפילה (תענית), רחמים,
ישראל.

XXXIV.15 (809:7 ff.)

[1] אז יבקע . . . תצמח . . . יאספך (:7 f.)—In the idea here that charity
will cause the World-to-Come to take place speedily, the other
concept embodied is גאולה. But in the idea that charity (צדקה,
810:1) will go before the doer and God will be his reward, the
concept of עוה"ב apparently then refers to the reward after death.
Also involved is גלוי שכינה (וכבוד ה', ibid.).

[2] שלח . . . בהדה . . . בהדה . . . בהדה (810:3)—Since the rabbinic complex is a pattern of value concepts, it allows one concept to be
emphasized at times above another. Here the concept of פיקוח
נפש, saving a life, is stressed above שקר, falsehood. It is not just
permitted but commanded to lie in this case (cf. מהרז"ו); thus it is
an example of the interrelation of Halakah and Haggadah.

[3] ליתן לך . . . נחמו בדברים . . . ותפק (5:)—The connotation of נחמה here is not to allay distress by means of words, but to indicate thus one's own distress at one's inability to help. This is felt to be a means of comfort since it signifies good will.

[4] ואדום . . . ר׳ טביומי . . . ונחך (811:1)—One third of the day God does צדקה and hence, by doing charity a person becomes like God. When the doing of charity is inspired by the idea of imitating God, there is also embodied the concept of קדושה.

XXXIV.16 (812:3 f.)

[1] ובנו ממך חרבות עולם (3:)—Both those who study the Torah and those who make it possible are the true builders of the world (cf. יפ״ת and מהרז״ו).

[2] עומדת לעד . . . ר׳ טרפון (3 f.:)—ר׳ טרפון, too, had in mind to use the money for תלמוד תורה, but limited to himself and ר׳ עקיבא, whereas ר׳ עקיבא used the same means in order to provide for a number of scholars. Not only was this achieved, but owing to ר׳ עקיבא, the reward for the charity of ר׳ טרפון "endures forever" (צדקתו עומדת לעד, 813:5) and it was thus a reward in this world as well. The concept of charity is here associated with that of תלמוד תורה.

[3] בפרץ לפניו . . . וקורא לך (6 f.:)—Poverty is not taken for granted but is regarded as an evil that God Himself should have remedied, and hence the man who gives charity is accounted as though he were Moses, God's "chosen," בחירו, (814:1), chosen to remedy the evil.

[4] שלום לי . . . משובב (814:1)—By giving charity to a poor man, a person rectifies the conditions which cause that poor man to complain that God has been unfair to him. He acts, so to say, as a peacemaker between that poor man and God; thus, the giver of charity causes the poor man not to feel excluded from God's love. The problem raised here is personal and valuational, whereas the explanation by רד״ל of the prooftext implies that the poor man—his wants now satisfied—is no longer compelled to wander from place to place (see מ״כ and מהרז״ו).

[5] שתקא . . . וקראתה (815:5 f.)—Halakah. The only faint connections between the text and the interpretations here indicate that these laws obviously existed before they were connected with this biblical verse.

Chapter XXXV

XXXV.1 (817:5 ff.)

[1] אל עדותיך . . . חישבתי (:5)—Daily, when he wishes to go elsewhere, willy nilly his feet bring him to synagogues and academies (places where God's laws are studied עדותיך, :8]). רד"ל ascribes this to habit. Emphasis is on תלמוד תורה.

[2] ר' בא . . . תלכו (818:4 f.)—In this interpretation the emphasis is on God's love, and the motive of prudence (adduced above) is absent. Indeed, the קללות can even be changed to ברכות.

XXXV.2 (819:3 f.)

[1] אמ' ר' חננה . . . בחוקותי תלכו (820:2)—This is a striking concretization of God's love, for here it is said that God's well-being is enhanced by Israel's observance of the מצוות. On the other hand, there are rabbinic statements which insist that when man observes the laws he does not thereby meet any need of God's, as in the Ne'ilah 'Amidah of Yom Kippur, which declares, "If he (man) be righteous what can he give Thee?" (after Job 35:7). (See the examples and discussion in S. Heinemann, טעמי המצוות, 3rd ed., p. 25.) We must say, therefore, that not only is our midrash here a concretization of the concept of God's love, but it is also an instance of indeterminacy of belief, since it is contradicted by other rabbinic statements. But if this midrash and the others like it represent beliefs that are indeterminate, then such beliefs cannot be epitomized in a hard and fast principle which declares that God has need of man.

XXXV.3 (820:6 f.)

[1] זקן תחילה . . . אבל הקב״ה (821:2)—The first part of this statement refers to מצוות in general, as can be seen clearly from the parallel in the Yerushalmi quoted by Margulies; the second part is thus only an example. Israel's observance of the מצוות is conceived here, accordingly, as the imitation of God. The concepts are: מצוות, God's love, Israel, and אבות (Abraham).

XXXV.4 (821:5 f.)

The very laws which are given to Israel by God were the means by which He made heaven and earth, the sun and the moon, the sea, sand and the deep, and this idea is derived by taking the word חוקותי (:5), "My laws," to relate to the "laws" spoken of in the Bible in regard to these phenomena. This is a purely mystical idea. It is also a purely rabbinic idea for in the Bible itself the laws connected with these phenomena refer to their respective functioning, not to their creation. The implication of the mystical idea is that the laws of the Torah are imbedded in the very structure of the world, and that the physical world and, so to speak, the moral law constitute a unity. The concepts are: חוקים, בראשית, and Torah. Value concepts are thus employed here to express a mystical idea, an idea which, in this case, does not directly involve conduct. In normal mysticism, however, the value concepts do involve conduct.

XXXV.5 (822:6 f.)

[1] Another interpretation of Lev. 26:3. God's laws control the יצר הרע. Evil impulses are also called "laws" here, apparently because of their power. און = עון, hence יצר הרע.

XXXV.6 ((823:4 f.)

XXXV.7 (825:1 f.)

[1] תשמרו (1:) again is study of אמ' ר' חננא . . . ועשיתם אתם [1] Torah. The study of Torah is, indeed, character molding (see "The Efficacy of Torah" in OT, pp. 68 ff.).

[2] רוח הקודש (4:)—(826:3) אמ' ר' אחא . . . לאיתן האזרחי [2] means here the capacity to find new interpretations of Torah, for משכיל (6:) refers to a Psalm, and the Psalms are conceived as having been written by men inspired by רוח הקודש.

XXXV.8 (826:7 f.)

Many of these instances refer only to Israel, although others do refer to the world in general. עולם, however, (827:1) can refer to either. By characterizing these matters as "gifts" of God, they are characterizing them as נסים. The list cannot, however, be regarded either as "everyday" נסים or otherwise (outside of normal, natural things), for sailing safely on the Mediterranean (הים הגדול, 827:5) is regarded as a "gift" whereby the natural order is overcome, whereas mercy (רחמים, ibid. :8) is a "natural" human trait. We have here an indication that the line between the two conceptual phases of נס is by no means distinct. The category of "gift" is thus not quite the same as the category of נס.

XXXV.9 (828:1)

Through Wednesday the falling rain does not interfere with providing for the Sabbath, but it does interfere on Thursday and Friday. Hence the blessing which speaks of rains in their seasons (בעתם, :1) refers to rain other than on Thursday or Friday. This midrash reflects the centrality of the Sabbath in the life of the Jew, making a living being secondary to preparation for the Sabbath. Furthermore, even in a long period of drought, rain on Friday is regarded as a curse. The concepts are: God's love and holiness (the Sabbath), although holiness is here felt as a goal rather than as an experience.

XXXV.10 (828:4 f.)

[1] ונתתי . . . שבתות (6:)—Since rain on Friday *nights only* interferes with nobody, it is the unmitigated blessing referred to in Lev. 26:4 and is thus a נס in reward for fulfilling the laws. The concepts of God's love and His justice in combination, as well as מצוות are also embodied here.

XXXV.11 (829:5)

XXXV.12 (830:1 ff.)

[1] אמ' ר' אבהו . . . תעשרנה (7:f.)—Though ordinarily there are at least two rainy periods. Yet when the people of Israel do the will of God, it is enough for one rainfall at His command for the earth to be immediately fruitful. The concepts of God's justice and נס are embodied here, and hence the midrash does not imply that this single rainfal is unusually heavy.

[2] ר' ברכיה . . . ולא לשדות (831:5 f.)—This midrash is related to the previous one, employing the same concept of זכות, but now emphasizing the individual, the emphasis on the individual being an emphatic trend of rabbinic thought. The difficulty is that the word זכות, often meaning "merit," is here used not only in relation to "one man" (6:) and thus used properly, but also, following that, in relation to "one plant" and "one field" (6:). Apparently, to meet this difficulty, the קרבן העדה to the parallel in J.T. Ta'an. III.2, 66d, explains, "Because of the זכות of one man who has one plant in one field." The version in B.T. Ta'an. 9b does not use the term זכות but it expresses the same idea more clearly and thus also the emphasis on the individual.

[3] There are (in 832:2) two partly contradictory definitions of what constitutes a ברכה of God, since according to the first opinion it is something concerning which one ought not to say, "It is enough," whereas according to the second opinion the ברכות are so abundant that people say, "We have enough of ברכות." This illustrates the fact that a value concept cannot be given a hard and fast definition. However, in both "definitions," the נס consists in

the unusual abundance of rain. A ברכה of God is thus an interpretation of an event, and this interpretation embodies the concepts of ברכה, God's love and נס.

[4] A ברכה of God is one of the two aspects or phases of the concept of
ברכה. The other phase consists of acts of worship, the saying of a
prescribed formula of thanksgiving in accordance with the type of
occasion involved. The concepts embodied in these ברכות depend
on the type of occasion to which they are a response, but all of
them include the concepts of ברכה (of course) and God's love.

Now, a phase of a concept shares with its other phases in the
ground supplied by that particular concept, as we demonstrated
elsewhere with regard to the concept of God's justice (see RM,
p. 17 and p. 161). Here the ground for the two phases is the
concept of God's love, although one phase is an interpretation of
an event and the other consists of acts of worship. We ought to
add that the description, "a ברכה of God," is our own designation
made for the sake of clarity. In our midrash here the terms used
are simply ברכה (4:) and ברכות (5:), for the conceptual term itself
can stand for only a phase of the concept (see RM, p. 161), and
phases differ from sub-concepts by not possessing designations
which apply to them alone (see ibid., p. 17).

A ברכה which has as its object another human being is, in
rabbinic thought, really a prayer, a בקשה. Thus, the Rabbis
interpret Pharaoh's plea, "And bless me also" (Exod. 12:32) to
mean "Pray for me. . . ." As far as rabbinic thought is concerned,
the concept of ברכה seems to be limited to the phases we have just
discussed.

Chapter XXXVI

XXXVI.1 (833:5 ff.)

XXXVI.2 (837:4 ff.)

[1] גפן ממצרים . . . ותטעה (4:)—This comment is exegesis, not interpretation. The metaphor is first enlarged upon and then explained
with reference to the biblical narrations. Ps. 80:9, the text com-
mented on, itself contains this mixture of metaphor (גפן, . . . תסיע,
4:), and reference to the biblical narrative (תגרש גוים, 5:), and the
comment does no more than quote the reference to the biblical
narrative.

[2] מה הגפן . . . צדיק . . . המדינות (838:5 f.)—Solomon is spoken of here
as a צדיק, a characterization entirely different from the biblical
view expressed in I Kings 11:1 ff. There are, however, also rabbinic
opinions in which Solomon is by no means regarded as a צדיק
(see Ginzberg, *Legends*, VI, p. 294, n. 59).

[3] מה גפן . . . חכמים (839:3)—The concepts embodied here are: תלמיד
חכם (4:), and עם הארץ (4:); also צדקה, the help which the
ignorant extend to the learned. But there is also a concept that
acts as a motive for the צדקה, namely, תלמוד תורה, and this
concept, too, is thus concretized here.

[4] צדיק בינוני . . . מה הגפן (4:)—The terms צדיק גמור and צדיק בינוני (5:)
represent sub-concepts of the concept צדיק. Obviously, however,
the צדיק גמור is superior to the צדיק בינוני, and hence the terms
also represent gradations in virtue. But the highest grade in
virtuous conduct is חסיד (see RM, p. 39). Such division into better
and still better types of good conduct undoubtedly bespeaks keen
ethical awareness and discrimination on the part of the folk, not
only on that of the Rabbis, for the terms characterizing the types
are value concepts, and value concepts are common terms in the

basic vocabulary of the people as a whole. Incidentally, צדיק גמור has an obverse in רשע גמור (see Ḳid., 40b).

[5] מה הגפן (5:)—He who knows more Torah ישראל . . . מחבירו than his fellows appears, because of his humility, to know less than they do. The concepts are: Torah and humility (ענותנות). But a phase of the concept of Torah is concretized as well: the efficacy of Torah, the idea that the knowledge of Torah has an immediate, though not inevitable effect on conduct. The knowledge of Torah in this case makes a man humble.

[6] תלמוד ואגדה . . . מה הגפן (7:)—The point is made, apparently, that while the divisions of Torah are related just as grapes and raisins are related, each division has its own character.

[7] לך שלום . . . מה הגפן (840:3)—If the purpose is to teach ברכות incumbent on the individual, what is primarily taught here is the first part of the midrash, namely that grapes require שלש ברכות.

[8] לעתיד לבוא (841:2)—Refers to the Days of the Messiah when Israel will be supreme.

והיו מלכים . . . עליון (3:)—The verses are biblical antecedents of the concept of ימות המשיח. All of the rabbinic value concepts are rooted in the Bible, have antecedents in the Bible. This is one of the indications that the Bible and rabbinic thought are in the same universe of discourse (on that subject see our comment at 801:2).

[9] לעתיד לבוא . . . מה הגפן (4:)—The words תחילה וסוף (5:) have their analogy in בעולם הזה and לעתיד לבוא (5:). The עולם הזה is regarded as the "beginning" and thus it is considered in its entirety as a single stage. The other stage is לעתיד לבוא. Following that is not another stage but the unending and enduring עולם הבא. If the entire עולם הזה is a single stage, there can be only events or happenings in this world but no development. This absence of development in history itself reflects the character of the organic complex of concepts which is felt to be the same throughout history. (See also TE, pp. 104 ff.)

[10] ארזי אל . . . מה הגפן (6 f.:)—Apparently refers to the nations paying tribute to the kings of Israel. A similar idea seems to be already implied in the biblical metaphor itself (see our next comment).

[11] שומר ישראל . . . מה הגפן (842:2)—The analogy of the watchman or "keeper" (השומר, 2:) enables the midrash to quote, "Behold, He that keepeth Israel doth neither slumber nor sleep" (Ps. 121:4). The ideas in this and the preceding midrash are contained primarily in the verses quoted from the Bible, again an indication that the Bible and rabbinic thought are in the same universe of discourse. The midrash (842:4) describes Israel as leaning upon the written Torah, the Torah written with a reed, entirely "leaning upon it" because the unwritten Torah, too, derives from it.

[12] יעקב . . . מה הגפן (5:)—"The Merit of their Fathers" supports Israel to this day. This concept implies a corporate personality, for the Patriarchs and their descendants are regarded as one personality. The midrash teaches here that they constitute a single personality in time, even though the Patriarchs are no longer living. Elsewhere the conception of a corporate personality underlies the interpretation of events involving the individual and those associated with him in the present. The conception of corporate personality also underlies the concept of "the Merit of the Children" (זכות בנים), which connotes that the fathers are rewarded for the future meritorious acts of their children (see 843:6 f. and 847:6 f., below).

XXXVI.3 (843:1 ff.)

[1] בשת פנים (5:)—A concept connoting: to be ashamed. A kindred concept is בושה, shame.

כיצד . . . שאין השכינה . . . את פניו (5 f.:)—According to יפ"ת, this may well mean not that he was ashamed but that he fled from the prophet to a place of uncleanness so that the prophet should not see him. (On the idea that the שכינה (6:) does not rest in an unclean place, see CA, p. 43.) However, it is possible that two ideas are expressed in this midrash, namely, that Ahaz went to an unclean place thinking that the prophet would not go there and that when the prophet did go there to speak to him, he was ashamed to face him.

ר' הושעיה . . . אחרי מנשה (844:5)—The concepts here are: Merit of the Fathers and Merit of the Children. Because in the case of Ahaz both were actualized, he was listed among the kings who were צדיקים. The corporate personality which involved Ahaz spanned, so to speak, three persons: his father, himself and his son.

[2] אמ' ר' פינחס . . . כלום (845:1)—A person performing a מצוה is here urged to make זכות אבות a matter of concern, a factor in his attitude in performing that מצוה. Usually זכות אבות is not something deliberately sought after, is not a consideration when performing an act but is an interpretation of an event which has already occurred.

כך אילו . . . בריתי יעקב (:3)—The prime example of זכות אבות is adduced in order to imply that it was the intention of the Patriarchs to have their descendants benefit from the מצוות (:4) which they, the Patriarchs, had performed. Similarity in style makes it likely that this is an intance of the idea given in our preceding comment, even though the authority here is not the same.

XXXVI.4 (846:1 ff.)

[1] ועתה כה . . . ר' פינחס . . . ישראל (:1)—The idea here that Jacob created the world is not meant seriously, of course. This very statement characterizes the world as God's (לעולמו, :2) and in it God says to the world, "My world, My world" (עולמי, עולמי, :2). What the idea does convey is a glorification of Jacob that goes even beyond hyperbole. In the light of the extravagant idea here, an idea not accepted seriously, our notion of indeterminacy of belief is to be seen as a sound psychological midrashic principle.

[2] א' ר' בניה . . . ראשית לו (847:3)—It was due to the merit which Moses would acquire that heaven and earth were created.

[3] אמ' ר' אבהו . . . יוצר הכל הוא (:4)—It was due to the merit which Jacob would acquire that everything was created.

[4] עשית . . . ורבנן . . . משל . . . ר' ברכיה (6 f.:)—The concept in both views here is זכות בנים. Unlike the preceding statements here, the זכות here involves the idea of a corporate personality. In זכות בנים the good deeds have not yet taken place, yet the ancestor, the first link in the corporate personality, is already rewarded. The idea of corporate personality is thus even more evident here than in the זכות אבות. An auxiliary idea, God's omniscience or fore-knowledge is in the service, as always, of a value concept, in this case the concept of זכות בנים.

The parable, as usual, is not wholly in accord with the application. In the parable it is the ruler who decides to execute the prisoner and then releases him, whereas in the application it is God, not Nimrod, Who saves Abraham against the ruler's (Nimrod's) wishes.

XXXVI.5 (849:1 ff.)

[1] למה נאמרו . . . בגינו (1:)—The text is somewhat awkward but the idea seems clear. In the order of succession, the Patriarchs are, of course, Abraham, Isaac and Jacob, but here the order is reversed. The lesson is drawn that זכות אבות does not refer to the merit of the Patriarchs as a group but to the merit of each of them individually, each Patriarch's merits being sufficient to reconcile God to Israel. The idea that there must be sufficient merit in order to bring about reward indicates that זכות אבות is a sub-concept of God's justice. There is an emphasis on the individual here at the same time that the idea of corporate personality is involved.

[2] גבי המזבח . . . ולמה נאמ' (3:)—There is undoubtedly a suggestion of the concept of vicarious atonement in the first opinion regarding Isaac, although it is given in the context of זכות אבות. There is a similar ambiguity in the second opinion. The concepts of vicarious atonement, כפרה, and זכות אבות are kindred concepts, the idea of corporate personality being the underlying idea in both concepts.

[3] צדיקים . . . ולמה נאמ' (5 f.:)—The word אף (5:), is taken as a deprecation. Only Jacob's sons were, all of them, righteous. The זכות of

Abraham and Isaac, on the other hand, is flawed because each of them had unworthy offspring. Here again, the ancestor and his descendants are viewed as a corporate personality, and the unworthiness of the descendants reflects on the ancestor.

[4] זכות אמהות (850:3)—אין לי . . . קברו וגו' is regarded as merit in their own right. It is not included in זכות אבות.

[5] ולמה מזכיר . . . והארץ אזכור (5 f.)—The parable indicates that the Land of Israel is regarded as having reared the Patriarchs, as having contributed to their character. The Land of Israel is holy, sensed as having a mystical quality whereby it belongs to God in a special sense, a mystical quality characteristic of what we have called the hierarchical phase of the concept of holiness (WE, pp. 216 ff.). But there is also a non-hierarchical phase of holiness which refers to moral conduct and refraining from sin. In the midrash here, the Land of Israel, though it concretizes hierarchical holiness, has a non-hierarchical, moral role as well, and thus the midrash also teaches incidentally that the two phases of holiness are not entirely separate. In what sense, however, does the Land have merit? It has merit, זכות, indirectly, by contributing to the merit of the Patriarchs. The parable here is vital to the midrash for without it the essential moral role of the Land would not be taught.

XXXVI.6 (851:3 ff.)

[1] גופא עד אימתי . . . המשרה (3 f.)—A number of authorities teach here that זכות אבות had a limited duration, although they set various limits to that duration. Since all these limits refer to the days of the First Temple, they all teach, by implication, that זכות אבות does not "function" in their day. Apparently they felt that by relying on זכות אבות there would be a tendency on the part of the folk to slacken in positive moral effort. However, the concept of זכות אבות was an element of the rabbinic complex of values; hence the view that it functioned only in the past met with opposition, as we shall see below [3].

[2] ר' יודן . . . לא ימוש (852:4)—This teaching agrees with the preceding

statements in the passage. Recognizing that זכות אבות is no longer
a factor, the individual ought to engage in deeds of lovingkindness. The word הדבק (:5), "cleave," suggests the imitation of God,
cleaving to Him by imitating His acts of lovingkindness, and the
word חסדי (:7) in the prooftext (Isa. 54:10), "My kindness," seems
to bear this out. (On imitating God's lovingkindness, see OT,
pp. 142 f.)

[3] אבותיך וגו' . . . אמ' ר' אחא (:7 f.)—A view which emphatically
declares that זכות אבות always "functions" and is to be invoked
in prayer (מזכירים, 853:1).

Chapter XXXVII

XXXVII.1 (853:5 ff.)

[1] בך חטא . . . טוב אשר (:5 f.)—Two differing halakic opinions embodying the value concept of נדר, vow. A third halakic statement also
embodying this concept is at 856:1.

[2] תמות . . . אשתו . . . יעקב . . . חונא ר' אמ' (854:1 f.)—In all these
statements, the concept of נדר is embodied (together with other
value concepts) in haggadic contexts. The concept נדר is thus not
limited to Halakah.

ר' שמואל בר נחמן . . . כאבים וגו' (:3 f.)—The three concepts here,
besides נדר and אבות, are the three cardinal sins. Because of the
idea of corporate personality, Jacob and his children being
members of a single personality, these sins are here attributed to
Jacob. The very heinousness of the sins, however, suggests that
the statement is hyperbole (see also יפ"ת). It was very likely subject
to indeterminacy of belief.

[3] לה' . . . אמ' ר' שמעון (856:1)—R. Simeon, in teaching that the prohibitions concerning a vow also apply to "valuation" of persons,
etc., evidently regards the latter as a form of vow. The text itself,

(Lev. 27:2) by using "vow" as the verb having "valuation" as its object, also implies that "valuation" is a form of "vow."

XXXVII.2 (856:4 ff.)

[1] נפשות לה׳ . . . ד״א כי פועל (860:5 f.)—This midrash seems to teach that had it not been for Moses the passage on "valuation" would not have been given. Because Moses adjusted the burdens so that a man carried a burden suitable to a man and so also in the case of a woman, etc., he was rewarded by being able to teach analogous divisions in "valuations." The concepts are: מתן תורה; תלמוד תורה; and מדת הדין.

XXXVII.3 (861:6 ff.)

[1] ששמו מבגיי . . . ושצפה (862:3)—רוח הקדש (:3) has here a connotation of clairvoyance but in relation to the learned. Elsewhere it has the more intrinsic connotation of divine inspiration resulting in new interpretations and laws (OT, pp. 37 ff.).

מפני הכשפים (:5)—This indicates that while magic was prohibited there was a belief in its efficacy.

[2] במה פתח לו (863:5)—He gave the man an opportunity to retract his vow by asking him if he knew how wrong it was to make a vow (see יפ״ת). This is implied in the statement of ר׳ יוחנן.

XXXVII.4 (864:4 ff.)

[1] והשיבן הקב״ה כהוגן (:4)—God answered them in a proper manner, that is, to their satisfaction. The concept here is God's love.

[2] במקומו . . . ולא היה יכול (866:7 ff.)—According to Jewish law the vow could have been retracted. That it was not, was due to Jephthah and Phineas, each of whom, because of his pride, refused to go to the other, and both were punished. The concepts are: נדר, מלכות, מדת הדין, גאוה, כהונה. This is an example of the interrelation of Halakah and Haggadah.

[3] אין לו . . . ר' שמעון . . . . ר' יוחנן 'ר (888:1)—According to Jewish law, the sacrifice was absolutely not permitted, vow or no vow. On that the two great authorities are at one, although otherwise their opinions differ. This is another example of the interrelation of Halakah and Haggadah.

[4] יבאו . . . א"ר יעקב (5:)—Elsewhere the idea that a man can make certain that his prayer will be answered is emphatically negated.

About the Author

Max Kadushin (1895–1980) was Visiting Professor of Ethics and Rabbinic Thought at The Jewish Theological Seminary of America. He received his B.A. from New York University and the degrees of M.A., Rabbi, D.H.L. and Litt. D. (*honoris causa*) from the Seminary. His other books include: *The Theology of Seder Eliahu, A Study in Organic Thinking* (1932); *Organic Thinking, A Study in Rabbinic Thought* (1938); *The Rabbinic Mind* (1952; 3rd ed., 1972); *Worship and Ethics, A Study in Rabbinic Judaism* (1964); and *A Conceptual Approach to the Mekilta* (1969). The latter three books are also available in later editions in paperback.

BROWN JUDAIC STUDIES SERIES

140001	*Approaches to Ancient Judaism I*	William S. Green
140002	*The Traditions of Eleazar Ben Azariah*	Tzvee Zahavy
140003	*Persons and Institutions in Early Rabbinic Judaism*	William S. Green
140004	*Claude Goldsmid Montefiore on the Ancient Rabbis*	Joshua B. Stein
140005	*The Ecumenical Perspective and the Modernization of Jewish Religion*	S. Daniel Breslauer
140006	*The Sabbath-Law of Rabbi Meir*	Robert Goldenberg
140007	*Rabbi Tarfon*	Joel Gereboff
140008	*Rabban Gamaliel II*	Shamai Kanter
140009	*Approaches to Ancient Judaism II*	William S. Green
140010	*Method and Meaning in Ancient Judaism*	Jacob Neusner
140011	*Approaches to Ancient Judaism III*	William S. Green
140012	*Turning Point: Zionism and Reform Judaism*	Howard R. Greenstein
140013	*Buber on God and the Perfect Man*	Pamela Vermes
140014	*Scholastic Rabbinism*	Anthony J. Saldarini
140015	*Method and Meaning in Ancient Judaism II*	Jacob Neusner
140016	*Method and Meaning in Ancient Judaism III*	Jacob Neusner
140017	*Post Mishnaic Judaism in Transition*	Baruch M. Bokser
140018	*A History of the Mishnaic Law of Agriculture: Tractate Maaser Sheni*	Peter J. Haas
140019	*Mishnah's Theology of Tithing*	Martin S. Jaffee
140020	*The Priestly Gift in Mishnah: A Study of Tractate Terumot*	Alan J. Peck
140021	*History of Judaism: The Next Ten Years*	Baruch M. Bokser
140022	*Ancient Synagogues*	Joseph Gutmann
140023	*Warrant for Genocide*	Norman Cohn
140024	*The Creation of the World According to Gersonides*	Jacob J. Staub
140025	*Two Treatises of Philo of Alexandria: A Commentary on De Gigantibus and Quod Deus Sit Immutabilis*	David Winston/John Dillon
140026	*A History of the Mishnaic Law of Agriculture: Kilayim*	Irving Mandelbaum
140027	*Approaches to Ancient Judaism IV*	William S. Green
140028	*Judaism in the American Humanities*	Jacob Neusner
140029	*Handbook of Synagogue Architecture*	Marilyn Chiat
140030	*The Book of Mirrors*	Daniel C. Matt
140031	*Ideas in Fiction: The Works of Hayim Hazaz*	Warren Bargad
140032	*Approaches to Ancient Judaism V*	William S. Green
140033	*Sectarian Law in the Dead Sea Scrolls: Courts, Testimony and the Penal Code*	Lawrence H. Schiffman
140034	*A History of the United Jewish Appeal: 1939-1982*	Marc L. Raphael
140035	*The Academic Study of Judaism*	Jacob Neusner
140036	*Women Leaders in the Ancient Synagogue*	Bernadette Brooten
140037	*Formative Judaism: Religious, Historical, and Literary Studies*	Jacob Neusner
140038	*Ben Sira's View of Women: A Literary Analysis*	Warren C. Trenchard
140039	*Barukh Kurzweil and Modern Hebrew Literature*	James S. Diamond
140040	*Israeli Childhood Stories of the Sixties: Yizhar, Aloni, Shahar, Kahana-Carmon*	Gideon Telpaz
140041	*Formative Judaism II: Religious, Historical, and Literary Studies*	Jacob Neusner

BROWN JUDAIC STUDIES SERIES

BROWN JUDAIC STUDIES SERIES

BROWN JUDAIC STUDIES SERIES